Praise for *Embodying Tara*

"Connecting with Mother Tara is one of the most powerful ways to bring peace and harmony to individuals and the world."
  —From the foreword by Khenpo Tsewang Dongyal Rinpoche, coauthor of *Tara's Enlightened Activity*

"Lopön Chandra offers the most accessible, in-depth, inspiring, step-by-step guide to embodying the twenty-one emanations of the great goddess, Tara, for the benefit of compassion in action for countless generations. A treasure and a classic is born from her living lineage with Lama Tsultrim and Tara Mandala as a companion for all on the path. Emaho!"
  —Shiva Rea, yogini and author of *Tending the Heart Fire*

"'I shall work for the benefit of sentient beings in a woman's body.' And here she is, Tara the savioress, a bodhisattva or a buddha—to me the essence of the divine mother or goddess we invoke in my Indian tradition by calling her forth through visualization, meditation, and mantra. Chandra's lyrical voice shares the history of Tibetan Buddhism and Tara, provides specific practice instructions, and illuminates Tara's qualities in modern-day women and the enlightened activities of communities around the world. With the blessings of her teachers and her long-standing deep sadhana, Chandra's book offers us a clear guide and inspiration to whirl in the mandala of Tara, so we may enter her mindstream ourselves."
  —Nina Rao, chantress and seeker

"How wonderful that at this time in the world, the goddess Tara is revealing her ever-deepening presence in the form of this book. Now we have in the most accessible yet deeply moving way all we need to find our way home to our compassionate mother, Arya Tara."
  —Krishna Das, American chant leader and Grammy nominee

"Tara has inhabited the royal seat of representation for the divine feminine for many ages. In this delightfully thorough book, Tara is explored in her twenty-one facets of unity. From her ancient roots in Asian folklore to living examples of her wisdom and compassion, Tara is made relevant for Buddhists and non-Buddhists alike. If we enter this book through the prism of the three wisdoms of Buddhism (listening, contemplating, and meditating) we are skillfully directed to nourish the radiant multidimensionality of Tara dwelling within each of us. I can't wait to share this beautiful book with my many Dharma sisters on the path of awareness."

—Sarah Powers, author of *Insight Yoga* and *Lit from Within*

"Chandra Easton's book gives clear and direct guidance on how to approach and choose the appropriate mindset; how to develop the technical skills to access the goddess; and how to experience her within the innermost depth of one's own soul."

—Emma Balnaves, teacher of Hatha Yoga and producer and director of *Agniyogana*

Embodying Tara

Twenty-One Manifestations to Awaken Your Innate Wisdom

CHANDRA EASTON

SHAMBHALA

Shambhala Publications, Inc.
2129 13th Street
Boulder, Colorado 80302
www.shambhala.com

Line drawings of the twenty-one Taras are reproduced
with permission by Tara Mandala International Buddhist Community.
The Vasudhara prayer that appears in "The Third Tara" is from *Buddhist
Goddesses of India* by Miranda Shaw, © 2006 by Princeton University Press.
Reprinted by arrangement with Princeton University Press.
A portion of the material in the Machig Labdrön section of "The Fifth Tara"
is from *Machik's Complete Explanation*, translated and introduced by Sarah
Harding, ©2003, 2013 by Tsadra Foundation. Reprinted by arrangement with
Shambhala Publications.
Cover art: "Green Tara" by Yoji Nishi
Cover design: Lauren Michelle Smith

9 8 7 6 5 4 3 2

Printed in the United States of America

Shambhala Publications makes every effort to print on
acid-free, recycled paper.
Shambhala Publications is distributed worldwide by
Penguin Random House, Inc., and its subsidiaries.

LIBRARY OF CONGRESS CATALOGING-IN-PUBLICATION DATA
Names: Easton, Chandra, author.
Title: Embodying Tara: twenty-one manifestations to awaken your innate
    wisdom / Chandra Easton.
Description: Boulder: Shambhala, 2023. | Includes bibliographical references.
Identifiers: LCCN 2023005439 | ISBN 9781645471141 (trade paperback)
Subjects: LCSH: Tārā (Buddhist deity)—Cult. | Tārā (Buddhist deity) |
    Buddhist goddesses. | Buddhist gods.
Classification: LCC BQ4710.T33 E27 2023 | DDC 294.3/4211—dc23/eng/20230206
LC record available at https://lccn.loc.gov/2023005439

Contents

Foreword

The gracious teacher Shakyamuni Buddha came to this world 2,600 years ago and turned the wheel of Dharma. His message of discovering one's innate treasure of the heart—of kindness, compassion, nonviolence, openness, and respect for all beings— spread from India to all of Asia. In the mid-eighth century, the great Tibetan Dharma king Trisong Detsen invited the great masters Guru Padmasambhava and Khenchen Shantarakshita to establish the whole body of Buddhism in Tibet. Ever since, Buddhism has been part of the lives and spiritual practices of Tibetans. The gracious Mother Tara has become one of the principal practices of Tibetan Buddhists. Over a hundred years ago, Buddhism began to take root in Western countries, and Tibetan Buddhism in particular came to the West in the mid-twentieth century.

There are many books and sadhanas translated into English on how to practice Tara. Chandra Easton, a brilliant scholar who is very devoted to Mother Tara, has completed a beautiful commentary on the root verses of *Praises to the Twenty-One Taras*, which is a famous tantra taught by the Buddha. Her commentary is based on the teachings of the great masters Taranatha, of the seventeenth century, Jigme Lingpa of the eighteenth century, and Ven. Khenchen Palden Sherab Rinpoche of the twentieth century. She is one of the first Western scholars and devotees to write a book on Tara. This book is not just a collection of intellectual essays—rather, it explains with devotion the power of Mother Tara according to the teachings of the uninterrupted lineage. It is a special book on Tara. It makes it easy for the modern reader to understand and connect with Tara, and to benefit from her practice, particularly now when so many challenges are happening in the world and signs of degeneration are manifesting. Connecting with Mother Tara is one of the most powerful ways to bring peace and harmony to individuals and the world.

I have been a practitioner of Tara for as long as I can remember because my family practiced Mother Tara every evening. Mother Tara has resonated in my heart ever since. I'm so happy and honored to write this short foreword. May it become a special tool to bring peace to everyone's heart. SARVA MANGALAM.

Khenpo Tsewang Dongyal
Padma Samye Ling
May 14, 2023—Dakini Day

Note on Translation

This book draws on Tibetan and Sanskrit Buddhist source materials. For ease of reading, I offer English translations of key Buddhist concepts along with Tibetan or Sanskrit phonetics. For simplicity, foreign words are rendered without diacritics, though seed syllables retain diacritics throughout—except when transliterated for ease of pronunciation in the guided meditations—and are set in small capital letters. All non-English terms in parentheses are Sanskrit, unless identified as Tibetan (Tib.). The Tara mantras are not classical Vedic mantras; therefore, adherence to the Vedic pronunciation system is not strictly required. However, since pronouncing the mantras with as much accuracy as possible improves their efficacy, I have transcribed them based on the original Sanskrit with the close guidance of Venerable Khenpo Tsewang Dongyal and Sanskrit scholar Dr. Vesna Wallace. In the appendix, I have prepared two lists of foreign names and terms that appear in this book. I show the Wylie transliteration for Tibetan names and terms and, for Sanskrit names and terms, the transliteration with diacritics according to the International Alphabet of Sanskrit Transliteration (IAST) system.

Preface

One clear fall day in 2018, while I was teaching courses at Tara Mandala Retreat Center in southwest Colorado, I asked my teacher, Lama Tsultrim, founder and spiritual director of Tara Mandala, for a meeting. I had a question that had been gnawing at me for a while, and I had finally gotten up the nerve to ask her for guidance. Her response was for me to come to her quarters in the Tara Temple that afternoon. So I went to the temple shrine room early to meditate before the meeting. When I entered the shrine room, I felt as though I had walked through a portal: The twenty-one Tara statues lining the walls of the inner sanctum enveloped me as if forming a fairy circle like the majestic old-growth redwoods of my home in Northern California. Sunlight filtered in through the long horizontal windows of stained glass along the upper walls. The half life-size Tara statues—representations of the twenty-one manifestations of the female buddha of compassion, Arya Tara—each consecrated with sacred substances, came alive with the flickering candlelight dancing upon their faces—some serene, some joyful, and some fiercely baring their sharp dakini canine teeth. A feeling of stillness permeated the space, beckoning me to sit down, to breathe. My mind relaxed into a state of reflection and clarity. The company of these awe-inspiring examples of feminine power crystallized the question I had come to ask.

When Lama Tsultrim invited me into her quarters, I told her that I knew it was time for me to write a book, to birth something of my own, but I was not able to bring any themes into focus. I said, "I feel like everything has already been written. What could I possibly have to share that would be meaningful?" Despite having studied and practiced Tibetan Buddhism and translated Tibetan Buddhist works in earnest for twenty-three years, I still felt unprepared to write a book on the Dharma. I had sat many retreats, both group and solitary, graced with meditative experiences that showed me the truth of my own nature. Like Lama Tsultrim, I had devoted much of my life to research and teaching about women in Buddhism. In 2015, my teachers had given me the title Dorje Lopön, which in the Tibetan Buddhist tradition means an esteemed teacher, equal to a doctorate degree in the West. Despite all of this, I still felt under-qualified. Who was I to write a book? I was feeling the effects of imposter syndrome: no matter how qualified I might be, I would never be worthy. It seemed like I was caught in a paralyzing dynamic of "never good enough."

Lama Tsultrim, who rode the first waves of Tibetan Buddhism coming to the West in the 1960s, who had weathered many a storm on the patriarchal waters of Buddhism, and who believed in me, looked at me with a glimmer in her eye and a compassionate smile and said, "Why don't you bring the twenty-one Taras to life? We have these beautiful statues in the temple, and yet we can do so much more to bring them alive." This idea resonated within my body, and I thought, "Of course!" My book's theme was right in front of me—or I might say, all around me—all along.

I'm what they call a Dharma brat: an American kid born in the seventies whose parents were swept up in the first wave of Dharma coming to the United States. It is not surprising that my relationship with Tara began with my mom, who first taught me the Tara mantra and to pray to her whenever I was afraid or in danger—which, during the years I was an avid rock and mountain climber, came in particularly handy! My mom taught me that Tara is *love*, the Great Mother, and that I could access her by reciting her ten-syllable mantra: OM TĀRE TUTTĀRE TURE SVĀHĀ. This was the first mantra I learned as a child.

Later, when I was twenty-six years old and pregnant with my first child, I often meditated on Tara, reciting her mantra and praying for the baby growing inside of me. In those meditations, I would sometimes have visions in which I was bathed in golden light coupled with blissful tear-filled states of meditative absorption. It seemed that Tara was incarnating as my child, for as soon as my baby was born, the visions stopped. It was for this reason that we decided to name our child Tara. (Our Tara is nonbinary and uses they/them pronouns.) Like my mom did for me, I taught them Tara's mantra as soon as they could speak. I encouraged Tara to feel the deity's loving power whenever they felt scared, alone, or in need of protection.

Up until that fateful day in Lama Tsultrim's quarters, I had studied the twenty-one Taras in depth. Yet despite having had this heart connection with Tara, I still felt the twenty-one Taras to be a bit out of reach, a bit esoteric. As I began to consider writing a book on the subject, I knew that I needed to find a creative angle—a way to engage with the themes and archetypes of these Taras that would help bring them alive for the modern reader. Through talking with friends and family, I realized integrating stories of diverse women throughout history—young and old, past and present, Buddhist and non-Buddhist—along with broader movements started by women who embody each of the Tara's qualities, could not only bring the Taras to life but also bring them down to earth so that their essence could be more palpable and relatable.

Women have always influenced culture and history, but their roles have been minimized and their stories untold. They are often portrayed as stereotypes of domestic competence and maternity or highly sexualized temptresses. For just one example, Cleopatra was a poet, philosopher, and gifted mathematician. Yet what we know of her is more a fictionalized seductress with large breasts. We need to actively look for women's stories and put them back into the historical narrative.

With regard to Buddhism, where gender bias exists due in large part to the normative gender hierarchies of South Asia from which the teachings arose, stories of women as spiritual masters are few and far between. In recent years some progress has been made thanks to books such as *Lives of Early Buddhist Nuns: Biographies as History* by Alice Collett, *Women of Wisdom* by Lama Tsultrim Allione, and *Stars at Dawn* by Wendy Garling, to name just a few. Through such writings, we can see that women did indeed play roles in the development of Buddhism. And by bringing these many forgotten stories of women to light, we begin to heal and correct the mistaken perception that women were of little import in our collective history; we begin to change misperceptions about all women and thus the course of the future.

In this book, you will learn about Tara's history, teachings, and enlightened qualities that can help sustain you in times of uncertainty and hardship as well as in times of calm and ease, no matter where you are in the world. This book will give you respect for the roots of these teachings on Tara and her twenty-one aspects while also showing you why they are meaningful for our time. For any spiritual tradition to be of benefit, it must adapt to its new soil and new cultural settings in ways that allow people to access it and bring it alive; otherwise it will wither and die by becoming irrelevant.

While I have been writing this book, the world has lived through the COVID-19 pandemic, and we have witnessed the renewal of autocracies, extremism, and white supremacy embodied by figures such as Donald Trump and his followers. The United States and the world have experienced cries for racial justice ignited by the killings of George Floyd, Breonna Taylor, and many other Black and Brown people. Extreme climate events have brought the climate crisis to our doorsteps. In California alone, we have had the worst fires in decades. Many have lost their homes, and some even their lives, during the fall fire seasons; and the air quality has been so bad at times that the daytime sky smoldered red-black, creating an apocalyptic environment. But amid the darkness, there is light. We must always look to the wisdom of those who are teaching liberation and fighting for justice. The real-life women and broader justice movements I share in this book do just this.

I hope the stories and teachings you encounter in the following pages show you how the twenty-one Tara archetypes are already manifesting in the world and provide you with strong female role models to guide you through difficult journeys. My hope is that this book inspires you to bring the Taras alive in yourself in new and creative ways. All of us, regardless of gender identity, help carry Tara's bodhisattva vow to be of benefit to others again and again.

My own journey of writing this book is complete; I've traveled (sometimes swiftly and sometimes slowly) through the currents of bringing the Taras to life, and I've seen where they lead—into the ocean of our primordially pure consciousness. Now it's your turn. Jump in and bring the Taras alive for yourself and let them bring you back home to your true nature. I release attachment to the outcome of my labors, knowing that while this book is complete, Tara's manifestations could (and will) never be captured in the pages of any book. Despite this, my prayer is that the Taras you encounter on these pages bring you joy, liberation, and inspiration to bring the Tara's enlightened activities alive in you for the benefit of beings everywhere.

Acknowledgments

First, I would like to thank my mother, Jeanine Kuhrts, who first taught me to love Tara as a female buddha and the wisdom within myself. Always seeking knowledge of the sacred, she inspired me to know Tara for myself and to believe in her blessings. She gave me life, and she gave me Dharma. Thanks to my father, Bob Easton, who always encouraged me to be a creative and innovative thinker, to believe in myself, to question authority and religious dogmatism, and to have a great time doing it. I thank my stepfather and Dharma dad, Eric Kuhrts, who has been a steady inspiration to live a life devoted to the Dharma, handing me Dharma book gems at just the right times throughout my life. Gratitude to my kids, Tara and Tejas, who have inspired me and demanded that I live the Dharma with authenticity, providing many opportunities to love and practice, for as the saying goes, "Patience is the essence of Dharma." Both kids witnessed what it took to bring this book into being, cheered me on, and put up with me for these five years. I thank them for helping me "keep it real."

Learning root languages and sitting at the feet of great teachers is a way to honor their generosity. In this way I hope that this book contributes to a cultural exchange like those that occurred when the Dharma traveled to Tibet, China, Japan, Vietnam, Korea, and other places around the world. I hope that this book pays respect to the tradition while also responding to and providing what is needed in our day and age, honoring those who will come next by offering them something that I have found useful and liberating. This book is a weaving together of the kind and wise Dharma teachings I have received from my teachers over the past three decades, channeled through the prism of these twenty-one Taras. Whatever faults found on these pages are solely my own.

I am ever grateful to my teacher Lama Tsultrim Allione for her guidance throughout the years, particularly with respect to elevating women's voices in the Dharma and bringing this book into being. Venerable Khenpo Tsewang Dongyal Rinpoche has been an invaluable guide and resource, providing support, advice, and encouragement along the way. He generously met with me periodically to clarify areas of uncertainty regarding the meaning and mantras of each of the Taras, encouraging me to write about Tara in ways that would be accessible to Western readers. He, like Lama Tsultrim, reviewed and approved of the meditations I wrote at the end of each chapter.

I am indebted to His Holiness the Fourteenth Dalai Lama, His Holiness the Sixteenth Karmapa, Gyatrul Rinpoche, Dr. B. Alan Wallace, Lama Pema Dorje Rinpoche, Gochen Tulku Sang-ngag Rinpoche, and Venerable Drupla Tsampa Karma (a.k.a. Drupön Lama Karma) for their invaluable teachings and embodiment of the Dharma. I extend my deepest gratitude to my Tibetan language teachers, Dr. B. Alan Wallace and the late Ngawang Thondup Narkyid (a.k.a. Kuno-la) for imparting their knowledge of Tibetan language to me with such skill. I am grateful for Sanskrit scholars Dr. Vesna A. Wallace, Dr. Cogen Bohanec, and Prof. Christopher Tompkins for their guidance on my translations of the twenty-one Taras' names and mantras. Gratitude to Dr. Robert Svoboda for clarifying the meaning of the Taras' Sanskrit names. Thanks to my graduate advisor at the Graduate Theological Union, Dr. Richard Payne, who read drafts of my chapters and gave invaluable feedback, and to Dr. Robert A. F. Thurman for his teachings on Tara and enthusiastic encouragement along the way.

I would like to thank all the friends, family, and colleagues who offered invaluable support and love throughout this time. In particular, deep thanks to Nina Rao and Genevieve Walker for their encouragement and commitment to bringing the Taras alive through devotional chants and melodies, working with me to create melodies for each of the Tara mantras that will inspire and help people to learn the mantras through our 21 Taras Collective (www.21taras collective.org). I thank Dr. Eve Ekman for her wise encouragement and Dharma sisterhood. I also give thanks to my dear friend Jennifer Burke for her helpful feedback regarding the overall approach to the book and the real-life Taras. To Stacy Zumbroegel, a wise Dharma teacher in her own right, for her insights and support over the years.

Gratitude to my editors Casey Kemp, Tasha Kimmet, and Peter Schumacher. Casey believed in this project from the beginning and helped me see my capacity to bring this book to fruition. Tasha breathed fresh air into my sails, ever insightful and encouraging every step of the way. Peter came in later in the process and helped steward this book across the finish line. Lee Mirabai Harrington gave invaluable editorial guidance as the book took shape and evolved. She was not just my editor; she was a mentor who helped me understand the craft of writing a book. Thanks to Shambhala Publications for recognizing that they were the perfect home for this book on embodying Tara in her twenty-one manifestations within the Nyingma tradition.

I'd also like to thank Paula Crossfield for helping me to organize the hundreds of real-life Tara options I gathered over the years. Thanks to Jenny Terbell, writing teacher and Dharma sister, for editing the Tara sadhanas. Gratitude to Kevin C. Smith for reading the chapters and giving invaluable input, encouraging me when life challenges arose, and for his work on the bibliography; to Erik Jampa Andersson for his insights into the nature of various nature spirits ("The Sixth Tara"); to Susi Lupiner with her input on Amma's biography ("The Fifteenth Tara"); and to Bodhi Stroupe for helping with the graphics and fonts. I thank Karla Jackson-Brewer, Lopön Charlotte Rotterdam, Ellen Booth Church, Jiyeon Anjel Van Slyke, Isabelle Bailey, and Lisa Erickson for their encouragement over the years and for their shared devotion to the twenty-one Taras. Finally, deep gratitude to all who attended my twenty-one Taras retreats over the years who gave insightful feedback and suggestions on real-life Taras and other content. You all helped this book take the shape it has today.

A large amount of the writing of this book occurred at Tara Mandala, in the Liberated Lion retreat cabin, in southwest Colorado, and at Esalen, Big Sur, Northern California. Thanks to these two organizations for supporting my work. Annice Kenan and Jesse Smith generously offered their beautiful home on the Northern California coast for my writing retreat. Lastly, I want to give thanks to the entire Tara Mandala community for their support while I stepped back from various roles and duties to focus on the book.

Embodying Tara

Introduction

Tara, the beloved Buddhist goddess and female buddha of compassion, manifests in twenty-one different forms—some peaceful, others fierce—with different enlightened qualities that can help us through the joys and hardships we experience. Just as a ray of light hitting a prism creates a rainbow, when Tara's enlightened intent illuminates the prism of your own mind, it manifests as a myriad of colors, sounds, symbols, and moods that reveal her compassionate power. The twenty-one Taras' iconography, mantras, and enlightened activities are expressions of different enlightened qualities all radiating from the same source—the Great Mother, the womb of totality.

As a fully awakened buddha, Tara emerged from the slumber of ignorance that kept her separated from her true nature, true power, and true potential. In Tara we may find themes similar to our own life and ways we have or can overcome obstacles to heal and embody our true wisdom and power. Tara's story helps us wake up to the ways we are asleep in our lives, dulled by an ignorance that clouds our luminous true nature. Understanding Tara's facets and history—the roots of her traditions and spiritual practices that originated in India and spread to Tibet and elsewhere—we are more able to appreciate, practice, and ultimately embody her wisdom and compassion in our lives.

Each pair of eyes that alight upon these pages will drift down the river leading to the great ocean of primordial consciousness. Like candles floating on tiny leaf boats pushed out onto the River Ganga in the Hindu ritual called *arta* (whereby the candle represents our consciousness, and the river, the bridge between our outer and inner worlds), as you read this book, you will set off on your own voyage with Tara, each of you drifting in different directions as your life's currents take you. Tara may appear differently to each of you, as she has for practitioners and artists who have depicted her through the ages. She may not always show up for you as she does in Buddhist ritual statues and paintings; she may come in dreams, visions, or as an internal voice of wisdom to guide you. Stay open to this—she is closer than you think.

In the following pages, you'll encounter each of the twenty-one Taras with their mantras, symbolic meanings, and meditations, as well as learn how real-life women and broader movements embody her enlightened activities. You will see how Tara is within and around all of us as expressions of compassionate action and wisdom in the world. Compassion, an important theme in this book and Buddhism as a whole, is the heart that quivers in the face of suffering. As *the* female buddha of compassion, Tara and her twenty-one manifestations are expressions of this quivering heart activated by the commitment she made long ago to help beings be free of suffering. Tara is also the heart of compassion within each of us, a heart strengthened and tenderized by life's challenges and the loving connections we experience in times of need.

The stories of women in history—such as Harriet Tubman, Dipa Ma, Qiu Jin, and Jetsun Pema—that align with each Tara show how her compassionate activities can manifest in the world through each one of us. We will see how each woman's commitment to liberation in its many forms—gender, social, racial, environmental, or spiritual—helped them overcome obstacles in their own lives. This book will invite you to consider how you might do the same. Like all of us, the real-life women you will meet in these pages are not perfect, but they convey how we too can embody Tara despite our imperfections. These women whose work and activities emulate each Tara can be seen as guides for how we might navigate the sometimes stormy waves of our life with Tara's skill and compassion.

Through their stories, you will see Tara in a unique, intriguing, and dynamic light, whether you are meeting her for the first time or already know and love her.

Who Is Tara?

Let me first introduce you to the unique historical and spiritual figure of Tara. By knowing the *one* Tara—her origins and history, her iconography and symbolism—we can begin to know the *many* Taras we will meet in this book. On a deeper level, understanding the ultimate meaning of Tara—which is synonymous with the enlightened nature of our own mind—we are able to grasp her myriad manifestations; to recognize her all around us, in others, in nature, and in ourselves.

Like us, Tara is many things all at once. Tara is commonly known as Arya Tara ("Noble Tara") in Sanskrit and Jetsun Drölma in Tibetan. *Tara* means "she who helps to cross to the other shore" or "she who saves," signifying her power to help beings traverse the ocean of suffering (*samsara*) to the far shore of liberation (*nirvana*). She is primarily known for saving beings from fear and misfortune. She is the "Savioress" who leads us to our destination, like the North Star guiding us home. In fact, Tara's name also means "star," and she is often depicted as ferrying beings across the night sky in her boat, signaling the metaphor of stars guiding beings across the ocean of samsara.[1] In this way, we can understand Tara to be the light of our internal North Star that helps us navigate home to our true nature. We can understand Tara in the following ways:[2]

· Tara is a legendary princess who became a bodhisattva—one who commits to liberation for the benefit of all beings.
· Tara is a fully awakened buddha, the "Blessed One, Noble Tara" (Bhagavati Arya Tara).
· Tara is the wisdom *dakini*, or *khandroma* in Tibetan, meaning "sky-goer"—the ultimate nature of mind as expressed by the fierce power of the divine feminine.

· Tara is the mother of all buddhas, called the Great Mother in Tibetan (Yum Chenmo), who is synonymous with Prajnaparamita, the Perfection of Wisdom.

· Tara emanates as the twenty-one manifestations of her limitless enlightened activities.

· Tara is a tantric deity who bestows blessings and invites us to unify our consciousness with her and recognize that she is us and we are her.

· Tara is you at your most essential inner core, beyond individual identity of your sex, gender, name, and form; she is your own pristine awareness[3]—the innermost nature of mind.

Yet all these identities are not the *actual* Tara because the actual Tara is beyond label or concept. You may well ask: If she is beyond label or concept, then why should we try to define her? We do so as with everything in this world—by naming something, we help to bring it into being, to bring it into the foreground of our experience. We give her names and epithets to honor and understand her, write poetry to her, meditate on her, chant mantras to her, and embody her—and in so doing we find meaning in our own lives and traverse the ocean of our suffering.

Tara's Origins

There are various origin stories regarding Tara's life, each beautiful in its own way, but the one that speaks most poignantly to me is the version of Tara as the princess Wisdom Moon.[4] According to this origin story, Tara was a woman before becoming a deity. Legend says that many eons ago, the princess Wisdom Moon lived in a world system called Manifold Light where the Buddha named Drum Sound[5] also resided. A devoted student with profound faith in the Dharma, Wisdom Moon developed the desire to take the bodhisattva vow after years of study and practice. The bodhisattva vow is the commitment to work tirelessly toward enlightenment for the benefit of all beings, not just for oneself. When she expressed this wish to the abbot and monks at Buddha Drum Sound's monastery, they rejoiced in her aspiration but told her that she should first pray to be reborn as a man so that she could benefit more beings. At that time, it was commonly believed that beings were not able to attain liberation in a female body but must first be reborn as a man to pursue liberation. Dismayed by their small-minded misogyny, she replied:

> Here there is no man, there is no woman,
> No self, no person, and no consciousness.
> Labeling "male" or "female" has no essence,
> But deceives the evil-minded world.

And then she made this vow:

> There are many who desire enlightenment in a
> man's body, but none who work for the benefit of
> sentient beings in the body of a woman. Therefore,
> until samsara is empty, I shall work for the benefit
> of sentient beings in a woman's body.[6]

And this is exactly what she did. Buddha Drum Sound gave her the bodhisattva vow, and she brought her spiritual practice to culmination and attained liberation. To this day, she is said to continually dwell in a state of concentration called "saving all sentient beings." As a result, Drum Sound Buddha gave her the name Tara, the Savioress. Tara is called a bodhisattva in Mahayana Buddhism (Great Vehicle) and a buddha in Vajrayana Buddhism (Diamond Vehicle) where women tend to have a more elevated status than in earlier forms of Buddhism.

Another popular yet less empowering origin story says that Tara appeared in another eon called "Without Beginning" and arose from the heart (or teardrop) of Avalokiteshvara,[7] the male buddha of compassion. In this myth, she is referred to as the daughter of Avalokiteshvara and is said to have benefited innumerable beings through her blessings.

Tara was already well established in eastern India by the onset of the Pala empire in the eighth century before she began to travel abroad. As Buddhist traditions in their many forms were transmitted from India to other parts of Asia, Tara's traditions and practices traveled there as well. Tara appears in statues as far south as Sri Lanka; as far east as Myanmar, Cambodia, Java, Thailand, and the Philippines; and as far north and northeast as Tibet, Mongolia, and China. For example, in Myanmar, Tara was worshipped by various tantric monastic and lay communities up until the Bagan era (ninth to thirteenth centuries) as evidenced by stone statues, terra-cotta votive tablets, and mural paintings.[8]

Tara is believed to have first arrived in Tibet with the Nepalese princess Bhrikuti, who brought a sandalwood statue of Tara with her when she married the first great Tibetan king, Songtsen Gampo (c. 617–650 C.E.).[9] However, Tibetans credit the great Buddhist teacher Atisha Dipamkara (982–1054 C.E.) for bringing Tara's devotional practices and texts to Tibet on a grand scale in 1042. For this reason, let's learn more about Tara's role in Atisha's life, and subsequently his role in her renown across all schools of Tibetan Buddhism.

Tara as Spiritual Guide to Atisha

Atisha was born to a royal family in East Bengal. One day while he was still a baby, he was sleeping in his cradle outside on the upper story of the palace when his parents heard beautiful music coming from the sky. The queen looked up and saw a lotus falling from the sky, and simultaneously, the little prince's face transformed into Tara's face. Because of this, everyone believed that Tara must have been his tutelary deity (ishtadevata) for many prior lifetimes.[10]

Tara continued to appear in Atisha's life as he grew into adulthood. One story tells how Tara advised him to avoid marriage and devote his life to the Dharma due to his strong karmic potential for becoming a great spiritual teacher. Based on this vision, he took monastic vows and went on to be one of most renowned teachers at Vikramashila, a prestigious Indian Buddhist monastery during the Pala dynasty.

Another story tells of a dream Atisha had in which Tara told him that enlightenment is unattainable without bodhichitta, the compassionate wish to awaken for the benefit of all beings. This caused him to seek out the great teacher Dharmakirti, who was renowned for his realization of bodhichitta. Atisha made an arduous trek over land and sea to Sumatra to find him, remaining with him for twelve years while studying and practicing meditation. Eventually he returned to India where he settled at Vikramashila monastery, planning to live out his life in peace and solitude. Dharmakirti's instructions on bodhichitta were to become the seeds of Atisha's famous Mind Training (Lojong) teachings that he brought to Tibet years later. Mind Training is a Tibetan practice focused on cultivating compassion for others and generating bodhichitta.

Meanwhile, the Tibetan empire was beginning to thaw from two hundred years of political fragmentation and religious persecution. The newly established Tibetan king Jangchub Yeshe Ö (c. 959–1040 C.E.) was intent upon reviving the Dharma in his country and had heard of Atisha's renown. The king invited him to Tibet three times. Atisha was reluctant to make the arduous journey, but upon receipt of the third invitation, he prayed to Tara for guidance. In response, she appeared to him in a vision and told him that if he went to Tibet, he would benefit many beings, yet his life would be cut short. He decided that benefiting beings by spreading the Dharma was more important than living a long life, and so finally, in 1042, Atisha crossed the Himalayas into Tibet.[11] As Tara predicted, Atisha spent only the last twelve years of his life there, playing an instrumental role in the revival of the Dharma through teaching and translating texts, many of them devoted to Arya Tara, particularly Green and White Taras.

Tara, Teacher of Female Buddhist Masters

Tara also influenced one of the greatest female figures in Tibetan Buddhism: Machig Labdrön (1055–1154 C.E.), the founder of the Chöd ("Severance") tradition. The core aspect of Chöd practice, called the "body offering," enables practitioners to cultivate generosity through releasing identification with the physical body as the "self." The meditator visualizes that their consciousness ejects out through the crown of their head and becomes the fierce dakini Tröma (Krodhakali)—an aspect of fierce Tara—who oversees the body offering. Machig Labdrön also taught on the nature of mind based on the great traditions of Mahamudra (Great Seal) and Atiyoga, known as Dzogchen (Great Perfection) in Tibetan. Interestingly, Machig was born a year after Atisha's passing.

One night in the spring of her forty-first year while she was on retreat, Machig had a vision during her evening meditation in which Tara appeared to her surrounded by dakinis and gave her numerous empowerments and blessings. In gratitude, Machig bowed to thank Tara and then asked her how she, an ordinary woman, could bring such teachings to fruition and help all beings. With a loving smile, Tara replied:

> Yoginī, do not feel discouraged! In the course of previous lives you have studied and mastered the meaning of the scriptures of sūtra and tantra....You are a mind emanation of the Great Mother Yum Chenmo: we are inseparable. You are the wisdom ḍākinī, the sovereign of the great expanse [*vajradhātu*] and the source of liberation of all phenomena. Don't lose heart. Keep your determination.

Machig, still filled with doubt, replied:

> How could I possibly be an emanation of the Great Mother, inseparable from you? And in what way am I the source of the liberation of all phenomena? And where is the residence of the Great Mother?

To this, Tara replied:

> Yoginī, although in your innermost heart there is a clear knowledge about the past, listen carefully and I'll explain it to you. The

one known as the primordial Mother Yum Chenmo is the ultimate nature of all phenomena, emptiness, the essence of reality [*dharmatā*] free from the two veils. She is the pure expanse of emptiness, the knowledge of the nonself. She is the matrix which gives birth to all the buddhas of the three times. However, so as to enable all sentient beings to accumulate merit, the Great Mother appears as an object of veneration through my aspirations and prayers for the sake of all beings.[12]

This final statement of Tara is deeply moving and profound. Tara speaks directly to Machig's essential self-worth, reminding her who she really is—an emanation of the Great Mother, the matrix who gives birth to all the buddhas of the three times of past, present, and future. As an emanation of the Great Mother as well, Machig too is emptiness, the "essence of reality free from the two veils" that obscure our liberation. These two veils, or obscurations, are the five poisons and cognitive obscurations, namely, grasping at phenomena as truly existent. Tara says the Great Mother is everywhere as "the ultimate nature of phenomena, emptiness." She is you; she is me; she is everyone and everything because all phenomena have the quality of emptiness, meaning everything is interdependent and empty of intrinsic existence. I imagine this moment as a great crowning for Machig, from one woman (buddha) to another (human), an invitation for Machig to take her seat as an emanation of the Great Mother herself.

Ultimate Tara: The Great Mother, Yum Chenmo

The articulation of the Great Mother principle, or Yum Chenmo in Tibetan, arises in the early Mahayana Buddhist literature within *The Perfection of Wisdom Sutras* (*Prajnaparamita Sutras*) (c. 100 B.C.E. to 600 C.E.). It is here that we find the first appearance of ultimate reality articulated as a feminine principle. The "perfection of wisdom" as the mother of all buddhas is the experience of wisdom (*prajna*) that all beings must birth through to become perfect (*paramita*) buddhas. Around the sixth century, the perfection of wisdom teachings took form as a deity called the Great Mother. In her book *Women of Wisdom*, Lama Tsultrim Allione states,

> The Great Mother principle is the space that gives birth to the phenomenal world...[the perfection of wisdom] is the quality of sharp perception which comes with the relaxation of the ego. Meditation, because it slows down the confused grasping aspect of the mind, allows the natural luminous clarity of the mind, prajñā, to come forth. This faculty of profound cognition is the source of, or the womb for the Buddhas to grow in and is therefore called "the womb of the Buddhas."[13]

This Great Mother principle is the interdependent, empty nature of all phenomena, or *shunyata*, which comes from the Sanskrit word *shunya*, meaning "empty." The suffix *ta* signifies "ness." Together they form "emptiness." Yet shunyata can also be translated as "openness" or "open dimension of being." A direct realization of the empty nature of all phenomena, including one's own mind, results in the perception of reality *as it is*, or "suchness" (*dharmata*),[14] which is said to be utterly beyond the realm of language or conceptual thought. Thus, even though the Great Mother and her expression as Tara are beyond language and concept, they appear from the pure expanse of emptiness as objects of devotion so that beings may revere them and accumulate merit. Merit—or simply put, positive energy—is like fuel for our road trip from suffering to liberation—that is, to nirvana. Without a gas tank filled with good positive energy, one's spiritual evolution will stall out on the side of samsara's highway.

Tara as Dakini

Tara in her many forms is often called a wisdom dakini, which is synonymous with a fully enlightened buddha. *Dakini* is a Sanskrit term that is associated with the Tibetan word *khandroma*, which means "she who travels through space" or simply "sky-goer" or "sky-dancer."[15]

In early Indian forms of tantra[16]—a philosophy and set of practices that developed around the sixth century C.E., which takes its name from sacred instructional texts that describe rituals for invoking deities—dakinis were understood to be wild, wrathful, flesh-eating goddesses who lived in charnel grounds. It wasn't until tantric Buddhist teachings were brought in earnest to Tibet in the eighth century C.E. that dakinis gained a more elevated status—without losing their unpredictable, wild character—as holders of the sacred Buddhist teachings and embodiments of the most profound wisdom that erupts into a blissful unmediated experience of enlightenment.

While the ultimate expression of the dakini is "primordially vast space," ungraspable and ineffable, these sky-dancers may manifest to us as our spiritual muse, our inspiration for awakening here and now, as a human being, a goddess, or our subtle energy. As subtle energy, the dakini represents the ever-changing flow of energy (*prana*) with which the yogic practitioner must work to become realized. Alternatively, dakinis may be perceived as the general play of perception of our phenomenal world.

Even though the dakini principle is often spoken of as feminine, dakinis are known as gender-inclusive (both male and female) and beyond gender (neither female nor male).[17]

What Is Deity Yoga?

Throughout this book, we will practice embodying Tara through meditations based on deity yoga. This form of spiritual practice, called *sadhana*,[18] is an important part of Vajrayana Buddhism that gives us the opportunity to open to the healing energy of deities like Tara. Sadhana is a spiritual practice focused on transcending, yet including, the sense of self or ego to experience the divine within, the universal self, so to speak. Since deity yoga may be unfamiliar to many Western meditators, especially those who are new to

Buddhism or more familiar with mindfulness, vipashyana,[19] or Zen practices, let's look at a brief explanation of the practice of deity yoga here.

Deity yoga helps transform our normal assumptions of who we are, as in "Oh, I'm just Chandra with all my hopes and fears." It allows us to transcend this conventional way of experiencing ourselves to activate qualities in our own psyche that can become our inner guides. Through deity yoga, we honor and embody enlightened qualities within ourselves and water the seeds of our positive qualities so that our wisdom nature can flower within us. In deity yoga, we in essence transform our small self into the big vast, loving, awakened self of a buddha such as Tara. By unifying our mind with the enlightened mind of the deity, we replace that small-mindedness with the vast limitless mind of our buddha nature.

Deity yoga is a way to realize the Buddha's teachings of nonself, called *anatman* in Sanskrit. To experience nonself means to release our fixation on our limited ego, to loosen the illusory bonds that hold together the false sense of a solidly existing self, called *atman*. Not only did the Buddha teach that no intrinsic separate self exists, but he also taught that there is no creator god that instead everything comes into being not because of a god but rather due to causes and conditions in an infinite interconnected web of dependent origination, or *pratityasamutpada*.[20] You may well ask: If the Buddha taught there is no god, then why are there deities in Buddhism? Buddhist deities are not gods in the way we might think of them from a Judeo-Christian, Muslim, Hindu, or pagan sense of the term. Instead, they represent the enlightened aspects of your own true nature, which is primordially pure and manifesting as ceaseless compassion. In the beginning we may pray to a deity "out there," but ultimately we come to understand that the deity is none other than our own awakened mind.

Deity yoga is the ultimate form of self-esteem. Even from a vipashyana perspective, which is the insight into the empty nature of self and phenomena, deity yoga is a very profound method (*upaya*) because it shows us that our identity—the labels we put upon ourselves, that our family and our culture put upon us—is empty of intrinsic existence. Deity yoga can also provide us a sense of potency, joy, and well-being. Through practice we learn how to embody unconditional love and compassion through a vaster perspective and an appreciation for the beauty of existence.

The term *yoga* points to an important aspect of this practice as well. *Yoga* is derived from the Sanskrit verbal root √*yuj*, meaning "to yoke" or "to unify." It has a wide array of meanings that range from "union" to "spiritual endeavor."[21] The practice of yoga is found in both tantric forms of Hindu and Buddhist traditions, wherein the practitioner implements postures (*asana*), breath work (*pranayama*), gestures (*mudra*), mantra recitation (*mantra japa*), sacred geometry (*yantra* or *mandala*) visualization, and meditation (*dhyana*) all for the purpose of awakening.

In a nutshell, deity yoga utilizes the many aspects of the practice of yoga to unify one's own mind with the enlightened mind of the deity—recognizing that they in fact have never been separate. This brings us to the understanding that the nature of the mind is divine.

The Nature of Mind Is Divine

The true nature of mind is divine because it is without suffering—it is supreme bliss. The bliss, joy, and happiness that we feel when we drop into deep states of meditation—when we come home to our deepest sense of ourselves—is different from the relative happiness we feel in the ordinary world conditioned by circumstances. This experience of the divine infused with bliss is not a transitory feeling. It is a joy and contentment that are inherently within your own mind beyond the duality and constructs of your thinking. It is like a gold nugget at the core of your being that may have mud around it. It may be hiding beneath your obscurations, but it is not sullied by them.

This genuine and immutable bliss *is* itself the deity. The experience of our true nature is said to be bliss and emptiness commingling. There is bliss together with recognition of the open, empty vastness of our own mind. It is not a solid thing, and therefore we cannot cling to or grasp it. Bliss-emptiness is the deity and the essence beneath all the beautiful forms of the mantras, visualizations, and meditations we do in Buddhist tantra and in this book. And perceiving this is why we practice deity yoga.

Experiencing the divine nature of your own mind is like stepping off the edge into the abyss, and when you finally do, you realize that the abyss is bliss so there is nothing to fear. Instead of falling to your death, you learn to soar, like dakinis, because you realize there is no ground below you; there is just infinite and loving space where all aspects of yourself are welcomed. This is the embrace of the Great Mother. I call this the *abliss*. When standing at the threshold of the small self's dissolution, remember that the abyss is bliss.

Even simply reciting Tara's ten-syllable mantra with an open heart available to possibilities and blessings yet free of expectation is a way to begin to move toward the edge of the abliss. It's such an enticing yet terrifying threshold. Tara ferries us over the edge and across the ocean in her cosmic boat to the other shore—which is liberation. In fact, Tara's power to help us is based on the force of our own devotion and trust. If we can open our hearts to her without doubt and apprehension, we are more likely to experience her blessings. Bokar Rinpoche, in *Tara the Feminine Divine*, says,

> The creative faculty of our mind is very strong. It is this strength that exerts itself in the fervent prayer addressed to Tara. Together with Tara's immense will to help beings, this strength makes possible the protection. The help that we receive is the fruit of the meeting of these two factors, the force of our devotion and Tara's compassion.[22]

In essence, because all phenomena are interconnected, phenomena have no reality in and of themselves, thus they are said to be "empty of intrinsic existence." It is because of this interdependent, empty nature of phenomena that transformation and awakening are possible. Because our perceptions—thoughts, feelings, emotions, appearances—are expressions of the deep conditioning of our own mind, they are interdependent, arising due to causes and conditions, and because of that, our conditioned perceptions can be changed. This points to a malleability of existence and our perceptions—a cocreation of our reality. When we turn toward Tara with an open heart, a sense of wonder, and devotion, she will meet us halfway due to the immensity of her vast compassion.

Dissolving Duality

Tara is an aspect of our own inner knowing, whether she is a peaceful longevity Tara or a fierce Tara who cuts through delusion. If we realize the true nature of our mind, the deities reveal themselves as being no different from our own mind. But if we don't understand our true nature, if we are locked in the duality of self and other, good and bad, right and wrong, and so on, then deities enter the play of that dualistic relationship of self and other. Due to this, we have visions of deities as external to ourselves and experience these two poles of manifestation: me here and deity over there.

Let's take the analogy of a dream. Imagine that you are in a dream in which you (the subject) have a vision of Tara (the object). If you are not lucid in the dream, you will reify the duality of self (you) and other (deity). But when you wake up, all those appearances dissolve back into your substrate consciousness[23]—a very subtle and neutral level of consciousness in which our karmic seeds are stored—and you think, "Oh, all of those appearances were just in my mind." In your dream, both the appearance of the deity and your own self were expressions of your mind. When you wake up to ultimate truth, it's like becoming lucid in a dream, where you realize "self" and "other" are constructs and not ultimately true. The distinction between self and other does not ultimately exist. When you are lucid in a dream, you realize that *you* are the deity. This harkens to the famous Sanskrit mantra, SOHAM, "I am that," meaning I am none other than divine consciousness.

I want you to understand this from the very beginning so you don't idolize Tara as a real being outside of yourself that you must call to and earn love from. Don't forget that she is an expression of your true nature, but for the time being, because you have forgotten who you really are, you must do a little dance, a little warm-up, to get ready for the meeting of you and your buddha nature—the ultimate love story. It's a beautiful dance that we can enjoy.

This is where devotion comes in as dedication to that divine truth that sometimes feels like it is far away. At times we long for it, and at other times, it is right here in our heart, and we realize it has never gone anywhere. This is the dance of deity yoga, and we can think of it as a divine play of consciousness rather than something we have to do in order to earn some reward from an external god.

Buddhas like Yum Chenmo, Tara, Amitabha, and Avalokiteshvara manifest as *sambhogakaya*, "complete enjoyment body" luminous beings for the benefit of beings to inspire us, uplift us, and heal us through their blessings and to help us along on our spiritual path. Because they are already liberated, they don't need our devotion. But because we are still stuck in the subject-object duality of samsara, we need them to help us; they play the role of the external deity out there to our subjective sense of self in here to inspire us to keep putting one foot in front of the other on our spiritual path and not get disheartened. Eventually we learn to recognize that we have never been separate from them—that we are them and they are us. This opens us to experiencing coemergent joy and liberation if we open our hearts to the possibility.

The Luminous Net of the Twenty-One Taras

Around the second half of the eleventh century in India, Tara's twenty-one manifestations appeared in a text called the *Praises to the Twenty-One Taras* (hereafter referred to as the *Praises*).[24] The text, considered a long mantra (*dharani*), arose at a time when Buddhist tantra, also called Vajrayana, was prominent in India—a time when women were believed to be embodiments of wisdom (prajna) and therefore deserving of reverence.[25] The *Praises* was brought to

Tibet in the late twelfth century where it became the most popular hymn to Tara—and possibly any deity within Tibetan Buddhism. In Tibetan monasteries and households around the world, it is recited several times a day. It is common for Tibetans, both lay or monastic, to learn it by heart as children and recite it as part of their morning and evening prayers, making offerings to images of Tara on their household shrines.[26]

The first twenty-one verses of the *Praises* consist of Shakyamuni Buddha's words in honor of each of the Taras, in which he pays homage to her, highlighting her various aspects such as her color, features, enlightened activity,[27] and expression—peaceful, fierce, or semifierce. The Buddha supplicates Tara by interchangeably drawing upon her three epithets of Tare, Tuttare, and Ture that also form the core of her ten-syllable root mantra: OM TĀRE TUTTĀRE TURE SVĀHĀ. These three epithets are expressed in the famous prayer that abbreviates the *Praises* into a single verse received by Atisha directly from Tara:

> OM I prostrate to Perfect Ārya Mother Tārā.
> I prostrate to Mother Tārā, the heroine TĀRE.
> The mother TUTTĀRA[28] eliminates all fear.
> The mother TURE brings all success.
> I completely pay homage to the syllables, SVĀHĀ.[29]

You will see these epithets echoed in the stanzas from the *Praises* that I include at the beginning of each of the twenty-one Tara chapters, along with an explanation of their meaning.[30]

The twenty-one Tara pantheon is a luminous net that captures many of the "greatest hits" of goddesses that appeared in the vast South Asian subcontinent within both Buddhist and Hindu tantric traditions. For example, the second Tara, Vajra Sarasvati, is akin to the Hindu goddess Sarasvati. In both traditions, Sarasvati is beloved as the goddess of wisdom—she bestows eloquence and is associated with speech, poetry, composition, and all forms of communication.

The Iconography of the Twenty-One Taras

Tara is frequently the subject of paintings, sculptures, and illuminated manuscripts used in ritual practice throughout Tibet. Much of Tibetan Buddhist art is used for ritual and meditation practice and therefore must follow strict guidelines for how it is made. This is essential for the efficacy of any given practice to Tara. The iconography for Tara, as well as other Buddhist deities, often has a textual basis and can differ depending on the lineage portraying her.

Three Main Iconographic Lineages

There are three main iconographic traditions of the twenty-one Taras all based on various interpretations of the root text, the *Praises*. The earliest[31] tradition—and the one most studied by Western scholars—comes from the eleventh-century Kashmiri tantric adept Suryagupta,[32] who was miraculously cured of leprosy through the blessings of Tara. Afflicted by the disease, he sealed himself in a hut and prayed to her day and night. After three months, she spoke to him through the statue of Tara on his shrine and bestowed him with the *Praises,* saying that anyone who prays to her will be granted their wishes as well as the common and uncommon attainments.[33] The Suryagupta school depicts each Tara as having different details such as posture, number of heads and hands, color, implements, and hand gestures. It is the most complex of the three main iconographic systems and most commonly, but not exclusively, followed within the Sakya school of Tibetan Buddhism.

The second iconographic lineage is the Atisha tradition,[34] primarily followed by the Kagyu and Gelug schools. This tradition is associated with both Atisha and Nagarjuna[35] in which each of the Taras differ only with respect to their color, expression, and the color of the flask each holds in their outstretched right hand. Unlike the Suryagupta lineage, this tradition depicts each Tara in the same position: the "posture of royal ease," seated with the right leg forward and the left leg folded in.

The twenty-one Taras in this book, however, are based on the third iconographic lineage: the Longchen Nyingtig (Heart Essence of the Vast Expanse) system of the Great Perfection (Dzogchen) tradition in the Nyingma school. This system began with Longchen Rabjam (1308-1363 C.E.) and was synthesized by the great treasure revealer (Tib. *tertön*) of treasure texts (Tib. *terma*) Jigme Lingpa (1730-1798), one of the greatest Dzogchen teachers of Tibet.[36] Jigme Lingpa revealed the teachings during a three-year solitary retreat in a cave at Chimphu, near Samye Monastery, central Tibet. The Longchen Nyingtig tradition depicts each Tara as the same except for their color, expression, and the symbols atop the lotus flower each holds in their left hand.[37]

In Venerable Khenchen Palden Sherab Rinpoche's commentaries to the *Praises*, four levels of interpretation known as the "four methods" (*tshul zhi* in Tibetan) are given for each of the twenty-one Tara stanzas. These four levels are the word-for-word translation, the general meaning, the hidden meaning, and the ultimate meaning. The first two levels provide a solid foundation for understanding each of the Taras and their deity yoga practice. I have intentionally focused on them as appropriate for an introductory book on this subject. The third and fourth levels are advanced and require the guidance of a qualified spiritual teacher. For example, the third level focuses on the yogic interpretation of each stanza, drawing parallels between the words of the stanza and their symbolic meaning related to the subtle body—namely, the channels winds, and essence drops. The fourth level focuses on the interpretation of the stanzas in relation to the two final stages of Dzogchen practice, *trekchö* and *togal*, which require pointing-out instructions and close communication and guidance from a qualified lama.

Longchen Nyingtig Iconographic Tradition

Let's explore Tara's iconography in the Longchen Nyingtig tradition in more detail so that you can connect with and understand the meaning behind her symbols.

POSTURE: Tara is seated in the "posture of royal ease," sometimes called the "horse dismounting posture," with her right leg slightly forward as if stepping into the world, symbolizing her compassionate activity within samsara. Her left leg is tucked in, with her heel close to her perineum, showing that she is fully seated and rooted in the supreme bliss of nirvana. Her position tells us that she holds both these truths within her at once. Her posture is fluid, and she is swaying at her waist, leaning a bit to her left. Nothing about Tara is stiff and static, for she is ever-moving and swift like the wind, ready to come to the aid of beings when called upon.[38]

HAND GESTURES: Tara's left hand is in the Three Jewels, or Protection, gesture (mudra) and holds the stem of a blue lotus (*utpala*) between her thumb and ring finger. The joining of the tips of these two fingers symbolizes the union of wisdom and compassion. The other three fingers fan out, upright, symbolizing the Three Jewels—the Buddha, Dharma, and Sangha—the objects of refuge in Buddhism. Taking refuge in the historical Shakyamuni Buddha, his teachings that lead beings out of suffering (Dharma), and the community of fellow practitioners on the path (sangha) is what defines being a Buddhist.

Tara's right hand is in the gesture of Supreme Generosity, with her palm up, resting on her right knee. This symbolizes her unending commitment to openly offer compassion and liberation to all beings without distinction. Sometimes there is a an eight-spoked dharma wheel (*dharmachakra*) on the palm of her right hand. The eight spokes representing the Noble Eightfold Path to enlightenment taught by Shakyamuni Buddha (see "The Ninth Tara"). This dharma wheel emits swirling rainbow wisdom light in all directions, protecting and liberating all beings from samsara, the ultimate gift.

ATTRIBUTES: Each Tara holds the blue lotus flower (utpala; *Nymphaea caerulea*), which signifies her enlightened mind. Upon each Tara's lotus is a symbol indicating her enlightened activity. For instance, the conch shell indicates the healing sound of the Dharma, the dharma wheel symbolizes the Noble Eightfold Path, the endless knot represents interdependence, and so on. The eight auspicious symbols of Buddhism are found in this system along with thirteen additional symbols.

COLOR: Each Tara's color signifies her connection with one of the directions in the buddha family mandala—which we will go over soon. For example, the fifth Tara Kurukulla is red and magnetizing like other deities who belong to the western dimension of the mandala.

EXPRESSION: Each Tara also has an expression or mood—peaceful, fierce, or semipeaceful/semifierce.[39] The latter can be understood in some contexts as joyful[40]—peace cojoined with fierce wakefulness. I will call deities with a semipeaceful/semifierce expression simply semifierce or joyful depending on the context. Generally, the expression of the deity represents the transmutation of one of the three poisons of Buddhism—ignorance, attachment, and aversion—into wisdom. Peaceful deities represent the transmutation of ignorance; fierce deities represent transmutation of aversion; and semifierce deities represent the transmutation of attachment.

EYES: At times Tara is depicted as having three eyes, with the third eye at the center of her brow. At other times, she is described as having seven eyes: her three eyes plus one eye on each of her palms and the soles of her feet, symbolizing her ability to see all the suffering in the world with great compassion. In fact, all the Taras have seven eyes, but they are not always emphasized in visual and written renditions.

JEWELRY AND ORNAMENTS: All sambhogakaya (complete enjoyment body) deities—buddhas like the twenty-one Taras who appear to those with high realization to teach them through visionary experiences—wear various garments and jewelry that have significance. These are classically called the Thirteen Sambhogakaya

Ornaments and include the eight jewel ornaments (crown, earrings, choker, long necklace, upper armlets, wrist bracelets, anklets, rings) and five silken ornaments (headband, upper garment, long scarf, belt, lower garment).

LOTUS THRONE AND MOON DISC: Tara, like most Buddhist deities, sits on a lotus-and-moon-disc throne. Generally, the lotus represents our human capacity, imbued with buddha nature, to grow from the muck of samsara and bloom into a fully awakened buddha, just like the lotus flower grows from the dark muddy waters toward the sun and blooms into a beautiful blossom. If the lotus does not have the sunlight to lure it toward the surface of the water, it does not "burst through" (another meaning of *utpala*) the water's surface. In this same way, the Buddha's teachings are like the sunlight that draws us up out of suffering, luring us to grow and mature into our potential as fully ripened, awakened beings—buddhas. All the Taras in the Longchen Nyingtig system are also seated upon a moon disc that represents bodhichitta.[41]

EIGHT OFFERING BOWLS: Eight offering bowls are shown placed on a shrine in front of Tara. Each bowl represents an offering that one would make to a spiritual teacher if that teacher were to come to your home or temple: washing water, drinking water, flowers, incense, candlelight, perfume, food, and music.

Tara and the Five-Buddha-Family Mandala

The iconography of the twenty-one Taras is connected to the system of the five-buddha-family mandala. The mandala is a sacred template for transforming our mental and emotional afflictions of the five poisons into wisdom through color, sound, and imagery to attain awakening. As sacred geography, the mandala consists of five dimensions—a center and four quadrants—each associated with a buddha family, creating the framework to move from fragmentation to wholeness. In Buddhist art, the mandala functions

EAST
Family: Vajra (adamantine)
Color: Blue
Element: Water
Poison: Anger, aversion
Wisdom: Mirror-like wisdom
Enlightened Activity: Pacifying
Symbol: Vajra

NORTH
Family: Karma (action)
Color: Green
Element: Air
Poison: Jealousy
Wisdom: All-accomplishing wisdom
Enlightened Activity: Subduing
Symbol: Double vajra or sword

CENTER
Family: Buddha (illuminated)
Color: White / crystal clear
Element: Space
Poison: Ignorance, delusion
Wisdom: All-encompassing wisdom
Enlightened Activity: Basis of all enlightened activity
Symbol: Eight-spoked wheel

SOUTH
Family: Ratna (jewel)
Color: Yellow
Element: Earth
Poison: Conceit, arrogant pride
Wisdom: Wisdom of equality
Enlightened Activity: Enriching
Symbol: Ratna

WEST
Family: Padma (lotus)
Color: Red
Element: Fire
Poison: Craving, attachment, desire
Wisdom: Wisdom of discernment
Enlightened Activity: Magnetizing
Symbol: Padma

The Five-Buddha-Family Mandala
(adapted with permission from Bodhi Stroupe)

as a meditative support, like a map of awakening and purification. Through meditating on the mandala, we gradually purify the five mental afflictions (*kleshas*), also called the five poisons, of ignorance, aversion, conceit, attachment, and jealousy and allow the five primordial wisdoms of all-encompassing wisdom, mirrorlike wisdom, wisdom of equanimity, wisdom of discernment, and all-accomplishing wisdom to reveal themselves. The deities associated with each of the families of the mandala correspond to the five primordial wisdoms manifesting as sambhogakaya deities.

Each of the twenty-one Taras' colors—and sometimes her symbols—relate to this buddha-family mandala symbolism. For example, Green Tara belongs to the northern karma (action) buddha family associated with the color green that represents the wind element. This is why Green Tara is said to be swift like the wind in aiding sentient beings in need. Often karma deities are shown in profile to signify that they are always moving, like the wind. You can learn more about each buddha family's symbolism in the five-buddha-family mandala diagram as well as throughout the Tara chapters.

The mandala structure pertinent to the twenty-one Taras comes from the Nyingma system in which the central buddha family color is almost always white—more accurately crystal clear, which is represented by the color white in paintings and statues—and the eastern vajra family color is blue. In other systems, like the Kagyu lineage, these two colors are reversed. Apart from this, the colors and their meanings are consistent throughout the lineages of Tibetan and Himalayan Buddhist iconography.

Embodying Tara through Deity Yoga

This book is all about embodiment. Many of us look to meditation in the hopes of relieving our suffering, not to mention attaining enlightenment. And perhaps the main type of meditation we know is a kind of emptying of the mind based on focusing on the breath and not attaching to any thoughts that arise. But another method of meditation we can employ is to embody deities such as Tara. Embodying deities through meditation, visualization, and mantra recitation helps us experience our true nature because we discover our mind is none other than the enlightened mind of the deity. The deity yoga we will learn in this book is the key through which embodiment occurs.

Mind Transforming Mind

Over the two decades I have taught meditation, I have noticed a common misperception that meditation is just emptying your mind and being as nondiscursive as possible. This is one way to meditate, and it has great merit, but it is not the only way. Psychonauts or inner space travelers of old, including Shakyamuni Buddha, saw the value of using the mind to transform the mind, employing meditations in which we consciously bring to mind images and feelings that help us cultivate certain beneficial qualities such as love, compassion, joy, and equanimity. Other forms of meditation may include reciting mantras and visualizing seed syllables (*bija mantra*), buddhas, or rays of light emitting from and reabsorbing into us and all sentient beings. We can understand these forms of meditation as *discursive* in nature, and they are mostly found in the Buddhist tantric form of meditative practice called deity yoga where we work with the creative capacity of our minds to bring about compassion, bliss, concentration, and wisdom.

Both discursive and nondiscursive meditations have been employed effectively by practitioners for centuries at various times in their life, depending on what is needed at any given moment. In this book you will experience both discursive and nondiscursive meditations as well. While deity yogas like the twenty-one Tara meditations fall within the discursive meditation category, all of them have nondiscursive aspects of simply resting in awareness, too. In this way, deity yoga practice is an exquisite balance of doing (discursive) and undoing (nondiscursive) approaches to meditation.

Shamatha and Vipashyana in Deity Yoga Practice

Most people who have some experience with Buddhism are familiar with calm-abiding (*shamatha*) and insight (*vipashyana*) meditations. Shamatha is both the name of the meditative technique and its result, which includes but is not limited to the popular practice of mindfulness of breathing, for cultivating relaxed, stable, single-pointed concentration. It prepares us for insight, or vipashyana, which is also the name of the meditative practice and its result. Insight is the experience of directly seeing into the empty nature of reality, including the nature of our own mind. When we experience the quiescence of shamatha, we experience the *blissful nature* of our own mind. When we realize vipashyana, we experience the *empty essence* of mind and appearances. Shamatha without vipashyana will not uproot the karmic seeds that keep us cycling around in samsara. Likewise, vipashyana without shamatha will slip through our fingers due to a lack of mental stability and only bring temporary benefits. The Buddha taught that shamatha is the basis upon which vipashyana occurs and that bringing these two practices to fruition is imperative for attaining liberation.[42]

In deity yoga, shamatha can be cultivated by means of visualization and mantra recitation. For example, in the Tara meditations, we will visualize ourselves as Buddha Tara, a body of light, not flesh and bone. As Tara, we will recite her mantra while imagining that light emanates from our hearts to all beings and reabsorbs back into us. This brings about a clear, single-pointed, and stable attention; thus, it is considered a method for cultivating shamatha. This phase of practice is called the creation stage,[43] whereby by we "create" ourselves as the deity using our imagination and purify obscurations veiling our buddha nature. While creation-stage meditation can lead to shamatha, it is also important and useful to augment deity yoga with the more foundational techniques of shamatha and vipashyana, such as mindfulness of breathing, common practices found in all Buddhist traditions.[44]

In terms of vipashyana in deity yoga, when we rest in the dissolution after the mantra recitation, we rest in the nature of the mind itself (*chittatva*).[45] The term *nature of mind* describes the true and natural state of mind, just as it is; it is synonymous with buddha nature. Resting in the nature of mind is the fruit of the practice and is called the completion stage,[46] whereby we release all effort and rest in the natural perfection of mind, where everything is complete as it is. This is the union of bliss and emptiness. This is the ultimate meaning of vipashyana, or insight.

Tara's Ten-Syllable Mantra

Mantra recitation is an essential element of deity yoga. In fact, Vajrayana is also called Mantrayana, the "Path of Mantra." Tara's ten-syllable mantra is one of the most recited mantras in Tibetan Buddhism. While each of the twenty-one Taras in this book has her own mantra, this main ten-syllable mantra may be recited for all the Taras as a "universal access" mantra. It is the basis upon which all the twenty-one Tara mantras are formed.

ༀ་ཏཱ་རེ་ཏུཏྟཱ་རེ་ཏུ་རེ་སྭཱ་ཧཱ།

OṂ TĀRE TUTTĀRE TURE SVĀHĀ

OM TARE TUTTARE TURE SVAHA

OṂ! Tara! Be swift, Tara! So be it!

Tara's Seed Syllable

TĀṂ ཏཱཾ

Seed syllables are the essential sounds that ignite the warmth of a particular deity in your consciousness. When we make the sound TĀṂ, we feel Tara come alive in us and the world; we connect with her ultimate meaning. TĀṂ is like the stem cell of Tara—the most direct route to access her and the source from which her blessings and manifestations come. TĀṂ symbolizes the unborn nature of all the Taras, the unconditioned nature of absolute, unmanifest space.

While both nirvana and samsara are, in essence, empty of intrinsic existence, they manifest differently according to our perceptions. Nirvana manifests as bliss, while samsara manifests as suffering. From the ultimate perspective they are the same, but from the relative perspective they are different: samsara is suffering based on ignorance, while nirvana is liberation based on an absence of ignorance. Tara's seed syllable represents the empty and unborn nature of samsara *and* nirvana.

Occasionally, various Taras will have alternative seed syllables. For example, the second Tara, Vajra Sarasvati, has the seed syllable HRĪM in her mantra. The twenty-first Tara, Marichi, has the BHRŪM syllable in hers. However, TĀM is the default seed syllable for all the Taras.

Three Samadhis: Emptiness, Compassion, and the Union of the Two

In the Nyingma tradition of Vajrayana Buddhism, deity yoga is practiced by means of the three samadhis or meditative absorptions:[47] samadhi of suchness (emptiness), all-illuminating samadhi (compassion), and the seed samadhi (union of emptiness and compassion).

The samadhi of suchness is the nature of emptiness, ultimate bodhichitta. It is the primordially pure *dharmakaya* (truth body) and the Great Mother Prajnaparamita beyond name and form. Deity yoga practice requires this foundation of emptiness to ensure that we do not stumble into the pitfall of reifying the deity and ourselves as intrinsically existing. Emptiness, like space, pervades all of existence. The fruition of meditating on emptiness in deity yoga, particularly the completion stage, is the experience of bliss, clarity, and nonconceptuality. In particular, this first samadhi is associated with nonconceptuality, as experienced when all appearances have dissolved and you rest in empty, luminous awareness at the end of each Tara sadhana.

The second—all-illuminating samadhi—is the cultivation of compassion; this is relative bodhichitta. The essence of emptiness *is* compassion. Emptiness and compassion are like two wings of the bird of enlightenment—we need them both to reach our destination. If we only have one of the two wings, we will fly in circles. Within the context of practice, we arouse the compassionate motivation to practice for the benefit of all beings, understanding that all beings desire happiness and freedom from suffering. When practicing deity yoga, meditating on emptiness is not enough. When we sincerely wish to be of benefit to others, that is the luminous aspect of emptiness manifesting as compassion. It is like the sun (emptiness) naturally manifesting light rays (compassion) to bring warmth to all beings.

The third—seed samadhi—is the union of emptiness and compassion. Dilgo Khyentse Rinpoche says, "Emptiness, which clears away the phenomenal world, and compassion, which arises for all beings who have not realized emptiness, are inseparable. Going to the core of compassion, we come to emptiness. There is no compassion other than emptiness. This nondual essence of emptiness and compassion takes the form of a seed syllable."[48] When practicing the creation stage in which we imagine ourselves as the deity, the seed samadhi is the seed syllable from which the deity arises; this is the seed samadhi *with* form. The seed samadhi *without* form is the very nature of our own mind, the union of emptiness and compassion.

The role of these three samadhis will become more apparent in the Tara sadhanas that follow. When we recite Tara's seed syllable TĀṂ three times, the first time we imagine that we arise as Tara; this is the *samayasattva*,[49] the "commitment being." The second time, we imagine sending rainbow wisdom light to numerous wisdom beings (*jnanasattva*[50]) in the sky above us. The wisdom beings are the twenty-one Taras, your lineage teachers, buddhas, bodhisattvas, dakinis, *dakas* (male counterparts to dakinis), protectors, and knowledge holders. The third time, we imagine that the wisdom beings send rainbow wisdom light back to us, blessing and empowering us, and we become fully activated as Tara. Embodying Tara, we imagine that a luminous and finely written TĀṂ syllable is in our heart center; this is called the *samadhisattva*,[51] the "meditative absorption being." This TĀṂ in our heart is the essence of the deity; it is our primary anchor in the meditation practice that brings about meditative absorption and union with our nature. As Tara, we recite her mantra and enact her enlightened activities through the visualization of rainbow light emanating to all beings and filling all of space.

If this feels challenging, don't worry, it will come. Over time, you will gain familiarity with the practice—its beauty and depth will reveal themselves to you. Be patient and open to the alchemy of these tantric meditative practices that have been passed down through centuries by realized masters who brought liberation to consummation through the practice of deity yoga.

How to Read This Book

The *Praises to the Twenty-One Taras*, which contains a stanza or praise about each of the twenty-one emanations of Tara, forms the basis for my discussion of the Taras in each chapter of this book. In the introduction to each Tara, I offer my own English translation of the original Tibetan stanza.[52] At the beginning of each chapter, I include a word-for-word English translation of the Sanskrit and Tibetan versions of each of the twenty-one Tara's names to illuminate her enlightened activities. In the appendix you will find her Sanskrit names with diacritics and her Tibetan names in Wylie transliteration. I also offer an easily readable version of each Tara's Sanskrit mantra (along with the Sanskrit diacritics for those who prefer that). These mantras appeared to Jigme Lingpa in meditative visions, called *terma*, and were subsequently transcribed into Tibetan from the original Sanskrit. Khenpo Tsewang Dongyal says that while it is optimal to receive empowerment and oral transmission, they are not needed to recite the twenty-one Tara mantras, and he encouraged me to include the mantras in this book.

Then we will explore each of the Taras from a number of perspectives. You will learn about their symbols, the meaning of their praises, and the facets of their expressions. You'll also meet real-life examples of the Taras that bring them into a modern perspective. Then you'll have the opportunity to reflect on how each Tara shows up in your own daily life or how you can bring that connection into being.

Finally, we'll practice deity yoga with each Tara. My aspiration is that by doing these meditations, you will come to know each Tara intimately. Unifying your mind with the enlightened mind of Tara, you will feel in your bones how to enact each Tara's enlightened activities. The meditations invite you to explore your identity by trying on the deities' clothes so to speak and letting your usual identity fade into the background. In so doing, you may feel for a short period of time what it would be like to be a buddha.

Note on the Meditations at the End of Each Chapter

Each Tara meditation structure is similar, with the goal of providing a basic framework for the practice of each Tara. These sadhanas are also a way to learn each Tara's characteristics, mantra, and enlightened activities so that you can draw upon them whenever you want. Feel the practice of deity yoga not as a creation of something foreign outside of you but as a coming home to who you really are deep within. Feel it as a simple, pure, and joyful endeavor, a reunion with your natural state.

The first Tara chapter includes the full-length deity yoga meditation for the first Tara. Think of it as your meditation template. The subsequent Tara chapters provide condensed versions for each Tara meditation. Use the complete sadhana in "The First Tara" as your framework for all subsequent Taras until you are familiar with the structure of the practice and no longer need it. If you would like to add your own personal opening and closing prayers to this practice, I encourage you to do so, though it is not necessary.

In addition to practicing the twenty-one Tara meditations, engage with the personal practice called "Journey with Tara" and a journaling exercise at the end of the book. I encourage you to do the Journey after all the Tara sadhanas to engage more intimately with Tara. You may also do the Journey as a stand-alone practice.

Now let's dive into the multifaceted world of the twenty-one Taras.

DRÖLMA NYURMA PAMO
(SKT. TARA TURAVIRA)

The First Tara

Tara the Swift Heroine

Homage to Tara, swift heroine
Whose eyes flash like lightning.
Born from the blooming pistil of the lotus face
Of the Lord of the Three Worlds.

Welcome to the world of the first Tara, whose power removes obstacles and increases bodhichitta, the compassionate wish to awaken for the benefit of oneself and others. As her name and homage imply, Tara the Swift Heroine is quick as the wind, protects beings from fear, and liberates them from suffering. She is red in color and has a semifierce disposition. She is fully activated dynamic energy, always infused with love and joy but never wrath. She is bliss and power manifest in a fantastic state of orgasmic potency arising from the dynamic collision of opposites: peace and fierceness/ferocity.

Tara Turavira in Sanskrit means "Savioress (*Tara*), the Swift (*tura*) Heroine (*vira*)." The Tibetan rendering of her name, Drölma Nyurma Pamo, means essentially the same thing: "Savioress (*Drölma*), the Swift (*nyurma*) Heroine (*pamo*)." Thus, we get Tara the Swift Heroine, or we could call her Tara the Swift Liberatrix.

Her Mantra

ༀ་ཏུ་རེ་ཏུ་རྟུ་རེ་ཏུ་རེ་བོ་དྷི་ཙིཏྟ་སྭཱ་ཧཱ།

OM TĀRE TUTTĀRE TURE BODHICITTA SVĀHĀ
OM TARE TUTTARE TURE BODHICHITTA SVAHA
OM! Tara! Be swift, Tara! Bodhichitta! So be it!

Her Symbol: The Conch Shell

Atop this Tara's blue lotus is the right-spiraling conch shell,[1] the first of the eight auspicious symbols.[2] This sacred conch is "self-blowing," meaning that there is a natural self-arising sound emanating from it that symbolizes the healing sound of the Dharma—the soothing words of the Buddha that awakens us from the slumber of ignorance, consoling and giving us hope, purpose, and perspective. In the early days of Buddhism, the conch became a logo of sorts for the Buddha's teachings.

The conch also highlights one of Tara Turavira's primary themes, bodhichitta, which is essential for the spiritual path. Bodhichitta has two aspects: relative and ultimate. Relative bodhichitta is the aspiration to awaken for the benefit of all beings. Ultimate bodhichitta is the direct realization of the empty interdependent nature of the mind and all phenomena. Hearing the sound of the conch, we remember our basic humanity, our innate goodness, our buddha nature, and our potential for awakening. We experience healing; our fears and anxieties are released; and we become more whole and satisfied in our life.

In Buddhist and Hindu traditions, the sound of the conch shell is an ancient calling to gather for ceremony, community, and practice. It also symbolizes purity and the triumph of good over evil. We might hear it say, "Come forth, here is something special, the sound of the Dharma, of truth, of justice, be healed through this sound." When we meditate on Tara Turavira, we imagine that the healing sound of the conch and Tara's love extend to all beings everywhere in all directions, feeling that every being is receiving this healing love.

Exploring the Facets of Tara Turavira

Now that you've met Tara Turavira, let's tease out the meaning surrounding her a bit more to bring her alive within the world and ourselves. She is the first to appear in this pantheon of the twenty-one Taras, bringing electrifying dynamism, bliss, and joy. Her red color indicates that she is connected to the lotus family of buddhas. The lotus energy magnetizes all good things; it allures beings toward ultimate satisfaction, which is liberation from the suffering of samsara. In tantra, red is the color of passion, blood, sensuality, and desire. The lotus family energy transforms the mental affliction of clinging into discerning wisdom.

Tara Turavira sees clearly with discernment, love, and passion for life and liberation. With furrowed brow, her eyes "flash like lightning," meaning that they are wide open, blazing with electrifying power. She bears witness to the world with all its suffering and joy, illuminating the darkness like a flash of lightning, and showing us that we too can be strong in the face of chaos, tragedy, and beauty.

The great compassion of Tara Turavira is seen in the next lines from the *Praises*: "Born from the blooming pistil of the lotus face / Of the Lord of the Three Worlds." This refers to the origin story for Tara in which she was born from Avalokiteshvara's tears when he witnessed the suffering of sentient beings. The "Lord of the Three Worlds" is an epithet for Avalokiteshvara who reigns over the worlds of the serpentine beings (*naga*)[3] below, the gods above, and the humans in the middle. In Jigme Lingpa's commentary on the *Praises*, he poetically states, "From [Avalokiteshvara's] eyes, which are like the center of the lotus flower of his beautiful face, appeared two tears of strong compassion for all sentient beings. From the tear of his right eye appeared white Tara and from the tear of his left eye appeared green Tara. I pay homage to you, Noble Lady Tara, with devotion, from my heart."[4] This stanza can be understood to celebrate Tara in all her many manifestations, colors, and expressions. Of greatest import is understanding how this first stanza highlights the connection between Tara and Avalokiteshvara as well as the lotus buddha family affiliation of both deities; like Tara, Avalokiteshvara is a "complete enjoyment body" emanation of the lotus family buddha Amitabha, the Buddha of Immeasurable Light, sometimes also called Amitayus.

Tara may at times appear in our dreams or meditations, swiftly and compassionately coming to our aid, as we saw with Suryagupta when he was cured of leprosy by praying to Tara. It can be beneficial to pray to Tara in times of great need to open to the potential of healing, though this by no means implies that we do not seek professional help when ill or struggling. For instance, when Kalu Rinpoche (1905–1989) had just sealed his boundaries for a three-year solitary retreat—once you have closed your retreat boundaries, you aren't supposed to come out even if you are dying—he got a tooth infection, which he knew could be deadly. One night, he had a dream of a red Tara in which she came to him and said, "If you recite 10,000 of my mantras, I will heal you. Even though you've never prayed to me before, I will heal you if you pray to me now." So he prayed to her and recited her mantra 10,000 times. After this, his tooth infection healed and he was able to complete his three-year solitary retreat.

This story shows us that we, too, may develop a connection with Tara through meditation, mantra recitation, and prayer. By so doing we create a bridge, an interconnection with Tara, to receive her blessings. Experiment with this, without having a transactional mindset of expecting anything in return, but rather keeping a sense of openhearted longing and devotion. I am not promising she will come to you and heal your aches and pains or bestow material boons, but rather I am encouraging you to open to the possibilities of Tara showing up in your life in ways you could never imagine and see what happens.

Real-Life Embodiments

We likely know women who embody the qualities of Tara Turavira: her swift fearlessness, her bodhichitta, her capacity to remove obstacles and help others. When I began looking, I found many historical and contemporary women with these qualities, two of whom I will share with you here.

Harriet Tubman

The primary embodiment of Tara Turavira that kept coming back to me loud and clear was none other than Harriet Tubman (c. 1822–1913). Tubman is an American icon of near-mythic proportions because she was instrumental in leading hundreds of enslaved people out of Maryland to safety in Pennsylvania on the 100-mile Underground Railroad from 1850 to 1860. Swift and compassionate like Tara Turavira, Tubman guided others out of suffering, removing their obstacles to freedom.

In 1849, at the age of twenty-seven, Tubman herself escaped from Maryland to Pennsylvania on the Underground Railroad. While there, she met William Still, the Underground Railroad agent famous for recording the stories of the freedom seekers who came through his state. Not content with her freedom alone, Tubman implored Still to allow her to join his organization and return to Maryland to liberate others. Tubman's nineteen journeys on the Underground Railroad, risking her own life and freedom, prove how she embodied Tara Turavira's compassionate wish to be of service to others.

While she was enslaved, Tubman experienced brutality and cruelty. She was rented out beginning at age six. At thirteen, she was hit with a two-pound weight aimed at a runaway slave, an injury that initiated the epileptic seizures she would suffer from the rest of her life. She also started experiencing visions and prophetic dreams in which God would tell her which way to go to avoid getting caught by slave owners.

While on the Underground Railroad, Tubman carried a gun, but not just for protection. If someone got scared and wanted to go back, she wouldn't allow it and was known for never losing a single person—no one was caught or killed under her watch. This reminds me of the fierce love of Tara Turavira, which may seem fierce at times but is always imbued with caring, passion, and discerning intelligence.

Being a woman did not hinder Tubman's determination to help

others find freedom, and by the end of the Civil War, she had escorted 700 men, women, and children out of slavery.

Later in her life, Tubman worked with Susan B. Anthony during the suffrage movement advocating for women's rights. When she was asked if she believed women should have the right to vote, she replied, "I suffered enough to believe it."

Susan Burton

Now let's look at someone representing the modern-day spirit of Tara Turavira. Susan Burton is founder and executive director of A New Way of Life Reentry Project, an organization that provides safe houses for women coming out of prison so that they can live with their children and families and get back on their feet. As a formerly incarcerated Black woman, Burton is a powerful leader for the movement to reform the criminal legal system in the United States.

Burton grew up in South Central Los Angeles, California, where she had a difficult childhood, experiencing abuse and neglect. After her five-year-old son was hit and killed by a police officer driving in front of her house, she self-medicated her pain with drugs and alcohol and cycled in and out of the prison system. Eventually, through her own recovery in a 100-day program in Los Angeles, she saw how she could break free from addiction and help others.

Burton learned to transform the affliction of addiction, another form of craving, into discerning wisdom—one of Tara Turavira's lotus family enlightened qualities. She shares this discernment through her advocacy work, teaching others how to make choices that will benefit themselves and their families. This is the very embodiment of compassion in action. Burton modeled A New Way of Life after the Alcoholics Anonymous (AA) 12-step program in which participants are guided to do their own inner inventory, looking back through their lives at those they hurt and those who hurt them, and by that introspection to begin to understand the causes and conditions of where they are today. Replicating the reentry model of A New Way of Life—which has a 97 percent success rate of women staying out of prison—Burton also created the SAFE (Sisterhood Alliance for Freedom and Equality) Housing Network.[5]

Burton has often been called a "modern-day Harriet Tubman" by those who have studied and written about her life, and she fittingly received the Harriet Tubman Legacy Award in 2022 for her work.

Further Contemplations

Now that you have met Tara Turavira and two women who embody her attributes, I invite you to think of other women you know with the qualities of discernment, compassion, swift action, and a commitment to help others who may be suffering. Contemplate how you might water these seeds within yourself as well. How might obstacles in your life become or be viewed as opportunities for growth and learning in your life? Journal about it, talk with friends, and explore ways to embody Tara Turavira—pray to her and find ways to step out, like Tara, into the world to help others.

The compassion practice, called *tonglen* (sending and receiving) in Tibetan, is a very powerful technique for cultivating bodhichitta. Like the popular Buddhist practice of loving-kindness, or *metta*[6] in the Pali language, tonglen promotes greater compassion and understanding in the practitioner. I encourage you to do the guided tonglen practice found in the additional resources section. When you practice the following meditations on the twenty-one Taras, let your practice be personal and intuitive. Enjoy finding creative, fresh ways to bring Tara alive within you.

First Tara:
Tara Turavira Embodiment Meditation

Before you begin, recall the three samadhis of emptiness, compassion, and the union of the two. Remember that all appearances of self and deity are empty of intrinsic existence, yet manifest as ceaseless compassion. This is the foundation upon which deity yoga is based.

Allow your eyes to close or remain open, and let your attention settle into your body. If the eyes are open, let them rest at a gentle downward angle. Breathe deeply into the abdomen and release any tension you feel with the exhalation. Take nine relaxation breaths: For the first few breaths, breathe into any physical tension in your body; then release it with the exhalation. For the next few breaths, breathe into any emotional tension in your body, then release it with the exhalation. For the last few breaths, breathe into any mental tension you are holding, feel where you may be carrying mental tension such as worries or concerns in your body, and then release it with the exhalation.

Then release any control of the breath and breathe naturally. Simply rest in the feeling of being in the moment with the breath in your body and let go of any thoughts with the exhalation. Spend as much time as you like here before continuing.

Front Visualization

Imagine that from luminous empty space Tara Turavira appears in the sky above you, about three arms' lengths in front of and slightly above the crown of your head. She is red and semifierce, smiling and passionate, with her canine teeth showing. Her eyes are wide open and flashing like lightning. She is seated on a full moon disc atop a lotus flower, surrounded by numerous wisdom beings,[7] including the other twenty Taras, buddhas, bodhisattvas, dakas, dakinis, protectors, wisdom holders, and so on. Imagine these wisdom beings filling the sky like masses of clouds across all of space. Tara and all the wisdom beings appear radiant yet empty of solidity like rainbows in the sky, smiling and gazing upon you with loving presence.

Tara Turavira is swift like the wind, liberating beings from the suffering of samsara. She increases the awakened heart of bodhichitta and removes obstacles to liberation. Her right leg is extended slightly, stepping down to help beings in samsara. Her left leg is close to her body, symbolizing resting in nirvana. Her left hand is at her heart in the gesture of the Three Jewels, holding the stem of a blue lotus that rises and blooms above her left shoulder. Upon the lotus is the self-blowing white conch shell, symbolizing the healing sound of the Dharma that brings love, joy, and compassion to all beings. Her right hand rests on her right knee, facing upward, palm open, in the gesture of Supreme Generosity.

Recite the Refuge and Bodhichitta Prayer

NĀMO
Noble Tara, the essence of all refuges,
you liberate beings from fear and suffering.
I take refuge in your vast, loving compassion.
In order to bring all sentient beings to the state of
enlightenment,
I generate the twofold bodhichitta of aspiration and action.[8]
(Recite three times.)

Self-Visualization

Now imagine that you become Tara Turavira by sounding her seed syllable TĀM three times:

First TĀM: As you sound TĀM out loud, long and slow, imagine that your body transforms into the body of Tara Turavira, red in color, semifierce, and wearing her sambhogakaya ornaments.[9] You are seated on a moon disc upon a red lotus flower. Your right leg is extended slightly, stepping down to help beings in samsara. Your left leg is folded close to your body, symbolizing resting in nirvana. Your left hand is in the gesture of Three Jewels, holding the stem of the blue lotus, which blooms above your left shoulder. Upon the lotus is the white conch shell that resounds the healing sound of the Dharma. Your right hand is resting on your right knee with an open, upward-facing palm in the gesture of Supreme Generosity. Your eyes are wide and flashing like lightning; your mouth is smiling yet fierce, teeth showing. Feel free to take this position or simply imagine it.

As Tara Turavira, your body is luminous and hollow like a balloon, empty of solidity. Imagine that in your heart center is an orb of red light the size of a walnut. Within this sphere is a white moon disc with a red TĀM syllable[10] in the center, standing upright. It is fine and effervescent, as if written with a single hair. Feel free to imagine the syllable in Tibetan, Sanskrit, or English script. I offer the Tibetan here.

Second TĀM: As Tara Turavira, sound TĀM a second time and imagine rainbow light emanating outward from the TĀM syllable at your heart. Feel that rainbow wisdom light, which is the purified essence of the five elements and five wisdoms, as an offering to all the wisdom beings in the space above you. They joyfully receive your offering. Let yourself truly sense this connection between you as Tara Turavira and all the wisdom beings in the sky above you.

Third TĀM: With the third sounding of TĀM, imagine that all the wisdom beings send rainbow wisdom light back to you, blessing and empowering you. Feel the light entering your heart and spreading throughout your entire body, filling you with illumination and bliss. This light fully activates you as the red Tara Turavira. Take your seat, and don't hold back. Truly feel what it would be like to be a fully awakened buddha, Tara Turavira, a being of radiant light and infinite love and capacity.

Mantra Recitation and Enacting Tara's Enlightened Activities

As you recite the following mantra, imagine it circles counterclockwise around the TĀM in your heart. The mantra garland (*mala*) stands vertically around the edge of the moon disc facing outward. If you were to look down into your heart from above, you would see the flat circular white moon disc, the top of the TĀM syllable, and the top of the mantra garland circling around the TĀM in a counterclockwise direction, like a locomotive going around the edge of the moon disc. All of this appears within a luminous orb of red light. Reciting the mantra causes the syllable TĀM and the mantra garland to vibrate, sending rainbow wisdom light in all directions, removing obstacles, bringing relief from suffering, and increasing bodhichitta. The healing sound of the conch shell soothes and releases beings from fear, consoles them, and brings them hope. See all beings become free from suffering and awaken to their true nature. The light and sound are expressions of Tara's love and compassion for all beings without exception.

OM TARA TUTTARE TURE BODHICHITTA SVAHA

Recite the mantra as many times as you like (but at least twenty-one times). Genuinely feel yourself as Tara Turavira.

Dissolution and Rest in Awareness

When your mantra recitation feels complete, dissolve the visualization. Imagine that the world and its inhabitants dissolve into blissful rainbow light and this light then dissolves into you as Tara Turavira. Then you yourself dissolve into light from the crown of your head and the soles of your feet, slowly converging at the sphere of red light at your heart chakra. Then the red sphere dissolves into the moon disc, the moon disc into the mantra garland, and the mantra garland into the TĀM. Lastly, the TĀM dissolves from the base all the way up to the flame atop the circle (*bindu*). Then everything becomes luminous emptiness.

Rest in spacious awareness—the vast, luminous, and wakeful nature of your own mind. Release into presence. When concepts arise, release them with the outbreath. Your eyes may be closed or open, gazing into space just above the horizon line. In either case, relax the muscles behind and around your eyes. Simply rest your awareness in its own nature. This is the very essence of Tara. Rest here as long as you like.

When you are ready, return to your form as Tara Turavira, and feel yourself fully integrated with her. Slowly open your eyes and look at the world with a new gaze through the eyes of Tara. As you move about your day, blend the meditative state with the post-meditative state, recalling the compassion and love of Tara Turavira within and all around you. You may find it easiest to do this by reciting or singing her mantra throughout the day.

Close your session by giving rise to a sense of gratitude to Tara and her blessings and to your teachers, ancestors, all beings, and the Earth that sustains us. Conclude by dedicating the positive energy from your practice with the following verse.

Dedication of Merit

>Through this virtue, may I quickly attain the state of Noble Tara.
>May I bring each and every being, without exception, to that state.
>May all beings be healthy, free from suffering and its causes, and may they awaken to their true nature.[11]

DRÖLMA LOTER YANG CHENMA
(SKT. TARA VAJRA SARASVATI)

The Second Tara

Tara the Melodious One, the Treasure of Intelligence

Homage to you, Mother [Tara] whose face is [like]
A hundred full autumn moons gathered.
A thousand stars clustered
Fully reveal your brilliant radiance.

Tara Vajra Sarasvati is the goddess of music, art, science, eloquence, and wisdom; thus, one could say she is the "Arts and Sciences Tara." Not only does she promote success among philosophers, scholars, and artists but she also leads one to the highest aim of all: supreme enlightenment. She blesses us with her gifts of insight, poetic inspiration, intuition, and artistic skill. Granting charming language and a beautiful voice, she also heals speech defects. She is white like "a hundred full autumn moons gathered." She is peaceful and smiling, an embodiment of "brilliant radiance," ablaze like a thousand stars. What a sight to behold. Who wouldn't want to meet—let alone embody—this majestic goddess?

Her Sanskrit name is Tara Vajra Sarasvati, translated as "Tara, She Who Is the Source of Flowing Adamantine [Wisdom]." *Vajra* means "thunderbolt," "diamond," "adamantine," or "indestructible." *Saras* means "anything flowing or fluid, a lake or pond." *Vat* is the possessive suffix referring to what came before. The *i* at the end is a long *i* (see appendix) and signifies the female gender. Thus, *Sarasvati* could also be translated as "she who is full of juice." Sarasvati is one of the earliest expressions of the divine feminine in South Asian cultures, with origins tracing back to the oldest known Sanskrit text called the *Rigveda* (c. 1500-1000 B.C.E.). Revered as the goddess of wisdom and learning, she is one of the most beloved deities in Buddhism and Hinduism.

In Tibetan, *loter* means "treasure of intelligence." *Yang* means "melodious," and *chenma* means "she who possesses." The translation I offer, "Tara the Melodious One, the Treasure of Intelligence," is based on the Tibetan version of her name since it is the Tibetan tradition upon which we are primarily basing our understanding of Tara.

Her Mantra

ཨོཾ་ཏུ་རེ་ཏུཏྟུ་རེ་ཏུ་རེ་པྲཛྙཱ་ཧྲཱིཾ་ཧྲཱིཾ་སྭཱ་ཧཱ།

OṂ TĀRE TUTTĀRE TURE PRAJÑĀ HRĪṂ HRĪṂ SVĀHĀ
OM TARE TUTTARE TURE PRAJNA HRING HRING SVAHA
OṂ! Tara! Be swift, Tara! Supreme wisdom! HRĪṂ HRĪṂ![1]
   So be it!

Her Symbol: The Ritual Mirror

In both the Hindu and Buddhist traditions, Sarasvati is often depicted playing a *vina*, an Indian lute or guitar. Yet in the context of this collection of the twenty-one Taras, she appears with a ritual mirror[2] atop her lotus flower. The ritual mirror represents the clear nature of mind that perceives phenomenal appearances as they are, free of obscurations or projections. In Mahayana Buddhism, perceiving appearances as they are means recognizing the empty interdependent nature of all phenomena, both outer (the environment) and inner (sensations, emotions, and thoughts). Like the mind, a mirror reflects appearances, yet it is unchanged by those appearances. In the same way, the essence of our mind, our pristine awareness,[3] is untarnished by appearances that arise and pass within the space of awareness. This experience—seeing into the empty, interdependent nature of all phenomena—*is* the experience of profound wisdom, prajna. The term *prajna*, found in Vajra Sarasvati's mantra, has great import in Buddhism for it is third of the

three trainings—ethics, meditative concentration, and wisdom—
and the sixth of the six perfections[4]—generosity, ethics, patience,
enthusiastic effort, concentration, and wisdom. In this way it is the
experience of wisdom that opens the doors to liberation.

The mirror is an important ritual implement in all major Tibetan
and Himalayan Buddhist traditions, ranging from the Kalachakra
(Wheel of Time) to Dzogchen (Great Perfection). For example, in
the ritual of Dzogchen pointing-out instructions, where the nature
of mind is pointed out to the student, the mirror is one of the primary symbols used. Symbols such as a flower, a crystal, or a mirror are shown to the student at the right time—when the student
is ripe, so to speak—to facilitate a direct experience of awareness
beyond concepts. Within the five wisdoms context, the mirror is
associated with the "mirrorlike wisdom" of the vajra family in the
eastern dimension of the mandala. Vajra Sarasvati Tara's mirror is
unique because the seed syllable HRĪṂ is written upon its surface.
Jigme Lingpa, in his commentary to the *Praises*, says that we should
visualize the HRĪṂ radiating wisdom rainbow light to all beings,[5]
inviting mirrorlike wisdom to dawn within all of us.[6]

Exploring Tara Vajra Sarasvati's Facets

Let's dive more deeply into the waters of Vajra Sarasvati Tara. Her
brilliant white color links her to the central buddha position of
the mandala structure, where the color symbolizes the element of
space and the transformation of the mental affliction of ignorance[7]
into the wisdom of *dharmadhatu*, or the realization of the absolute truth—emptiness. This refers to the gnosis that understands
the way things truly exist, the quality of all phenomena: empty
of intrinsic reality yet appearing like an illusion. The wisdom of
dharmadhatu directly experiences and knows this on a visceral
level and opens us to complete liberation from the bonds of dualistic clinging to self and phenomena as inherently real. This gnosis
brings the liberation from suffering that true insight imparts, which
is the ultimate superpower of Vajra Sarasvati Tara.

In Buddhist tantra, Sarasvati manifests in many forms, primarily as a white but also as a red deity. In her white forms, like in Hindu traditions, she is the goddess of wisdom and learning. In her red forms, she retains her identity as the goddess of wisdom, but she is also associated with the lotus magnetizing enlightened activities, like other red deities such as Tara Turavira, Vajrayogini, Red Manjushri, Amitabha, and Kurukulla (fifth Tara).[8] Both red and white Sarasvati are often considered the counterpart of the male deity Manjushri, who is also associated with wisdom and appears in both white and red forms.

Sarasvati's importance in Buddhist and Hindu religious traditions evidences the sometimes-blurred boundaries between them. In medieval Buddhist tantra—the era in which the *Praises* appears— the distinctions between Buddhist and Hindu deities were not always pronounced. Occasionally one deity is represented by two different names, such as the well-known Buddhist deity Vajrayogini, who is known as Chinnamasta in Hindu traditions. Here, Sarasvati and Vajra Sarasvati Tara are another such instance.

In the Vedas, Sarasvati is associated with the Sarasvati River. In the *Vamana Purana,* one of the eighteen primary religious Hindu texts, she is said to move through the clouds and produce rain.[9] Sarasvati is also linked with a ritual drink of immortality called *soma*, implying that she represents the underlying sap of vitality necessary for all beings, thus nourishing and promoting fertility.[10] In later commentaries on the Vedas called the Brahmanas, Sarasvati became associated with the goddess of speech Vac. Sarasvati thus became known as "creative sound," having the power to give rise to the essential human quality of existence: speech. Eventually she became more commonly associated with eloquence and less associated with the eponymous river. Considered the embodiment of peace (*sattva guna*[11]), Sarasvati also represents the themes of purity, transcendence, and spiritual perfection, as is further supported by the animal-vehicle (*vahana*) that carries her—the swan. She represents grace, beauty, virtue, and the potential for artistic inspiration and philosophical insight that enables human beings to transcend the limitations of the natural world.

While Sarasvati is best known as the goddess of culture and learning, her numerous epithets also suggest she is of a primordial, absolute nature: Jaganmata (mother of the world), Shaktirupini (whose form is power), and Vishvarupa (containing all forms within her). Professor of religion David R. Kinsley states that "it is through her association with our human superior power of intellect that she is equated with the highest powers of the cosmos."[12]

When Sarasvati is worshipped as the goddess of innate knowledge, or Jna, she has the power to grant the wisdom that reveals our enlightened qualities. Hindu traditions believe that there are three ways of attaining liberation: devotion (*bhakti*), action (*kriya*), and knowledge (*jnana*). Those who follow the path of knowledge worship Sarasvati as a means to liberation from samsara. Praying to and embodying Sarasvati is the direct route to reach this destination. This circular path leads us right back to where we are, but with the clear vision to recognize that we are divine and have never been separate from that divinity.

I also see Tara Vajra Sarasvati's enlightened activity as teaching us how to make connections. Sarasvati allows us to see patterns so that we can have the aha moment that brings us to revelations, innovations, scientific breakthroughs, artistic expressions, and full-blown insight into the nature of our mind and the phenomenal world around us—which is the ultimate meaning of wisdom in Buddhism.

Real-Life Embodiment
Ani Choying Drolma

This real-life Tara Vajra Sarasvati highlights the qualities of eloquence, melodious expression, and compassionate wisdom, all in the service of benefiting others. The Tibetan Buddhist nun and devotional singer Ani Choying Drolma is known for her inspiring voice and her many humanitarian efforts, including the education of women, medical services for the underprivileged, and care for the elderly. The daughter of Tibetan refugees, she was born in Kathmandu, Nepal, in 1971. As a youth, she escaped an abusive father by taking refuge in a Buddhist nunnery called Nagi Gompa in the foothills outside Kathmandu. There she met her teacher, the renowned late Dzogchen master Tulku Urgyen Rinpoche, who oversaw her education and spiritual training.

Ani Choying Drolma trained in Buddhist meditation, chanting rituals, and ceremony performance, quickly advancing to become Nagi Gompa nunnery's chant leader. Her vocal talent was recognized by the well-known American guitarist Steve Tibbetts, who asked her if he could record her singing. With the blessings of her teacher, she worked with Tibbetts, who helped her develop her vocal skills. Tulku Urgyen Rinpoche saw her voice as a channel for the blessings of Tara. He knew that she could benefit many beings through these mantras, exposing prayers to people who otherwise would never hear them. In 1997, Ani Choying Drolma and Steve Tibbetts released their first album called *Chö* (*Severance*), named for the spiritual practice taught by the eleventh-century Tibetan female teacher Machig Labdrön, our real-life fifth Tara.

To benefit other Tibetan refugees, Ani Choying Drolma established two philanthropic organizations. The first is Arya Tara School for Women and Nuns, where both Western and Buddhist curricula are taught—the first of its kind in Nepal. The second is the Ani Foundation through which she raises money for the welfare and advancement of Tibetan Buddhist nuns in the Himalayas. In 2014, she was named UNICEF goodwill ambassador to Nepal, enabling her to amplify UNICEF's work to protect Nepali children and adolescents from violence, creating safe and happy environments where they can grow up to become healthy, responsible adults. In this way, she continues to use her voice to bring the issues of women and children to the forefront.

Choying Drolma has set an example for a new generation of Tibetan Buddhist nuns to be leaders in their community and has given many the direct opportunity to do so through her education programs. She thus connects intention with compassionate action. She reflects Sarasvati's qualities both in terms of her artistic inspiration and her cultivation of both secular and religious educational opportunities for women and girls.

Further Contemplations

Now that you have met Tara Vajra Sarasvati and one woman who embodies her qualities, I encourage you to think of other people who do as well. Celebrate them by reading their writings, listening to their music, or embracing their other artistic creations and then share their stories with others. Ponder how you might develop these qualities within yourself. Take a class on a topic of interest, pick up a classic novel, or take a poetry, singing, or language course. Try something new that stimulates your intellect. Pray to Sarasvati and remember to call upon her for inspiration. Like Jamyang Khyentse Chökyi Lodrö, ask her to "enter the milky lake" of your mind and grant you "the brilliant light of wisdom." Be open to receive her gifts. Lastly, find ways to share her qualities in the world around you—volunteer at a library or school or donate to an organization that does work like the ones founded by Ani Choying Drolma.

Second Tara:
Tara Vajra Sarasvati Embodiment Meditation

Before you begin, recall the three samadhis of emptiness, compassion, and the union of the two. Remember that all appearances of self and deity are empty of intrinsic existence yet manifest as ceaseless compassion.

Settle into a comfortable meditation seat and take nine relaxation breaths, breathing into any physical tension, then any emotional tension, and finally any mental tension and releasing it all with your exhalations.

Front Visualization

Imagine that from luminous empty space Tara Vajra Sarasvati appears in the space in front of and slightly above you, peaceful and white in color, glowing with the brilliant light of a hundred full autumn moons. She unlocks the treasures of music, art, wisdom, and knowledge. Upon her lotus is a *melong*, a mirror marked with the seed syllable

HRĪM, which radiates light in all directions, dispelling ignorance and gathering back wisdom and beauty.

Recite the Refuge and Bodhichitta Prayer (3 times)

NĀMO
Noble Tara, the essence of all refuges,
you liberate beings from fear and suffering.
I take refuge in your vast, loving compassion.
In order to bring all sentient beings to the state of
    enlightenment,
I generate the twofold bodhichitta of aspiration and action.

Self-Visualization

Sound Tara's seed syllable TĀM three times.

First TĀM: Imagine that your body becomes Tara Vajra Sarasvati, white in color and peaceful. Your body is luminous and hollow, with the TĀM in your heart center.

Second TĀM: As Tara Vajra Sarasvati, send offerings of rainbow wisdom light to the wisdom beings. Let yourself truly sense this connection between you and them.

Third TĀM: Wisdom beings send rainbow wisdom light back to you, empowering you as Tara Vajra Sarasvati, fully activating you. Truly feel what it would be like to be the awakened buddha Tara Vajra Sarasvati, a being of radiant light and infinite love and capacity.

Mantra Recitation and Enacting Tara's Enlightened Activities

As you recite her mantra, imagine that the mantra garland, seed syllable TĀM, and the HRĪM on the mirror atop your lotus emanate rainbow wisdom light in all directions, dispelling ignorance and unlocking the treasures of music, art, wisdom, and supreme enlightenment for all beings without limit.

OM TARE TUTTARE TURE PRAJNA HRING HRING SVAHA

Recite the mantra as many times as you like—but at least twenty-one times. Genuinely feel yourself as Tara Vajra Sarasvati.

Dissolution and Rest in Awareness

When your mantra recitation feels complete, dissolve the visualization: first the world and its inhabitants, then you as Tara Vajra Sarasvati converging at the TĀM in your heart center. Then everything becomes luminous emptiness.

Rest in spacious awareness—the vast, luminous, and wakeful nature of your own mind. Release into presence. When you are ready, return to your form as Tara Vajra Sarasvati and feel yourself fully integrated with her. As you move about your day, recall the compassion and love of Tara Vajra Sarasvati within and all around you.

Close the session with a sense of gratitude to Tara and her blessings.

Dedication of Merit

Through this virtue, may I quickly attain the state of Noble Tara.

May I bring each and every being, without exception, to that state.

May all beings be healthy, free from suffering and its causes, and may they awaken to their true nature.

DRÖLMA SERMO SÖNAM TOBKYE
(SKT. TARA VASUDHARA / TARA PUNYOTTAMADA)

The Third Tara

Tara the Golden One Who Bestows Merit

Homage to the Golden Mother, whose hand is
Is adorned with a blue water-born lotus
And whose sphere of activity is generosity, enthusiastic effort,
*   asceticism,*
Peace, patience, and concentration.

Enter the abundant, prosperous, and bountiful world of the third Tara, whose power increases all that is good and virtuous in the world. Tara Vasudhara is peaceful and the color of "refined gold."[1] She bestows both material and spiritual wealth upon all beings. Her warmth, like the golden rays of the rising sun, catalyzes growth of positive qualities within the world.

In Sanskrit she is called Tara Vasudhara ("flow of wealth") or Tara Punyottada ("she who grants supreme merit"), and in Tibetan, Sermo Sönam Tobkye. *Sermo* means "golden," *sonam* "merit," and *tobkye* "give rise to power." Often *sermo* is left out, and she is referred to as Drölma Sönam Tobkye. In line with the Tibetan, I have translated her name as "Tara the Golden One Who Bestows Merit."

Her Mantra

ཨོཾ་ཏུ་རེ་ཏུཏྟ་རེ་ཏུ་རེམ་ཧཱ་པུཉྩེ་སྭཱ་ཧཱ།

OM TĀRE TUTTĀRE TURE MAHĀ PUṆYE SVĀHĀ
OM TARE TUTTARE TURE MAHA PUNYE SVAHA
OṂ! Tara! Be swift, Tara! Bestow great merit! So be it!

Her Symbol: The Wish-Fulfilling Jewel

Upon Tara Vasudhara's lotus flower is a wish-fulfilling jewel[2] that grants all forms of material and spiritual wealth. We should consider our teachers and even Shakyamuni Buddha wish-fulfilling jewels because they offer us the riches of the Dharma, the priceless teachings that lead us to liberation. However, the ultimate wish-fulfilling jewel and the true teacher is our very own buddha nature, the seed within us that gives rise to peace, satisfaction, and liberation from the cycle of birth and death (samsara). In Mahayana Buddhism, buddha nature is *tathagatagarbha*, a Sanskrit term meaning "embryo of the thus gone."[3] *Tathagata* means "one who has gone beyond," and *garbha* means "embryo," "womb," or "interior of anything." Thus, buddha nature is that embryo or seed within all sentient beings that grows into true freedom and enlightenment when the right conditions are present.

Exploring Tara Vasudhara's Facets

In her form as Vasudhara, Tara is the goddess of prosperity and abundance, much like golden Lakshmi in the Hindu tradition. Vasudhara is revered across South, Southeast, and East Asian religious traditions and lineage boundaries, highlighting the wide and inclusive net of the twenty-one Tara pantheon. She is popular in predominantly Theravada Buddhist countries in Southeast Asia, such as Myanmar and Thailand, as well as in the Himalayan Buddhist regions of Tibet, North India, and Nepal, where she has the strongest following in the Newar Buddhist traditions of the Kathmandu Valley. She is often identified with the Hindu earth goddesses Bhumidevi and Prithvi, who have similar iconography, each the color of gold and holding jewels. The Sakya tradition—one of the four main schools of Tibetan Buddhism—celebrates her in the following prayer.

> Holy lady, source of all blessings and well-being,
> Queen of riches and glory, Vasudhārā,

Bestower of all desired good fortune,
I bow to you, noble lady, wish-fulfilling mandala...
Beautiful as a golden mountain,
Adorned by two hands–wisdom and skillfulness,
Bestower of endless treasure to living beings,
I worship you, sublime Vasudhārā.[4]

Vasudhara's two hands—like those of all deities and people for that matter—are potent symbols of action. The left hand is associated with wisdom that sees into the empty interdependent nature of all things, and the right hand symbolizes skillful means infused with compassion. The left hand and wisdom are associated with the enlightened feminine principle, and the right hand and skillful means are associated with the enlightened masculine principle. The commonly taught hand gesture for meditation called the gesture of meditative equipoise—where the right hand rests atop the left and the two thumbs meet—reminds us that wisdom should always be the foundation and support for compassionate action. We don't want to have what's called "idiot compassion"—that is, uninformed and unbalanced, a kind of bleeding heart that gives to the point of exhaustion. Conversely, we don't want to have a stark cold wisdom that feels no care for the world. The two thumbs joined together in a circular fashion signify the unification of both wisdom and skillful means.

Some people might think that it is un-Buddhist to pray for material abundance. I would beg to differ. There are many Buddhist rituals for abundance. Why? Because with abundance and having our basic human needs met, we have the freedom to practice the Dharma and benefit others. Basic human needs are relative depending on what lifestyle you lead. If you are monastic, these needs will be much simpler than those of a layperson. But regardless of our situation, we can pray for abundance with a motivation to benefit others, free of self-centeredness and with a quality of nonattachment to the outcome of our actions. Uproot assumptions within you that limit your mindset, and think, "May I and all beings experience abundance and have what we need to thrive." When you experience wealth or good merit, you could think, "May all beings also experience this abundance." You will begin to see the fruits of this mindset in your life, as both spiritual and material abundance are possible depending on circumstances.

In the five-buddha-family mandala framework, Tara Vasudhara belongs to the southern ratna buddha family. Like all ratna buddhas, such as Prajnaparamita and Ratnasambhava, Tara Vasudhara is associated with the earth element and the qualities of stability, firmness, fertility, fecundity, wealth, royalty, and abundance. Ratna deities' enlightened activity is to increase and enrich all that is good and beneficial in the world.

The ratna family obscuration or mental affliction is conceit, the transformation of which brings about the wisdom of equanimity. Often, beneath conceit lies a feeling of unworthiness. We might overcompensate to hide this insecurity, which can often come across as arrogance. Having a grounded sense of pride and purpose is very important. Feeling proud helps us to have confidence in who we are and what we want. In fact, the wisdom of equanimity is an aspect of balanced pride because we are stable and rooted in our self-worth and thus have the capacity to integrate the ups and downs of our life. We can be confident without conceit.

Another phrase used to elucidate the wisdom of equanimity is "one taste."[5] This comes from the four yogas of Mahamudra, one of the main Buddhist tantric lineages that traveled from South Asia to Tibet. One taste is the state of dissolving appearances and mind into each other or dissolving all perceptual appearances into emptiness—the union of shamatha and vipashyana. A more vernacular understanding of one taste is the capacity to respond to the highs and lows in our life with balance and perspective. It does not mean that everything is bland and tastes the same but rather that we experience the full range of feelings and experiences with maturity and a keen sense of perspective. Understanding that all things are impermanent and ever-changing, we should not get caught up in the extremes of labeling some things "good" and others "bad." In this way, we find equanimity amid the dramatic swings of life. One taste teaches us to relate to the world free of bias and experience it in all its tragic, comedic glory. It is a sign of maturity, a fruition of one's spiritual practice. Embodying Tara Vasudhara's qualities of wise compassion cultivates that maturity. Tara Vasudhara enriches our lives on all levels from the mundane to the ecstatic. She is the stable earth beneath our feet in times of turmoil and upheaval as well as in times of peace and bliss when appearances dissolve into mind itself (chittatva), which is the experience of one taste.

Six Perfections and Tara Vasudhara

In her stanza within the *Praises*, the Buddha says that Tara Vasudhara's "sphere of activity" is the six perfections—generosity, asceticism, enthusiastic effort, patience, concentration, and peace—which differ slightly from the list commonly associated with the six perfections that replaces asceticism with ethics and peace with wisdom.

Tara Vasudhara's association with the six perfections is an exquisite opportunity to explore bodhichitta in more depth. Why? Because the six perfections are an important aspect of bringing bodhichitta into our lives, which is essentially the whole point of Dharma practice—at least from the Mahayana point of view in which bodhichitta is of utmost importance. In the context of the first Tara, we learned that bodhichitta has two primary aspects: relative (compassion) and ultimate (wisdom). And relative bodhichitta also has two aspects: bodhichitta in aspiration and action. The first, bodhichitta in aspiration, refers to the wish to benefit all beings including ourselves through training in the four immeasurables[6] of loving-kindness, compassion, empathetic joy, and equanimity. They are called immeasurables because the intention is to cultivate these states beyond limits—to make our love, compassion, empathetic joy, and equanimity for all beings infinite in scope. The second, bodhichitta in action, lays out how we bring our aspirational bodhichitta into the world, to live it out loud and be of service in the world. Bodhichitta in action consists of the six perfections listed above. These are the noble qualities to be practiced associated with the bodhisattva vow—the commitment to awaken and act for the welfare of all beings as made by the Tara-to-be, Wisdom Moon, so long ago.[7]

Let's meet a real-life woman who intersects with many of Tara Vasudhara's enlightened activities.

Real-Life Embodiment
Vandana Shiva

Dr. Vandana Shiva is an embodiment of Tara Vasudhara in her dedication to securing the biodiversity of our seeds and thus the welfare of humanity, since without seeds we won't have food and without food we cannot exist. Born in Dehradun, India, in 1952, Dr. Shiva is a physicist, scientist, writer, scholar, environmental activist, and food-sovereignty advocate who promotes preserving the ancient wisdom of seed cultivation and particularly the insight of the women who have harvested crops in India and around the world for millennia. The seed is a beautiful example of Tara's wish-fulfilling jewel that both gives life and holds the genetic memory for future generations.

In particular, Dr. Shiva is leading the fight to keep seeds free of the greed that comes when large corporations with unregulated political power try to control and patent them. When corporations genetically engineer "terminator seeds" that make it impossible for farmers to reproduce their own seeds, this creates a genocidal and ecocidal system that hinders the capacity for farmers to continue to grow their own crops. It is a shortsighted approach that limits bio-diversity and leads to food shortages, bankruptcy, and even farmer suicides, as seen in India in recent decades. Dr. Shiva enacts the second paramita of ethics, when she invites us to see how eating is an ethical, ecological, and political act; the more biodiverse our food is, the more we break down the boundaries between farmers and those who eat the food. When we eat the original grains, millets, vegetables, and dahls that have been cultivated over generations, we become partners with the farmers and embodiments of Tara

Vasudhara's enlightened activities of abundance, balance, prosperity, and equality.

In her book *Sacred Seed*, Dr. Shiva links the notion of karma—cause and effect—with the material and spiritual significance of the seed: "In a spiritual context, a seed is seen as the ideological beginning of a thought....The Buddha likened types of seeds to wrong or right views, which means your perspective or your motivation.... Therefore, possessing the right view is a very important seed for cultivating the path to final awakening."[8] We reap what we sow. If we water the seeds of contempt and hatred within ourselves, we will experience correlative negative states. And if we water the seeds of compassion and equanimity within ourselves, we will experience the sweet fruit of such qualities. This teaching on the seed and its fruit is a beneficial way to understand the link between our motivation (seeds) and the results (fruit) of our actions.

These humble and tiny seeds are life-giving gems strewn all around us that contain thousands of future seeds, thousands of potential lives of abundance and beauty. With her reverence for the seed, soil, and humanity, Dr. Shiva embodies bodhichitta in action, working tirelessly for the welfare of current and future generations.

Further Contemplations

Now that you have met Tara Vasudhara, think of people you know who embody her rich, golden, earthy qualities. Talk to them, read about them, learn about their challenges and triumphs. Then begin to cultivate abundance, enrichment, and equanimity in your life. You can do this by walking barefoot on the earth, spending time in nature, wearing yellows and golds, practicing generosity, and meditating on Tara Vasudhara to bring about the qualities of both spiritual and material abundance you seek in your life. Remember that the greatest wish-fulfilling jewel is within you. It is your buddha nature, your true home, and your resource of joy and happiness.

Third Tara:
Tara Vasudhara Embodiment Meditation

Before you begin, recall the three samadhis of emptiness, compassion, and the union of the two. Remember that all appearances of self and deity are empty of intrinsic existence yet manifest as ceaseless compassion.

Settle into a comfortable meditation seat and take nine relaxation breaths, breathing into any physical tension, then any emotional tension, and finally any mental tension and releasing it all with your exhalations.

Front Visualization

Imagine that from luminous empty space Tara Vasudhara appears in the area in front and slightly above you, peaceful and golden yellow like the light of the rising sun. She bestows both material and spiritual wealth for all beings without limit. She liberates beings through the six perfections of generosity, ethics, patience, enthusiastic effort, concentration, and wisdom. Upon her lotus is a wish-fulfilling jewel that increases merit and prosperity. She is surrounded by numerous wisdom beings.

Recite the Refuge and Bodhichitta Prayer (3 times)

NĀMO
Noble Tara, the essence of all refuges,
you liberate beings from fear and suffering.
I take refuge in your vast, loving compassion.
In order to bring all sentient beings to the state of
    enlightenment,
I generate the twofold bodhichitta of aspiration and action.

Self-Visualization

Sound Tara's seed syllable TĀṂ three times.

First TĀṂ: Imagine that your body becomes Tara Vasudhara, golden yellow in color and peaceful. As Tara Vasudhara, your body is luminous and hollow, with the TĀṂ in your heart center.

Second TĀṂ: As Tara Vasudhara, send offerings of rainbow wisdom light to the wisdom beings. Let yourself truly sense this connection between you and them.

Third TĀṂ: Wisdom beings send rainbow wisdom light back to you, empowering you as Tara Vasudhara, fully activating you. Truly feel what it would be like to be the awakened buddha Tara Vasudhara, a being of radiant light and infinite love and capacity.

Mantra Recitation and Enacting Tara's Enlightened Activities

As you recite her mantra, imagine the TĀṂ and the mantra garland at your heart and the wish-fulfilling jewel upon your lotus emanate rainbow light in all directions, increasing merit and prosperity and bringing abundance to all beings through the enactment of the six perfections.

OM TARE TUTTARE TURE MAHA PUNYE SVAHA

Recite the mantra like the buzzing of bees as many times as you like—but at least twenty-one times. Genuinely feel yourself as Tara Vasudhara.

Dissolution and Rest in Awareness

When your mantra recitation feels complete, dissolve the visualization: first the world and its inhabitants, then you as Tara Vasudhara converging at the TĀṂ in your heart center. Then everything becomes luminous emptiness.

Rest in spacious awareness—the vast, luminous, and wakeful nature of your own mind. Release into presence. When you are ready, return to your form as Tara Vasudhara and feel yourself fully integrated with her. As you move about your day, recall the compassion and love of Tara Vasudhara within and all around you.

Close the session with a sense of gratitude to Tara and her blessings.

Dedication of Merit

Through this virtue, may I quickly attain the state of Noble Tara.

May I bring each and every being, without exception, to that state.

May all beings be healthy, free from suffering and its causes, and may they awaken to their true nature.

DRÖLMA TSUGTOR NAMGYALMA
(SKT. TARA USHNISHA VIJAYA)

The Fourth Tara

Tara, Victorious Queen of Crowning Light

Homage to the Mother, Crowning [Light] of the Tathagata
  (Thus Gone One),
Whose actions are limitlessly victorious,
[And who is] venerated by the spiritual heirs of the Conqueror
Who have attained every single perfection.

Ushnisha Vijaya is one of the most beloved Buddhist goddesses across Asia because of her ability to bestow health and long life. Tara Ushnisha Vijaya, Ushnisha Tara for short, is golden yellow and peaceful. She balances the five elements of earth, fire, water, air, and space within us and the world. Ushnisha Tara conquers negativity, illness, elemental imbalances, and untimely death. She is also known as the Tara who has accomplished immortality; thus, we can nickname her "Immortality Tara."[1] She also protects beings from mental afflictions and from taking rebirth in unfavorable circumstances within the six realms of existence.

Her Sanskrit and Tibetan names mirror each other: *Ushnisha* (Tib. *tsugtor*) means "crown protuberance" and refers specifically to one of the thirty-two signs of the enlightened qualities of a buddha, symbolized by the light that emanates from the crown chakra, or crown energy center, of a fully enlightened being. *Vijaya* (Tib. *namgyalma*) means "victorious queen." We may translate her name as "Tara, Victorious Queen of the Crown Protuberance," but I prefer the more poetic yet still accurate "Tara, Victorious Queen of Crowning Light."[2]

Her Mantra

ༀ་ཏུ་རེ་ཏུ་ཏུ་རེ་ཏུ་རེ་ཨཱ་ཡུར་དྡ་དེ་བྷྲཱུྃ་སྭཱ་ཧཱ།

OM TĀRE TUTTĀRE TURE ĀYUR DĀDE BHRŪM SVĀHĀ.

OM TARE TUTTARE TURE AYUR DADE BHRUM SVAHA

OM! Tara! Be swift, Tara! Bestow longevity, BHRŪM! So be it![3]

Her Symbol: Vase of Immortality

Upon her lotus flower is a vase of immortality[4] overflowing with ambrosia, which purifies the five elements, returning beings and the world to their natural equilibrium and revitalizing their life force.[5] Her healing ambrosia purifies our mental afflictions, destructive emotions, and physical ailments, protecting us from diseases and transforming them into wisdom and vitality.

Exploring Ushnisha Tara's Facets

In her stanza, she is called "Mother, Crowning [Light] of the Tathagata (Thus Gone One)." Thus Gone One is an epithet for the Buddha.[6] A popular Buddhist legend says that while Shakyamuni Buddha was giving teachings to his disciples, Tara arose from the crown of his head and expounded the *Ushnisha Vijaya Dharani Sutra*,[7] which is said to bestow longevity and freedom from suffering if we recite or even just hear it.

Some versions of Ushnisha Tara's origin story say that she appeared from the Buddha's crown as the goddess Prajnaparamita, thus her golden color and association with Yum Chenmo in this twenty-one Tara pantheon. When the stanza says that the spiritual heirs of the Conqueror revere her, this refers to the disciples of the Buddha, who have attained every perfection, which is short for the six paramitas laid out in the third Tara chapter.

Balancing the Five Elements

Ushnisha Tara protects us from our mental afflictions and their myriad offshoots—anxiety, depression, fear, despair—that cut short our life force and pull us into negative states. Many of our modern-day diseases are caused by stress, poor diet, and environmental toxins. Traditional Indian medicine, called Ayurveda (which we will explore in the real-life Tara section), and Tibetan medicine, called Sowa Rigpa, both teach that our bodies consist of the five elements: earth, water, fire, air, and space. When these elements are out of balance, we experience disease. For example, bones are associated with the earth element as they are stable, firm, and strong. Blood, lymph, and fluids are like water—the currents that flow through us, bringing nutrients and cleansing toxins. The fire element is our metabolism and our digestive fire, which break down material, separate what the body needs, and eliminate what it does not need. The wind element is the motility factor in the body. It is the nervous system and the energy that moves through the channels in the subtle body. Lastly, the space element exists between the cells and between and within our organs and tissues. Space pervades our body: within every atom, there is 99.99 percent space. The mandala diagram in the introduction shows how the five elements relate to the five directions, five wisdoms, five mental afflictions, and five lights.

A Psychological Interpretation of the Six Realms

A more modern interpretation of "unfavorable circumstances" popularized by the Tibetan Buddhist teacher Chögyam Trungpa Rinpoche (1939-1987) shows us how to understand the six realms of existence and their associated mental afflictions in a more psychological and less literal light. For example, the lowest of the realms— the hell realms—are linked to the affliction of anger. When we are burning with anger, hatred, and aversion, we often feel like we are trapped in hell. The next realm up—the hungry ghost realm—is associated with greed and the constant dissatisfaction that it brings. Hungry ghosts are depicted as having large, distended bellies, needle-thin necks, and large gaping mouths. No matter how hard they try, they cannot satiate their hunger and thirst. Can you see how our modern consumer culture that preaches to "buy, buy, buy and you will be happy" has made us like hungry ghosts? The animal realm is linked with ignorance in part because animals do not have the capacity for complex reasoning, complex language, difficult problem-solving, and introspection. A common Tibetan way of reasoning this is by saying, "If we were to say to an animal, 'Recite the Tara mantra and you will be free of suffering,' they would not be able to do it," no matter how cute, cuddly, and special they are. That is not to say that animals do not deserve the same degree of love and protection as humans.

The three higher realms are also interpreted in terms of states of mind: The human realm is associated with desire and grasping. The jealous god realm is associated with, you guessed it, jealousy. Finally, the god realm is associated with bliss. You might think, "Well what's wrong with bliss?" Of course, bliss can be pleasurable and a great motivation for practice; however, it can also be a hindrance because the ego can be sneaky and identify with bliss, reify it, cling to it, and then long for it again and again. When you experience states of bliss, investigate the nature of that bliss. Who is feeling it? Ask and then observe and rest in the experience of awareness that pervades that bliss. Recognize that the bliss, however powerful, is empty of intrinsic existence, just like other feelings and thoughts—like everything, in fact. Let the bliss just be, without clinging to it; it's not so easy to do. Notice the subtle forms of clinging to pleasure and pushing away pain, and release more deeply into the bliss-emptiness experience, which is the nature of your mind manifesting. This is when you "meet the Buddha" as Thai Buddhist monk and teacher Ajahn Chah (1918–1982) has said. Buddha meets buddha, and you realize you have never been separated from the source. In fact, that separation was an illusion; you have never been and will never be separate from the ground of your being: the Great Mother, Yum Chenmo, God, Buddha, Brahma,

Allah, Yahweh, Krishna, Devi—in this space they are all one, and you are one with them.

Lastly, ponder this: Each moment is a rebirth. The past has passed, and the future is yet to come. We are in a process of birth and death with every moment, every thought, every breath. In this way, whether we take rebirth in heaven or hell depends on our own mind. Ushnisha Tara's gift is to remind us of this, and in that way, we can say that she helps us not get pulled down into negative circumstances and mental states such as depression, anger, despair, regret, self-loathing, and self-hatred.

Real-Life Embodiment

Maya Tiwari

As a teacher of the ancient Indian science of Ayurveda, humanitarian, health activist, and author, Maya Tiwari is a powerful example of Ushnisha Tara, helping to create the conditions for health and longevity in others. Tiwari was born in 1952 in Guyana, on the north coast of South America to parents of South Asian descent. She moved to the United States at the age of eighteen to study and became a successful fashion designer with a boutique called Maya on Madison Avenue in New York City.

Tiwari became a leader in the field of Ayurveda and making it more accessible to those who might not usually have access to it after her own life took a turn in her early twenties when she learned she had cancer. Over time, she was able to heal herself through natural lifestyle changes, food, and herbs that connected her to her South Asian heritage. In 1981, she established the Wise Earth School of Ayurveda, the first of its kind in North America. In 1998, on Mother's Day, Tiwari founded the Mother Om Mission (MOM), a nonprofit organization that brings Ayurvedic wisdom and practices to at-risk communities in New York's inner-city neighborhoods and Guyana.

Later she started the Peace Mandala movement, leading hundreds of people worldwide to create peace mandalas made from seeds and grains to help generate inner harmony by reconnecting to nature's seed-memory of wellness and love. We see a parallel theme with Vandana Shiva's advocacy on seed biodiversity and commitment to food cultivation. To further promote peace in the world through individual discovery of inner harmony, Tiwari started the Living Ahimsa World Peace Tour and Oath. Hundreds of thousands of people have taken this oath to engage in a daily practice of meditation and mantra recitation and live a life of nonviolence.

Tiwari embodies Ushnisha Tara's enlightened activity of balancing the five elements within us, channeling this life-sustaining ambrosia, and sharing practices that we can all do using herbs, food, lifestyle practices, yoga, and meditation. These practices bring balance to our physical and emotional bodies, helping us to not feel powerless in the face of disease and thus less likely to be pulled down into suffering, even if there is disease and pain. In this way, Tiwari utilizes Ushnisha Tara's loving longevity nectar.

Further Contemplations

Learning about Ushnisha Tara is an invitation to focus on your health and well-being. Often we neglect our health due to work or family obligations. I encourage you to spend some time learning how to bring balance and healing into your life in a way that feels right and good to you. Perhaps this is through holistic food preparation, self-care practices like self-massage, or using the wisdom of Tara to transform some of your destructive emotions. I encourage you to seek inspiration and guidance in Maya Tiwari's teachings, podcasts, and books in which she offers many home remedies and practices that are affordable and accessible. Learn to intuit what is healthy for you and your body at any given moment while also consulting trustworthy mentors and medical practitioners when needed.

As you engage in the meditations on Ushnisha Tara, you may find that through visualization, mantra recitation, and resting in a relaxed natural state of mind, you will begin to feel her ambrosia flow inside of you. It may seem like the nectar is descending from the crown of your head, filling your body, and bringing healing to places in you that are out of balance or in pain. For example, if you are burned out and your adrenals and kidneys are taxed due to overwork, caffeine, and lack of sleep, you may imagine her soothing golden nectar flowing over and soaking those areas, suffusing them with healing and replenishment. When you embody her, you may feel the crown of your head opening to a higher spiritual power, receiving healing and guidance from that dimension of light (sambhogakaya) that is the domain of the Taras. Like all the Taras, Ushnisha Tara is ultimately within us. She is also all around us and can manifest to us if our so-called veils of perception are thin. Trust yourself and open your mind to the potential of healing on all levels of your being.

Lastly, Ushnisha Tara is the bridge via the crown chakra from everyday life to the transcendent yet inclusive experience of spiritual realization; this is the meaning of the *ushnisha*, or topknot. It is transcendent because as we awaken to our true nature, we move past duality and ignorance. It is inclusive because when we experience transcendent states, we must bring along all aspects of ourselves; we don't leave this plane to go somewhere better, and we must attend to our good health and well-being, as well as the well-being of our family and community. Spanning the mundane and the spiritual, Ushnisha Tara is the realization of the nondual nature of the two; unifying heaven and earth, she is the victorious queen who reigns with compassion and is there when we open to her.

Fourth Tara:
Tara Ushnisha Vijaya Embodiment Meditation

Before you begin, recall the three samadhis of emptiness, compassion, and the union of the two. Remember that all appearances of self and deity are empty of intrinsic existence yet manifest as ceaseless compassion.

Settle into a comfortable meditation seat and take nine relaxation breaths, breathing into any physical tension, then any emotional tension, and finally any mental tension and releasing it all with your exhalations.

Front Visualization

Imagine that from luminous empty space, Tara Ushnisha Vijaya appears in front and slightly above you. She is peaceful and golden yellow like the Great Mother Prajnaparamita. She bestows longevity and protects beings from taking rebirth in unfavorable circumstances. She gives shelter from unvirtuous activities and disturbing emotions. Upon her lotus is a vase of immortality overflowing with healing nectar, which balances the energies of the five elements and revitalizes our life force. She is surrounded by numerous wisdom beings.

Recite the Refuge and Bodhichitta Prayer (3 times)

NĀMO
Noble Tara, the essence of all refuges,
you liberate beings from fear and suffering.
I take refuge in your vast, loving compassion.
In order to bring all sentient beings to the state of
enlightenment,
I generate the twofold bodhichitta of aspiration and action.

Self-Visualization

Sound Tara's seed syllable TĀM three times

First TĀM: Imagine that your body becomes Ushnisha Tara, golden yellow and peaceful. Your body is luminous and hollow, with the TĀM in your heart center.

Second TĀM: As Ushnisha Tara, send offerings of rainbow wisdom light to the wisdom beings. Let yourself truly sense this connection between you and them.

Third TĀṂ: Wisdom beings send rainbow wisdom light back to you, empowering you as Ushnisha Tara, fully activating you. Truly feel what it would be like to be the awakened buddha Ushnisha Tara, a being of radiant light and infinite love and capacity.

Mantra Recitation and Enacting Tara's Enlightened Activities

As you recite the mantra, imagine that the TĀṂ and the mantra garland at your heart emanate rainbow light in all directions. The vase of immortality overflows with healing nectar that purifies the five elements and revitalizes the life force of all beings everywhere, without limit. Through this healing nectar and rainbow light, all beings become free from suffering and awaken to their true nature.

OM TARE TUTTARE TURE AYUR DADE BHRUM SVAHA

Recite the mantra as many times as you like—but at least twenty-one times. Genuinely feel yourself as Ushnisha Tara.

Dissolution and Rest in Awareness

When your mantra recitation feels complete, dissolve the visualization: first the world and its inhabitants, then you as Ushnisha Tara converging at the TĀṂ in your heart center. Then everything becomes luminous emptiness.

Rest in spacious awareness—the vast, luminous, and wakeful nature of your own mind. Release into presence. When you are ready, return to your form as Ushnisha Tara and feel yourself fully integrated with her. As you move about your day, recall the compassion and love of Ushnisha Tara within and all around you.

Close the session with a sense of gratitude to Tara and her blessings.

Dedication of Merit

> Through this virtue, may I quickly attain the state of Noble Tara.
>
> May I bring each and every being, without exception, to that state.
>
> May all beings be healthy, free from suffering and its causes, and may they awaken to their true nature.

DRÖLMA WANGDU RIGJE LHAMO
(SKT. TARA KURUKULLA)

The Fifth Tara

Tara, Magnetizing Goddess of Knowledge

Homage, Mother, who with tuttara and HŪṂ
Fills the desire realm and all directions throughout space,
Trampling the seven worlds underfoot,
[You] possess the strength to summon all.

Tara Kurukulla is red and joyful. She overpowers negativity and magnetizes all that is positive and beneficial. Her magnetizing power is a charismatic force that draws people, things, and ultimately spiritual realization toward whoever engages with her. Her blissful yet ferocious smile beckons us, piquing our curiosity and magnetizing us to her.

Tara Kurukulla also has the power to enact the other three enlightened activities: pacifying, enriching, and subduing. In this regard, she pacifies aggression, enriches favorable circumstances, subdues negativity, and, as we have learned, magnifies all that is beneficial. She summons all these enlightened activities in service of helping beings attain the supreme knowledge that is none other than the direct realization of the nature of reality and your own mind.

Kurukulla is another example of a goddess who plays a role in both the Buddhist and Hindu traditions, at times appearing directly as herself or as aspects of other deities such as Kali, Amitabha, or as we see here, Tara. Before her association with Tara, Kurukulla was most likely an Indian tribal goddess associated with enchantment and subjugation.[1]

Her Sanskrit name has a mysterious etymology not reflected in her Tibetan name. Often her name is simply linked to her place of origin—the Kurukulla Mountains of Latidesha, Gujarat, India. In statues and paintings, she is often depicted inside her mountain grotto. *Kuru* is the imperative of the verbal root √kṛ, meaning "to do," but it is not clear if that has significance to her name here. In the *Monier-Williams Sanskrit-English Dictionary*, *Kurukulla* is listed as meaning "belonging to the kuru race."[2] During India's Iron Age (1500–200 B.C.E.), Kuru was an important Vedic Indo-Aryan tribal union in north India.

In Tibetan, Wangdu Rigje Lhamo means the "magnetizing (*wangdu*) goddess (*lhamo*) of knowledge (*rigje*)." *Wang* means "power," and *du* means "to gather." Thus, the compound word *wangdu* means having the "power to gather," "power to summon," or more commonly, "to magnetize"—the enlightened activity of all padma family deities including Kurukulla. We could translate *rigje* as "knowledge causing" because *rig* means "knowledge" or "awareness," and *je* is a verb meaning "to do," "to make," or "to cause." According to the Khenpo brothers, her shortened name of Rigjema means "she who precisely understands everything."[3] "Omniscient Magnetizing Goddess"[4] could be another all-inclusive way to translate her name.

Her Mantra

ༀ་ཧྲཱི༔ཏུཏྟཱ་རེ་ཏུ་རེ་ཀུ་རུ་ཀུལླེ་ནྲི་ཧྲཱུྃ་ཧ༔

OM̩ TĀRE TUTTĀRE TURE KURU KULLE NR̩JA SVĀHĀ

OM TARE TUTTARE TURE KURU KULLE NRIJA SVAHA

OM̩! Tara! Be swift, Tara! Kurukulla, who is born from a lotus![5] So be it!

Her Symbols: Bow and Arrow

Tara Kurukulla's ritual implements are a bow and arrow[6] draped in a garland of red lotus flowers, symbols of her magnetizing power, and the five colored ribbons indicative of the five wisdoms. The arrow[7] itself represents the energy of the individual and is often used in tantric Buddhist ritual and teachings to signify the realization that comes when the arrow of nondual awareness hits its mark in the heart of duality. Like Cupid's bow and arrow in Western classical mythology, Tara Kurukulla's arrow pierces the heart of beings with an irresistible magnetic potency. Yet there is a more transcendent element to her charm because it captivates us into the highest state of release: enlightenment.

Exploring Tara Kurukulla's Facets

Tara Kurukulla's iconographic elements—the bow and arrow, her red form, the red lotuses, and her semifierce expression—point to the uninhibited display of her power to arouse compassion and bliss in her devotees.[8]

In the *Praises*, Tara Kurukulla is honored as the mother who fills all space, especially the human desire realm, with her powerful mantric words: *tuttare* and the seed syllable HŪṂ. *Tuttare* can be understood as an epithet to Tara. HŪṂ is a powerful seed syllable that represents the enlightened mind, the unchanging nature of great bliss.

In "trampling the seven worlds underfoot," Tara Kurukulla rules over the seven higher realms that consist of the earth and the heavenly realms above as laid out in various Puranas and the *Atharvaveda*.[9] The final line of her stanza, "[You] possess the strength to summon all," points to Tara Kurukulla's enlightened activity of magnetizing all that is good in the universe. Tara Kurukulla aids meditators in transforming perceptions—notions of self and identity, emotions, and desires—through a contemplative alchemy that brings about the transcendent bliss of nondual wisdom. This alchemical element is key to Buddhist tantric praxis because it permits the space in our spiritual life for passion, love, connection, magnetism, and sensuality as a means to liberation.

Bringing It Home

Do you know someone charismatic because of their warmth, compassion, and discerning intelligence? Perhaps a mentor, family member, or public figure? I think of His Holiness the Fourteenth Dalai Lama, whose charisma is undeniable and yet he can be very discerning and even fierce at times. Charismatic people are enjoyable to be around. Padma deity wisdom can feel like playing in the delightful relational field with others without losing our sense of discernment, who we are, and where our boundaries lie. I had a teacher who, in her group retreats, would lead us through dyad work where two people would sit face-to-face and practice being open and seen around a given topic or phrase, such as, "I am willing to include my... (fear, anger, heartbreak—you get the picture)." One person would speak that phrase and then share how it felt to express it. The listener's role was to be present with mindfulness, minimizing head nods and facial expressions—the normal social cues for connection—and bear witness with full presence. The brilliant element was the teacher's instruction to both the speaker and the listener to remain 60 percent within our body, within our own experience, and 40 percent available to the person in front of us. I like to call this practice "60/40," and it's something that I do a lot in my everyday life. I see the ability to rest in 60/40 in the discerning yet magnetizing wisdom of Tara Kurukulla because we learn to be present and awake, discerning, while also feeling connected and warmhearted without aloofness or judgment. When we embody this kind of discerning wisdom, we don't lose ourselves to the other; we don't need to uproot ourselves to give and receive love and attention. We can have deep connections and feel empowered by them. When the padma wisdom is alive in us, our inner warmth and joy are contagious. This warmth brings a deep feeling of satisfaction while also attracting positivity, making us open and ready to engage in the divine expression of Tara Kurukulla's blissful play.

Real-Life Embodiments
Machig Labdrön

Machig Labdrön[10] (1055-1154) is one of the most famous female teachers in Tibetan Buddhism. Known for her distinctive teachings on Chöd and Mahamudra, she pioneered a unique, authentic style of Dharma based on her studies, her visions of Tara, and her meditative experiences. Machig is a great example of a real-life woman with Tara Kurukulla's power to summon and magnetize people toward the healing potential of the Dharma through her innovative teachings. She overcame (the Tibetan *wangdu* can also be translated as "overcome") the limitations of being a woman in medieval Tibet within the patriarchal structure of Buddhism—no small feat then, and no small feat even now.[11]

As a young girl in a family of devoted Buddhist practitioners, Machig showed a proclivity for the Dharma, so her parents enrolled her in the local village monastery to receive the best education available in rural Tibet. While a nun, she memorized many sacred Buddhist texts, most notably the Mahayana sutras of the *Perfection of Wisdom* genre. Her studies of these sutras catalyzed an experience of awakening that would change the course of her life. While reading a passage on the nature of demons and gods, she understood that they were none other than appearances of her own mind. This epiphany, along with her first encounter with the great Indian teacher Dampa Sangye, eventually gave rise to her unique teaching style.

Machig met Dampa Sangye when he was on one of his many trips to Tibet. Having seen through his clairvoyance that Machig had been an Indian pandit in a past life who had taken rebirth in Tibet, he was magnetized to find her, curious to discern what had become of this great master. Prior to Dampa Sangye's surprise visit, Machig had a dream of a white dakini who told her that a "black acharya"[12] would come to see her the next day. The next morning as she stepped outside her door, she saw Dampa Sangye on the stone path of her monastery and began to prostrate to him. As he approached, he stopped her and touched foreheads with her—a symbol of mutual respect and recognition. She said, "Dampa Rinpoche, how wonderful that you have come to Tibet."

Dampa replied, "Drönma, dakini of timeless wisdom, it is even more wonderful that you have come to Tibet to benefit beings. That is cause for rejoicing."

"How will I help beings?" she asked.

Then Dampa made this prophecy: "Child, expose your hidden faults. Overcome hesitation. Carry what you dare not. Cut your fetters. Give up attachments. Keep to haunted places. Know that beings are as vast as the sky. In haunted places, seek the buddha within yourself. Your doctrine will arise like the sun in the sky."[13] Eventually she gave up attachment to the comforts of the monastery and her identity as a celibate nun. She entered the life of a wandering yogini with a group of wandering yogins who practiced in nature and cemeteries, rarely staying in one place for long, and she began to develop her unique teachings on Chöd, well known for its beautiful liturgies accompanied by the bell, double-sided drum, and human thigh-bone trumpet. It was during this time, at the age of twenty-three, that she met Topa Bhadra, an Indian tantric adept, who became her spiritual consort and the father of her four children.[14]

At thirty-seven, she established her monastery of Zangri Khangmar, the Red House of the Copper Mountain, in central Tibet. Embodying Tara Kurukulla's power to attract, Machig magnetized many who came to study with her from all over Tibet, Mongolia, and even Nepal. "All the lamas, masters, and students developed indisputable faith in her and requested her teachings, saying that she was the real Tara."[15] Machig even caught the eye of pundits in India who heard that she claimed her Dharma teachings originated in Tibet. This was unheard of because India was universally believed to be the only legitimate source of authentic Dharma teachings. These pundits sent three yogis to travel to Tibet by "fast walking," whereby yogis float above ground, to challenge her in debate to make sure she wasn't a charlatan, or worse, a demoness who could poison the Dharma and bring her strange teachings to India. Now if this isn't a sign of Machig's charismatic power, then I don't know what is. She won every single debate in the presence of hundreds of thousands of witnesses, and as a result, the Indian yogis accepted her teachings as authentic, as is customary when losing a debate, and invited her to teach in India. She declined, saying that her karma was to remain in Tibet.

Machig embodied Tara Kurukulla's power to influence and magnetize people toward the Dharma. She also had a charismatic talent for sharing it, summoning us to engage in the greatest journey of our lives: the path to enlightenment.

Lama Tsultrim Allione

Fast-forward a thousand years to another powerfully magnetic woman in Lama Tsultrim Allione (b. 1947), who, like Machig Labdrön, has overcome obstacles as a female Dharma practitioner and teacher. Lama Tsultrim—herself an emanation of Machig—has worked for decades to bring Machig's teachings to the West and to elevate the voices of women in Buddhism. With her padma-like magnetic charisma and empowering teachings, Lama Tsultrim Allione has drawn thousands of people to practice and find healing and refuge in the Dharma.

As a teenager, Lama Tsultrim became interested in Buddhism and mandalas, inspiring her to travel to India and Nepal where she began studying Tibetan Buddhism. She became the first American to be ordained by His Holiness the Sixteenth Karmapa, but she later gave back her monastic vows and began teaching on the Dharma under her teacher Trungpa Rinpoche (1939-1987). The tragic death of one of her young children in the 1980s catapulted her into a deep despair that eventually led her to seek solace and guidance in the life stories of Buddhist women. Publishing and teaching on this subject, Lama Tsultrim embodies Tara Kurukulla's power to subdue negativity and draw in that which is healing and beneficial. Notably, she developed a pioneering technique based on Machig's famous Chöd lineage called Feeding Your Demons that teaches us to nurture the parts of ourselves we usually fight or resist. She furthered this mission in helping others on their spiritual paths by cofounding Tara Mandala Retreat Center in 1993. This 700-acre retreat center in southwest Colorado is dedicated to the divine feminine in Buddhism and is to this day the hub of a flourishing international Buddhist community, at the center of which is a beautiful temple devoted to Machig and the twenty-one Taras. In this way, Lama Tsultrim enacts the enlightened activities of Tara Kurukulla—pacifying, enriching, magnetizing, and subduing—for the benefit of others' spiritual paths.

Further Contemplations

Let Tara Kurukulla and these two real-life women inspire you to draw in your heart's deepest and most authentic desires. Perhaps all you need to do is pick up the phone and call someone to say hello. Perhaps this means speaking your passions fearlessly, unashamed of what you want and who you are. How about something playful, like adding more red color in your house or wardrobe? Embody Tara Kurukulla's vibrancy through dance, song, and art. How might you invite more positivity and joy in your life? Find ways to step out and shoot your own arrow in the direction you wish to go. On a deeper level, let Tara Kurukulla's loving arrow pierce the heart of your own ego fixation and liberate you into the warmth of nondual bliss, union with the divine, wholeness, the Great Mother—however you feel it. Let Tara Kurukulla's blessings crack open your heart and become one with the divine love that has always been around and within you.

Fifth Tara:
Tara Kurukulla Embodiment Meditation

Before you begin, recall the three samadhis of emptiness, compassion, and the union of the two. Remember that all appearances of self and deity are empty of intrinsic existence yet manifest as ceaseless compassion.

Settle into a comfortable meditation seat and take nine relaxation breaths, breathing into any physical tension, then any emotional tension, and finally any mental tension and releasing it all with your exhalations.

Front Visualization

Imagine that from luminous empty space Tara Kurukulla appears in the space in front and slightly above you, joyful and red in color. She magnetizes the essence of everything that is beneficial, effortlessly accomplishing the four enlightened activities of pacifying, enriching, magnetizing, and destroying. Upon her lotus is a five-colored bow and arrow poised to shoot red wisdom light in all directions, dispelling ignorance that reifies dualistic concepts of self and other. She is surrounded by numerous wisdom beings.

Recite the Refuge and Bodhichitta Prayer (3 times)

NĀMO
Noble Tara, the essence of all refuges,
you liberate beings from fear and suffering.
I take refuge in your vast, loving compassion.
In order to bring all sentient beings to the state of
    enlightenment,
I generate the twofold bodhichitta of aspiration and action.

Self-Visualization

Sound Tara's seed syllable TĀṂ three times

First TĀṂ: Imagine that your body becomes Tara Kurukulla, red and semifierce. Your body is luminous and hollow, with the TĀṂ in your heart center.

Second TĀṂ: As Tara Kurukulla, send offerings of rainbow wisdom light to the wisdom beings. Let yourself truly sense this connection between you and them.

Third TĀṂ: Wisdom beings send rainbow wisdom light back to

you, empowering you as Tara Kurukulla, fully activating you. Truly feel what it would be like to be the awakened buddha Tara Kurukulla, a being of radiant light and infinite love and capacity.

Mantra Recitation and Enacting Tara's Enlightened Activities

As you recite the mantra, imagine that the TĀṂ and the mantra garland at your heart, as well as the bow and arrow upon your lotus, emanate rainbow wisdom light in all directions, magnetizing the essence of all that is beneficial for the world and its inhabitants.

OM TARE TUTTARE TURE KURU KULLE NRIJA SVAHA

Recite the mantra as many times as you like—but at least twenty-one times. Genuinely feel yourself as Tara Kurukulla.

Dissolution and Rest in Awareness

When your mantra recitation feels complete, dissolve the visualization: first the world and its inhabitants, then you as Tara Kurukulla converging at the TĀṂ in your heart center. Then everything becomes luminous emptiness.

Rest in spacious awareness—the vast, luminous, and wakeful nature of your own mind. Release into presence. When you are ready, return to your form as Tara Kurukulla and feel yourself fully integrated with her. As you move about your day, recall the compassion and love of Tara Kurukulla within and all around you.

Close the session with a sense of gratitude to Tara and her blessings.

Dedication of Merit

Through this virtue, may I quickly attain the state of Noble Tara.
May I bring each and every being, without exception, to that state.
May all beings be healthy, free from suffering and its causes,
and may they awaken to their true nature.

DRÖLMA JIGJE CHENMO
(SKT. TARA MAHABHAIRAVA)

The Sixth Tara

The Great, Awe-Inspiring Tara

Homage to you Mother [Tara], revered by Indra,
Agni, Brahma, Maruts, and Shiva.
All the Bhutas, Vetalas,
Gandharvas and Yakshas praise you.

The sixth Tara, aptly named "The Great Awe-Inspiring Tara," is the first of our fierce Taras, whose dynamic power will move you, push your boundaries, and challenge your assumptions about yourself and the world around you. She destroys all negativity, particularly the negativity born of confusion, misperception, memory loss, amnesia, and mental illness. Her red color signifies she belongs to the padma family, and the dark hue represents her extremely fierce power.

Tara Mahabhairava's name is another instance in which the Tibetan and the Sanskrit monikers line up. In Sanskrit, Tara Mahabhairava means "Tara the Great (*Tara maha*) Terrifying One (*bhairava*)."[1] For the Tibetan Jigje Chenmo, *jigje* means "terrifying," and *chenmo* means "great one" in the feminine gender as signified by the *mo* suffix. Thus, we might also translate Jigje Chenmo as the "Great Terrifying Tara." Rather than viewing this terrifying aspect with a sense of horror or fear, however, we should emphasize the awe-inspiring aspect of her name, a tremendous power she wields to help us break free of our limitations and confusion.

Her Mantra

ༀ་ཏུ་རེ་ཏུཏྟ་རེ་ཏུ་རེ་སརྦ་བིགྷྣན་བྃ་ཧཱུྃ་ཕཊཿསྭཱ་ཧཱ།

OM TĀRE TUTTĀRE TURE SARVA VIGHNĀN BAM HŪM PHAṬ
SVĀHĀ

OM TARE TUTTARE TURE SARVA VIGHNAN BAM HUNG PHAT
SVAHA

OM! Tara! Be swift, Tara! Let all obstacles be dissolved! BAM
HŪM PHAṬ! So be it![2]

Her Symbol: The Ritual Dagger

Tara Mahabhairava's symbol is a black ritual dagger,[3] which in Himalayan shamanic traditions represents the central axis of the universe—the axis mundi. Sometimes, the ritual dagger is associated with the World Tree—a colossal tree that connects the heavens to the terrestrial world and the underworld. In this sense, Tara Mahabhairava uses her ritual dagger to connect heaven and earth, to stake down the wisdom of all the ages. Ritual daggers also demarcate the boundaries of ceremonial sites and hold down negative energies—so-called demons—so they cannot cause harm while shamans perform healing ceremonies.[4]

Exploring Tara Mahabhairava's Facets

Tara Mahabhairava has the power to overcome any ill inflicted on beings by the different gods because, as we learn from her praise, she is revered by many of the most important gods and spirits in Hindu mythology. These include Indra, the king of the gods associated with the sky, lightning, storms, and war; Agni, the god of fire; Brahma, the god of creation; and Shiva, the god of destruction and transformation. She is also honored by Maruts, the Vedic gods of wind, and the bhutas, supernatural beings who are sometimes benevolent but more often malevolent. Vetalas are like zombies, a class of harmful spirits that haunt cemeteries and charnel grounds and have the power to possess corpses.[5] Gandharvas are celestial beings skilled in music, singing, and dance. Yakshas, literally, harm-bringers, are semidivine beings that either haunt or protect natural places and cities. When malevolent, they steal our vitality and radiance, particularly the vitality of the sick. When benevolent, they bestow wealth and worldly boons, as well as guard the god realms such as that of Mount Meru, the center of the universe in Buddhist cosmology, echoing the power of the ritual dagger to protect and connect heaven and earth. In the positive sense, yakshas may also be understood as nature spirits, tree spirits, nymphs, or dryads. In this capacity, Tara Mahabhairava is another example of the syncretic history of the Hindu and Buddhist spiritual traditions with its sharing of deities, teachings, and practices.[6]

Tara Mahabhairava's ability to overcome ills inflicted by gods and malevolent spirits can also be understood as pacifying our hopes (gods) and fears (demons) that limit our liberation. In Buddhist thought, "gods" are analogous to the hopes that, while seemingly harmless, block our authentic relating to reality as it is. Of course, hope is an important aspect of life and often a lifeline in times of despair. Yet in this context, hope can also be understood as a limitation. Why? Well, for example, if we are consumed with our hope of finding a perfect partner, that "special one," we might miss the beauty of the imperfect yet lovable and loving person right here before us. On a spiritual level, if we get caught up in spiritual materialism—hoping for renown because of our meditative prowess—this is considered one of the greatest pitfalls to spiritual realization. Before we know it, we have lost our way and become muddled in worldly ambition. Conversely, demons can be understood as our fears. (The role fear plays in our spiritual life is discussed in depth in "The Ninth Tara.") In this way, Tara Mahabhairava calls us in to heal our personal gods and demons, opening the way for the realization of our true nature, free of oscillating between hopes and fears.

Tara Mahabhairava Is Calling Us In

Like the Buddha's teachings 2,600 years ago, Tara Mahabhairava incites the courage and commitment needed to overcome ignorance in the pursuit of justice. I can hear her sounding the alarm—"calling us in" to remember our humanity, undo our unconscious ways of thinking, and awaken our buddha nature. *Dharma* literally means "truth," "justice," and "righteousness." In this way, awakening is not just about attaining nirvana; it is about waking up to our misperceptions of reality and our uninvestigated ways of seeing the world and seeing others. The Buddha taught that we suffer because we have *forgotten* our true nature and that Dharma practice is simply a path to *remembering* our inherent goodness. Therefore, let us meet an extraordinary woman who, like Tara Mahabhairava, helped to bring heaven down to earth, articulating the ideals of equality into our everyday life, particularly for women, through her writing and activism.

Real-Life Embodiment

Nawal El Saadawi

Dr. Nawal El Saadawi (1931-2021), an Egyptian feminist, humanitarian, writer, educator, and psychiatrist, embodies the fierce fire of Tara Mahabhairava with her commitment to exposing and healing the negativity born of delusion, amnesia, and mental illness, particularly seeking to heal the psychological imbalances that result from oppression and abuse. Dr. Saadawi has published extensively on issues faced by women in Egypt, refusing to shy away from the controversial topics of prostitution, domestic violence, female genital mutilation (FGM), and religious fundamentalism. Saadawi asks all of us to overcome oppression by seeing and naming it.

Although she was raised in a progressive household and received an education, at the age of six, Saadawi's family forced her to undergo female genital mutilation, whereby a girl's external genitalia are cut off to "preserve her modesty." This experience is reflected in her work. She attended medical school, became director of the Ministry of Public Health in Cairo, and completed her master's degree in public health at Columbia University. In 1972, she published her first book, *Women and Sex*, which exposed abusive practices such as FGM in Egypt. While it became a foundational text for second-wave feminism in the West, in Egypt it caused an uproar, leading the Egyptian government to dismiss her from her position. As a result, she turned toward women's psychological health, namely the topic of neurosis, and became the United Nations' Advisor for the Women's Programme in Africa (ECA) and the Middle East (ECWA) from 1979 to 1980.[7]

Dr. Saadawi continued to write, wielding her mighty pen like Tara Mahabhairava's ritual dagger to call for gender equality in Egypt, critique President Anwar Sadat's alleged democracy, and openly discuss the trauma of her female circumcision. She has described ways in which women lost rights they had in ancient Egyptian and African civilizations when patriarchal systems took over. She brought ideas of justice down from the unmanifest dimension of hope (heaven) into the manifest world (earth). She reminds us that writing helps us to retrieve our memories and to bring those missing parts of our narrative back to make us whole again.[8] Dr. Saadawi carried within her the tireless passion and ferocity needed to work for women's rights in Egypt and abroad, a dynamic power that reminds me of Tara Mahabhairavs's enlightened activities to heal ignorance.

Further Contemplations

Take some time to write about the ways Tara Mahabhairava and her counterpart Nawal El Saadawi have opened your mind to new ways of seeing—stake your thoughts with the ritual dagger of your pen. Invite Tara Mahabhairava to help you uncover and transform your negative thoughts and misperceptions into illuminating wisdom. Embody her enlightened activity through her meditation, then engage with her journey and journal practices at the end of the book.

Keep in mind that we need a community around us as we peel away these layers of negativity and misperceptions—our own and those we encounter. Perhaps you are involved with an organization that promotes equity, justice, or mental health; if not, consider finding one you want to support and get connected. Talk to your friends and family about these issues, and collectively search for solutions to injustices around you. Read some of the books and engage with the other resources offered in the additional resources section.

Sixth Tara:
Tara Mahabhairava Embodiment Meditation

Before you begin, recall the three samadhis of emptiness, compassion, and the union of the two. Remember that all appearances of self and deity are empty of intrinsic existence yet manifest as ceaseless compassion.

Settle into a comfortable meditation seat and take nine relaxation breaths, breathing into any physical tension, then any emotional tension, and finally any mental tension and releasing it all with your exhalations.

Front Visualization

Imagine that from luminous empty space, Tara Mahabhairava appears in the space in front and slightly above you, fierce, awe-inspiring, and dark red in color. Her tremendous power overcomes all inner and outer negative forces, particularly those born of ignorance, misperception, memory loss, amnesia, and mental illness. Upon her lotus is the ritual dagger, sparkling with wisdom flames that fill all of space with radiant light. She is surrounded by numerous wisdom beings.

Recite the Refuge and Bodhichitta Prayer (3 times)

NĀMO
Noble Tara, the essence of all refuges,

you liberate beings from fear and suffering.
I take refuge in your vast, loving compassion.
In order to bring all sentient beings to the state of enlightenment,
I generate the twofold bodhichitta of aspiration and action.

Self-Visualization

Sound Tara's seed syllable TĀṂ three times.

First TĀṂ: Imagine that your body becomes Tara Mahabhairava, fierce and red in color. Your body is luminous and hollow, with the TĀṂ in your heart center.

Second TĀṂ: As Tara Mahabhairava, send offerings of rainbow wisdom light to the wisdom beings. Let yourself truly sense this connection between you and them.

Third TĀṂ: Wisdom beings send rainbow wisdom light back to you, empowering you as Tara Mahabhairava, fully activating you. Truly feel what it would be like to be the awakened buddha Tara Mahabhairava, a being of radiant light and infinite love and capacity.

Mantra Recitation and Enacting Tara's Enlightened Activities

As you recite the mantra, imagine the TĀṂ and the mantra garland at your heart emanate rainbow wisdom light in all directions. Your ritual dagger sparkles with blazing wisdom flames, illuminating darkness and bringing about liberation for all beings everywhere.

OM TARE TUTTARE TURE SARVA VIGHNAN BAM HUNG PHAT SVAHA

Recite the mantra as many times as you like—but at least twenty-one times. Genuinely feel yourself as Tara Mahabhairava.

Dissolution and Rest in Awareness

When your mantra recitation feels complete, dissolve the visualization: first the world and its inhabitants, then you as Tara

Mahabhairava converging at the TĀM in your heart center. Then everything becomes luminous emptiness.

Rest in spacious awareness—the vast, luminous, and wakeful nature of your own mind. Release into presence. When you are ready, return to your form as Tara Mahabhairava and feel yourself fully integrated with her. As you move about your day, recall the compassion and love of Tara Mahabhairava within and all around you.

Close the session with a sense of gratitude to Tara and her blessings.

Dedication of Merit

Through this virtue, may I quickly attain the state of Noble Tara.

May I bring each and every being, without exception, to that state.

May all beings be healthy, free from suffering and its causes, and may they awaken to their true nature.

DRÖLMA ZHEN GYI MITUBMA
(SKT. TARA APARADHRISHYA)

The Seventh Tara

Unassailable Tara

Homage to Mother [Tara], who crushes enemies' magical devices[1]
With [the seed syllables] TRAṬ *and* PHAṬ.
Radiant Mother, with your right leg bent and left leg extended,
You dance within a blazing wildfire.

Tara Aparadhrishya is unlimited love and compassion manifesting as unbridled protective power. She is fierce and blue-black like the color of "a dark rain cloud."[2] She pacifies negativity, violence, and natural disasters including lightning, thunder, and hail. She tramples outer and inner "artifices" or "magical devices" that cause harm and destruction. Outer artifices refer to harmful man-made weapons and machines, whereas inner artifices are the machinations of the mind such as ignorance, anger, conceit, attachment, and jealousy. Her blue-black color signals that she is a fierce deity belonging to the eastern vajra family in the mandala, which is associated with the mental affliction of anger transmuted into mirrorlike wisdom.

Our seventh Tara's Sanskrit name, Tara Aparadhrishya, means "She Who Is Unassailable." In Tibetan, her name Zhen Gyi Mitubma implies the same meaning, but with minor differences. *Zhen* means "others," *gyi* an instrumental marker signifying "by," and *mitubma* "unassailable" or "unconquerable." Thus, she is the Tara who is "Unassailable by Others."

Her Mantra

ༀ་ཏུ་རེ་ཏུཏྟཱ་རེ་ཏུ་རེ་བཛྲ་ཏ་ཀ་ཧ་ན་ལི་ཙ་ཕཊ་སྭཱ་ཧཱ།

OM TĀRE TUTTĀRE TURE VAJRA TA KA HA NA LI CA PHAṬ
SVĀHĀ

OM TARE TUTTARE TURE VAJRA TA KA HA NA LI CHA PHAT
SVAHA

OṂ! Tara! Be swift, Tara! VAJRA TA KA HA NA LI CA[3] PHAṬ! So
be it!

Her Symbol: Sword of Wisdom

Tara Aparadhrishya's symbol is the double-edged sword of wisdom[4]
blazing with flames. This sword of wisdom represents the sharp
wisdom that cuts the root of ignorance. The sword also represents
justice, equity, love, and creativity.[5]

Exploring Tara Aparadhrishya's Facets

Tara Aparadhrishya's Sword of Wisdom and the Heart Sutra

Tara Aparadhrishya's blazing sword of wisdom cuts through the ignorance that clings to self and other—that is, to duality. Shakyamuni
Buddha taught that we suffer because we misperceive the way we
exist. For example, we reify a sense of self when there is none, and
we take that which is impermanent to be permanent. While we may
feel that we exist as a separate independent "I" or self, under deeper
analysis there is no actual self to be found. Instead, what makes
up this sense of self are various qualities called the five aggregates
(*panchaskandha*)—form, feeling, perception, karmic volition, and
consciousness—that converge to create the illusion of a separate
individual.

In the *Heart Sutra*—perhaps the most well-known text of the
Prajnaparamita Sutras genre—we find teachings on nonself encap-
sulated in this tetralemma:[6] "Form is emptiness. Emptiness is form.
Form is none other than emptiness. Emptiness is none other than

form."[7] If Tara's sword of wisdom could speak, that is what it would say. Why? Because her sword of wisdom cuts through our mind's tendency to (a) assert things exist, "form is emptiness"; (b) deny things exist, "emptiness is form"; (c) assert both a and b, "form is none other than emptiness"; or (d) assert neither a nor b, "emptiness is none other than form." We get stuck in duality when we try to establish something as being real or solid—"form is real"—or conversely if we try to establish the opposite—"emptiness as real." These two extremes of clinging to the permanence of form and clinging to the nihilism of emptiness are philosophical and practical pitfalls that keep the mind circling around and around in samsara. Thus, the sword of wisdom cuts through the impulse to establish, negate, do both, and do neither. Instead, the experience of emptiness helps us to find what the Buddha taught as the Middle Way beyond the two extremes of establishing and denying anything.

Insert the other four skandhas in the place of "form" in the tetralemma and you have the Buddha's teachings on the emptiness of self. For example, "Feeling is emptiness, emptiness is feeling," and so on. It is in this middle space between extremes where realization dawns, the "cave of duality" collapses (as is said in Dzogchen), and we find ourselves in a direct experience of the interconnected, empty fullness of reality. This unmediated direct experience of the empty nature of self and other is called insight (vipashyana).

In fact, this ability to hold things with an open palm, creatively finding ways to bring the feeling of emptiness into your everyday life, is a sign of maturity on the path. Recall the union of emptiness and compassion explained in the three samadhis we discussed in the introduction. Emptiness alone is not enough. The interconnectedness we feel with the world upon understanding emptiness brings us to the experience of compassion for others. Conversely, when we feel the depth of compassion, we realize emptiness, for we see that everything and everyone is interconnected. In this way, we understand that emptiness and compassion are not two separate things and yet they are not the same, like the sun (emptiness) and the warmth of its rays (compassion). When we have the sincere wish to benefit others, that is the luminous aspect of emptiness manifesting as compassion.

In my experience, these teachings on emptiness are also effective for overcoming and healing hierarchical, patriarchal, and dualistic ways of thinking. When we can be comfortable in the gray areas between right and wrong, we are able to approach life's challenges and paradoxes with more grace and creativity. We are more able to be humble yet confident, to cocreate solutions with others, and to make opportunities out of life's challenges rather than become defensive or entrenched in the stagnant illusion of a self to defend and protect. Whenever possible, challenge yourself to notice when you get pulled into the assumption that there is only one right way to do things. Instead, move into that liminal in-between space, where there are infinite potentials. In this middle ground, we find our way to balance, creativity, integration, nuance, subtlety, intelligence, and healing. When we directly perceive our empty, luminous, true nature, which is that experience of wisdom, we are wielding Tara Aparadhrishya's sword of wisdom.

Magical Diagrams

Tara Aparadhrishya's stanza says "Homage to Mother [Tara], who crushes enemies' magical devices / With [the seed syllables] TRAṬ and PHAṬ." The TRAṬ seed syllable essentially means "crack!"—it is an interjection, a calling. PHAṬ has a similar meaning, bringing about the feeling of cutting through concepts and delusions (see "The Sixth Tara," endnote 2). "Magical devices" is a translation of the Tibetan word *trulkhor* (*yantra*). *Trul* means "illusion," "delusive," and "imitative" when used as an adjective and "altering something from its natural state" when used as a verb. *Khor* means "wheel," which also implies a continual movement, like an engine. Thus, *trulkhor* means a continuous artificial activity. In Tibet, trulkhor refers to modern machinery such as engines, weapons, cars, trains, planes, watches, etc.

In yoga practice, *trulkhor*, or *yantra yoga*,[8] refers to practices that utilize movement, breathing, and concentration to purify and prepare the body and mind for deep states of meditative absorption. Trulkhor in this context is a series of yogic movements that work with the subtle body to prepare the yogin for the practice of inner heat (*chandali*; Tib. *tummo*). *Chandali* literally means the "wrathful mother" and is associated with kundalini shakti.[9]

On an inner level, trulkhor represents the internal machinations of mental and emotional states that go round and round. These mental and emotional states are considered an "artificial" use of the mind because they are not our true nature but rather habits born from ignorance. For most of us, we cycle through the same old reruns of hopes and fears. This becomes evident when we meditate and see the machinations of our mind. Anyone who has tried to sit quietly in meditation while attending to the breath or focusing on a mantra will have realized that the mind tends to churn round and round, repeating habits of grasping and rejecting, oscillating between hopes and fears. This conceptual mind[10] is not to be mistaken for our "natural state" of the mind, which is pristine awareness.[11] When habitual thoughts begin to quiet down and we have a sense of the gaps between one thought and the next, we begin to experience the space in which our innate clarity and wisdom shine through. This is the experience of Tara Aparadhrishya's sword of wisdom that compassionately cuts with blade ablaze through the foggy delusion of our habitual mind again and again until we release into our natural state. We become free of artifice (trulkhor), and we experience the clarity that has been there all along, like the sun ever shining despite occasional cloud cover.

On a more playful note, if I were to choose a Tara for the first-ever Tara sci-fi movie, I would pick Tara Aparadhrishya. With her explosive power, sword ablaze with wisdom flames, she is like a superhero who pacifies the negativity and evil of the machine age (trulkhor). I would love to see Tara Aparadhrishya prevail through her unbridled love and compassion manifesting as fierce wisdom.

Real-Life Embodiment
Wangari Maathai

Tara Aparadhrishya pacifies violence, natural disasters, and machinations—such as bulldozers, chain saws, politics, and abusive behavior—that harm the environment and those who live in it. Our modern-day Tara straddles these themes. Born in Kenya, Africa, Dr. Wangari Maathai (1940-2011) wielded the sword of wisdom through intelligence and compassion, changing people's lives through her passion, joy, and fearless commitment to protecting the rights of women and the environment. The first woman in East and Central Africa to earn a doctorate, Dr. Maathai was active in the National Council for Women of Kenya, helping to improve the lives of women and children throughout her home country. In 1977, she founded the Green Belt Movement, an environmental nongovernmental organization devoted to environmental conservation, planting trees, and women's rights. Dr. Maathai taught women and men how to conserve the land, rivers, and trees, bringing about increased harvest and food for their community. She particularly focused on preserving the Karura forest, an urban forest in Nairobi, as well as several others in Kenya. She not only planted trees but she also planted ideas empowering people to tackle big problems and to heal the environment no matter what opposition they met. In 2004, she won the Nobel Peace Prize for sustainable development, democracy, and peace. As a woman who owned her power and danced in the flames in order to oppose the trulkhor generated from corporate greed and political corruption, she was an embodiment of Tara Aparadhrishya.[12]

Further Contemplations

When you practice Tara Aparadhrishya's meditation, particularly in the dissolution phase after the mantra recitation, notice your internal trulkhor, the mental and emotional states that cycle round and round in your mind, and cut them loose sounding the seed syllables TRAṬ! and PHAṬ! Then rest in the experience that follows. You may notice the clouds of concepts parting to reveal the sky-like quality of pristine awareness.

How can you wield your own sword of wisdom when needed? Can you employ it to help address issues like climate change, natural disaster relief, and promoting peace? We don't need to win Nobel prizes like Dr. Maathai to have an impact. Be true to yourself and claim your right to take up space in this world, wherever you find yourself. Engage in Tara Aparadhrishya's meditation and the Journey with Tara at the end of the book as ways to begin to embody her enlightened activities.

Seventh Tara:
Tara Aparadhrishya Embodiment Meditation

Before you begin, recall the three samadhis of emptiness, compassion, and the union of the two. Remember that all appearances of self and deity are empty of intrinsic existence yet manifest as ceaseless compassion.

Settle into a comfortable meditation seat and take nine relaxation breaths, breathing into any physical tension, then any emotional tension, and finally any mental tension and releasing it all with your exhalations.

Front Visualization

Imagine that from luminous empty space Tara Aparadhrishya appears in the space in front and slightly above you, fierce and dark blue in color. She is true love and compassion manifesting as limitless, unbridled protective power. She destroys all internal artifices of negative mental and emotional states and vanquishes the external artifices of machineries of war and environmental destruction. She also pacifies natural disasters such as storms, lightning, earthquakes, and hurricanes. Upon her lotus, a sword blazes with the flames of wisdom. She is surrounded by numerous wisdom beings.

Recite the Refuge and Bodhichitta Prayer (3 times)

NĀMO

Noble Tara, the essence of all refuges,
you liberate beings from fear and suffering.
I take refuge in your vast, loving compassion.
In order to bring all sentient beings to the state of
    enlightenment,
I generate the twofold bodhichitta of aspiration and action.

Self-Visualization

Sound Tara's seed syllable TĀM three times.

First TĀM: Imagine that your body becomes Tara Aparadhrishya, blue-black and fierce. Your body is luminous and hollow, with the TĀM in your heart center.

Second TĀM: As Tara Aparadhrishya, send offerings of rainbow wisdom light to the wisdom beings. Let yourself truly sense this connection between you and them.

Third TĀM: Wisdom beings send rainbow wisdom light back to you, empowering you as Tara Aparadhrishya, fully activating you. Truly feel what it would be like to be the awakened buddha Tara Aparadhrishya, a being of radiant light and infinite love and capacity.

Mantra Recitation and Enacting Tara's Enlightened Activities

As you recite the mantra, imagine rainbow light from the TĀM and mantra garland at your heart, and wisdom flames from your blazing sword, emanate outward to all beings, pacifying internal negativity and external machines of war, environmental destruction, and natural disasters. As Tara Aparadhrishya, feel that your love and unbridled protective power safeguards all beings from harm and restores peace.

OM TARE TUTTARE TURE VAJRA TA KA HA NA LI CHA PHAT
SVAHA

Recite the mantra as many times as you like—but at least twenty-one times. Genuinely feel yourself as Tara Aparadhrishya.

Dissolution and Rest in Awareness

When your mantra recitation feels complete, dissolve the visualization: first the world and its inhabitants, then you as Tara Aparadhrishya converging at the TĀM in your heart center. Then everything becomes luminous emptiness.

Rest in spacious awareness—the vast, luminous, and wakeful nature of your own mind. If you notice internal trulkhor, thoughts cycling round and round, cut them loose sounding the seed syllables TRAṬ! and PHAṬ! Then rest in the experience that follows. Release into presence and let concepts dissolve into the sky-like quality of awareness.

When you are ready, return to your form as Tara Aparadhrishya and feel yourself fully integrated with her. As you move about your day, recall the compassion and love of Tara Aparadhrishya within and all around you.

Close the session with a sense of gratitude to Tara and her blessings.

Dedication of Merit

Through this virtue, may I quickly attain the state of Noble Tara.

May I bring each and every being, without exception, to that state.

May all beings be healthy, free from suffering and its causes, and may they awaken to their true nature.

DRÖLMA ZHEN MIGYALWAI PAMO
(SKT. TARA APARAJITA)

The Eighth Tara

Tara, Invincible Heroine

Homage to Mother Ture, the great fearsome one,
Who annihilates Mara's most powerful warriors.
With a lotus face and furrowed brow,
You are the slayer of every foe.

Let me introduce you to the "Invincible Heroine," Tara Aparajita, who is dark red and fierce. Her superpower is to dismantle and obliterate injustice. I call her the Justice Tara. She protects beings from aggression, conflict, violence, and lawsuits. She is our go-to Tara for overcoming all forms of injustice: racial, social, gender, voting, labor, environmental—you name it.

In Sanskrit, *aparajita* means "unbeatable," "unconquerable," or "invincible." In Tibetan, Zhen Migyalwai Pamo literally means the "heroine (*pamo*) who is invincible by (*migyalwai*) others (*zhen*)," but a more concise translation is the "invincible heroine."

Her Mantra

ཨོཾ་ཏུ་རེ་ཏུཏྟཱ་རེ་ཏུ་རེ་དྷ་པ་ཙ་ཧཱུྃ་ཕཊཿསྭཱ་ཧཱ།

OM TĀRE TUTTĀRE TURE DAHA PACA HŪM PHAṬ SVĀHĀ
OM TARE TUTTARE TURE DAHA PACHA HUNG PHAT SVAHA
OM! Tara! Be swift, Tara! Incinerate! HŪM! PHAṬ! So be it![1]

Her Symbol: Vajra

One of the most iconic symbols in Buddhist tantra, the *vajra* or ritual scepter [2] sits atop Tara Aparajita's lotus flower. The Sanskrit word *vajra,* like its Tibetan equivalent *dorje,* means "thunderbolt," "indestructible," or "adamantine," symbolizing the indestructible nature of mind—our buddha nature.

The vajra appears in the earliest known Sanskrit Vedic text, the *Rigveda* (c. 1500 and 1000 B.C.E.), where it is the weapon of the rain and thunder deity, Indra. According to Indian mythology, the vajra is one of the most powerful weapons in the universe, appearing as a ritual implement in Buddhism, Jainism, and Hinduism. The Indian mystics attributed the vajra to the quality of indestructibility; modern science has revealed that a bolt of lightning is five times hotter than the sun.

In Buddhist tantra, the vajra symbolizes the enlightened masculine principle associated with skillful means, compassion, and bliss. It is often paired with the ritual bell,[3] which symbolizes the wisdom that realizes emptiness—the enlightened feminine principle. The sound of the bell invites us into an unmediated experience of emptiness. No matter our gender identity, we all have both masculine and feminine aspects within us, according to tantric Buddhist philosophy.

Exploring Tara Aparajita's Facets

In her praise, Tara Aparajita is honored as "Mother Ture, the great fearsome one, / Who annihilates Mara's most powerful warriors." *Ture,* which means "swift," is another epithet for Tara as found in her mantra. She is said to be swift like the wind when in service to beings in need. Her "great fearsome" character signals that she is one of the fierce Taras in this pantheon. She takes no prisoners, she "annihilates Mara's most powerful warriors," and she is the "slayer of every foe." What does this mean?

Shakyamuni Buddha encountered Mara many times before and

even after his enlightenment. Mara was the voice of Buddha's psyche, expressing his doubt at various vital junctures on his path to enlightenment. Most notably, Mara appeared to the young Buddha-to-be, Prince Siddhartha, shortly after he set off on his spiritual quest, leaving behind his palace, royal status, wife, and young son. Mara tried to tempt the Buddha to abandon his search for freedom from suffering, promising him royal power and fame as a universal monarch if he were to turn back. But the prince recognized Mara for what he was—his own doubt—and said, "Mara, I see you." In response, Mara vanished into thin air. On the eve of the Buddha's enlightenment, Mara appeared again but this time with his armies of warriors and beautiful daughters to disrupt the Buddha just before he achieved complete liberation. As before, Siddhartha recognized this assembly for what they were—apparitions of his own mind—and because of that, they faded away.

Maras, or "demons," are thoughts, emotions, and physical states that block the experience of freedom in our lives.[4] They include mental afflictions of ignorance, aversion, conceit, attachment, and jealousy. While these so-called demons feel real, the Buddha taught his disciples to consider them phantoms, illusions, or mirages that lack any substantial existence. Self-clinging or ego is the core mara that gives rise to the whole host of "Mara's warriors," meaning the myriad other mental afflictions. Liberation threatens the ego because it signals its imminent doom. When ego-clinging falls away through meditative insight or other peak experiences, we have the visceral experience of being a part of something greater than our individual identity. Often these insight experiences bring about the dissolution of the separate self and open us to the somatic experience of the universal self. It is as if the ceramic container of our ego shatters, and we realize that the space inside the container and the space outside the container are—and always were—the same. Separation was an illusion.

When you experience low self-esteem, for instance, welcome the feeling in, but ask yourself: Is this true? A thought like "I am unlovable" feels very real, but is it true? You will find that it is not.

Parents, family, and friends have loved you. You are lovable, and you can rewire neuronal pathways away from negative states toward positive states through contemplation, prayer, meditation, therapy, journaling, and so on. Doubt, too, is a powerful mara because it is particularly effective at casting a shadow over our confidence and fortitude to fulfill our destiny, our dharma. We can unlearn this negative self-talk and replace it with something truer—our essential goodness and lovability. Building this capacity helps us to love others more fully. It is a significant first step to be able to say, "Mara, I see you. I may even love you, but it's time for you to chill out." Sometimes loving our maras isn't possible yet, so instead we might say, "Mara, I see you. You can go over there for a while. I'm not able to welcome you home just yet." Over time, your capacity to allow these fragmented aspects of yourself back home will grow stronger.

Real-Life Embodiment
Ruth Bader Ginsburg

Our real-life Justice Tara is the late U.S. Supreme Court justice Ruth Bader Ginsburg (1933-2020), who embodied justice on many levels and overcame obstacles on her journey to greater equality for American citizens. Born in Brooklyn, New York, she was a lawyer, a jurist, and the second woman to be appointed to the Supreme Court where she served from 1993 until her death in 2020. While Ginsburg had a mixed early record on issues such as criminal justice, race, and Indigenous rights, her understanding of and approach to issues evolved, permitting her to advance better legislation for groups who did not always have fair representation. Her willingness to learn, acknowledge errors, and move forward in the pursuit of justice and civil rights is why I chose to highlight her as a real-life example of Tara Aparajita.

Ginsburg brings qualities of Tara Aparajita into the world through her fierce yet compassionate methodical advocating for the advancement of gender equality and women's rights. Ginsburg spent much of the 1970s advocating as a volunteer lawyer for the American Civil

Liberties Union. As one of its general counsel, she focused specifically on the ACLU's Women's Rights Project, which she cofounded in 1971. During this time, she showed her capacity as a modern Tara Aparajita to obliterate injustice by winning multiple victories litigating cases persuading the Supreme Court to scrutinize sex discrimination under the Fourteenth Amendment. Concurrently, she developed a case for the Equal Rights Amendment, which aimed to explicitly enshrine gender equality in the Constitution.

Ginsburg achieved great strides in bringing justice to the United States. She understood the threats to liberty, equality, and justice for all amid political and social unrest. She upheld the ideal of an indestructible "vajra-like" commitment to fighting for progress. She called for all those concerned with equality and justice to come together for the welfare of our country. In this way, she is a palpable embodiment of our Justice Tara's fierce ability to overcome the maras that obstruct our experience of freedom.

Marsha P. Johnson

Marsha P. Johnson (1945-1992) was a transgender, gender-nonconforming person of color who stood for justice for other individuals like themself when few rights were acknowledged for LGBTQ+ people. Johnson fought on the front lines to dismantle injustices that were little known at the time, notably helping to catalyze the modern LGBTQ+ rights movement that began with the famous Stonewall Uprising of 1969 in response to a police raid of the New York City gay bar called the Stonewall Inn. The first Pride parade was held the following year in June to commemorate that moment. An outspoken advocate for people with AIDS, transgender people, and homeless youth, Johnson cofounded the first LGBTQ+ youth shelter organized by trans women of color in the U.S. called Street Transvestite Action Revolutionaries (STAR) House. Standing up for what is right and giving voice to those who have none is an important way we can enliven and embody Tara Aparajita's enlightened activity, like Marsha P. Johnson.

Further Contemplations

By embodying Justice Tara, reciting her mantra, and resting in her wisdom, you allow her to reveal the unique ways you can skilfully help free others of the first mara of ego-clinging. Take a journey with her and ask her how you might address justice and inequality. Even on a small scale, we can set an example for others with our integrity and fairness. If you are in a position of privilege, I would encourage you to find ways to help others who may not have those same advantages—speak out, march, advocate for anyone marginalized due to their race, gender, or religious beliefs. Perhaps volunteer to help secure voting rights for all citizens or advocate for the LGBTQ+ community. You might learn nonviolent communication skills to help resolve conflict more effectively or explore other methods such as restorative justice and therapies that help you speak your truths even in the face of adversity. Tara Aparajita guides us to act without expecting anything in return and to center those in need rather than focusing on ourselves. This is true Dharma practice.

Sometimes it is a great challenge to "love your maras" or, as the Bible says, "love your enemies,"[5] in the context of major issues like injustice, oppression, violence, and the fear that comes from legitimate threats. Sometimes the snake *is* a snake, not a rope. Our fight-or-flight response is there for a good reason. It is right to stand up to injustice, feel righteous anger, speak out, or simply walk (or run) away. There are also times when we need the counsel of those who understand our rights and can help us advocate for them. Know when to seek that help. Other times we need to learn how to step out of the stress response that keeps us hypervigilant even when we don't face a true threat—meditation can help us to see the mara as a mara or the rope as a rope. This is imperative for our health and well-being. Know when to put down the burden. Pray to Tara Aparajita and ask for her protection and love. Go on a journey with her.

Eighth Tara:
Tara Aparajita Embodiment Meditation

Before you begin, recall the three samadhis of emptiness, compassion, and the union of the two. Remember that all appearances of self and deity are empty of intrinsic existence, yet manifest as ceaseless compassion.

Settle into a comfortable meditation seat and take nine relaxation breaths, breathing into any physical tension, then any emotional tension, and finally any mental tension and releasing it all with your exhalations.

Front Visualization

Imagine that from luminous empty space Tara Aparajita appears in the space in front and slightly above you, dark red and fierce. With compassion as swift as lightning, she annihilates all illusions. Her fierce, loving power resolves conflict, injustice, violence, and lawsuits. Upon her lotus is a vajra blazing with flames of wisdom. She is surrounded by numerous wisdom beings.

Recite the Refuge and Bodhichitta Prayer (3 times)

NĀMO
Noble Tara, the essence of all refuges,
you liberate beings from fear and suffering.
I take refuge in your vast, loving compassion.
In order to bring all sentient beings to the state of
    enlightenment,
I generate the twofold bodhichitta of aspiration and action.

Self-Visualization

Sound Tara's seed syllable TĀM three times.

First TĀM: Imagine that your body becomes Tara Aparajita, dark red and fierce. Your body is luminous and hollow, with the TĀM in your heart center.

Second TĀM: As Tara Aparajita, send offerings of rainbow wisdom light to the wisdom beings. Let yourself truly sense this connection between you and them.

Third TĀM: Wisdom beings send rainbow wisdom light back to you, empowering you as Tara Aparajita, fully activating you. Truly feel what it would be like to be the awakened buddha Tara Aparajita, a being of radiant light and infinite love and capacity.

Mantra Recitation and Enacting Tara's Enlightened Activity

As you recite the mantra, imagine the TĀM and the mantra garland at your heart emanate rainbow wisdom light in all directions. This light and the wisdom flames from the vajra annihilate all illusions and resolve all conflict, including violence, arguments, and lawsuits.

OM TARE TUTTARE TURE DAHA PACHA HUNG PHAT SVAHA

Recite the mantra as many times as you like—but at least twenty-one times. Genuinely feel yourself as Tara Aparajita.

Dissolution and Rest in Awareness

When your mantra recitation feels complete, dissolve the visualization: first the world and its inhabitants, then you as Tara Aparajita converging at the TĀM in your heart center. Then everything becomes luminous emptiness.

Rest in spacious awareness—the vast, luminous, and wakeful nature of your own mind. Release into presence. When you are ready, return to your form as Tara Aparajita and feel yourself fully integrated with her. As you move about your day, recall the compassion and love of Tara Aparajita within and all around you.

Close the session with a sense of gratitude to Tara and her blessings.

Dedication of Merit

Through this virtue, may I quickly attain the state of Noble
Tara.

May I bring each and every being, without exception, to that
state.

May all beings be healthy, free from suffering and its causes,
and may they awaken to their true nature.

DRÖLMA SENGDENG NAG
(SKT. TARA KHADIRAVANI)

The Ninth Tara

Tara of the Acacia Forest

Homage to Mother [Tara], whose fingers grace
Her heart in the mudra symbolizing the Three Jewels.
She is adorned with wheels that radiate
dazzling light in all directions.

Tara of the Acacia Forest is *the* Green Tara, the most well known of the twenty-one because she is said to be the source from which all the Taras emanate. Think of Green Tara as the queen of the twenty-one-Tara pantheon. She has a peaceful disposition and is blue-green like an emerald. Her color and her name demonstrate her connection to the interconnected web of the natural world with its forests, flowers, and trees. Her name in Sanskrit is Tara Khadiravani, and in Tibetan it is Sengdeng Nag. In Sanskrit, *khadira* means "acacia tree,"[1] and *vani* means "forest"; thus she is called "Tara of the Acacia Forest." In Tibetan, *sengdeng* means "acacia tree," and *nag* means "forest." She resides in the Khadira Vani (Acacia Forest) within her pure land called Turquoise Leaves,[2] a paradise of verdant forests, mountains, lakes, waterfalls, birds, and wildlife.[3]

She is our Nature Tara because she is associated with life and the full repeating cycle of creation, sustenance, and cessation. Her green color also links her to the karma family in the northern dimension of the mandala associated with the element wind. Tara Khadiravani is swift like the wind, ready to come to our aid in a moment's notice. She is compassion in action, ever-present and available to those who call upon her. Her superpower is to liberate beings from the "eight great dangers," meaning she protects beings from the various ways fear manifests in our lives. Buddhist tradition teaches that each of these dangers has an outer and inner meaning; they are the (1) elephant of ignorance, (2) fire of anger, (3) lion of conceit, (4) water of clinging, (5) snake of jealousy, (6) thief of false views, (7) demons of doubt, and (8) prison of greed.

Her Mantra

ཨོཾ་ཏུ་རེ་ཏུཏྟུ་རེ་ཏུ་རེ་དུ་ན་ཏྲ་ཡ་སྭ་ཧཱ།

OM̐ TĀRE TUTTĀRE TURE DĀNA TRAYA SVĀHĀ
OM TARE TUTTARE TURE DANA TRAYA SVAHA
OM̐! Tara! Be swift, Tara! Bestow the threefold gift! So be it!

Tara Khadiravani's mantra contains the Sanskrit words *dana*, meaning "gift" or "generosity," and *traya*, "threefold." Thus, *dana traya* means "threefold generosity" or "threefold gift"—Tara offers the gift of refuge in the Buddha, Dharma, and Sangha with her "fingers [that] grace her heart in the mudra symbolizing the Three Jewels."[4] As we recite her mantra, we imagine that we, as Tara Khadiravani, bestow on others the gift of refuge and protection from suffering and fear.

Her Symbol: Dharma Wheel

The dharma wheel[5] atop her lotus is one of the most important symbols in Buddhism—its eight spokes represent the Noble Eightfold Path,[6] Shakyamuni Buddha's first teaching after he attained enlightenment. The Noble Eightfold Path consists of the following:

1. Correct view: Have an accurate understanding of the nature of reality, principally the Four Noble Truths on the nature of suffering and the path to liberation.[7]
2. Correct intention: Have an intention motivated by compassion; abandon thoughts motivated by ignorance, aversion, and clinging.

3. Correct speech: Speak with kindness; refrain from harmful speech, such as lying, and speech that is divisive, harsh, and meaningless.
4. Correct action: Preserve and respect all life; abstain from killing, stealing, and sexual misconduct.
5. Correct livelihood: Engage in honest work; avoid work that directly or indirectly harms others, such as selling weapons, humans, animals for slaughter, intoxicants, or poisons.
6. Correct effort: Apply yourself with diligence; let go of negativity and sustain positive mental states.
7. Correct mindfulness: Cultivate awareness of your body, feelings, thoughts, and phenomena (the four applications of mindfulness).
8. Correct concentration: Cultivate single-pointed concentration, samadhi.

This list of the eight "correct" ways of being in the world is meant to show us how to live a life imbued with integrity, wisdom, and awareness. It is not meant to perpetuate a perfectionistic ideal but to clarify that when we correctly walk the path of the Dharma, we can live a life of love and service and die without regret.

From a Buddhist perspective, turning the wheel of Dharma is the greatest gift our teachers can give us and the greatest gift we can give others because Dharma practice is the only medicine that can heal the deep wound that keeps us cycling in samsara. This wound is the dissatisfaction we feel that is born of grasping at a separate sense of self and keeps us looking to external stimuli for happiness. Dharma shows us that ultimate satisfaction is within us and each of us can tap into that wellspring by dissolving the illusory bonds that keep us ignorant of our buddha nature. When we taste the nectar of the Dharma, we are refreshed, like drinking from a mountain spring, and our journey back home doesn't feel so long. In fact, we realize that we never left home; we were here all along. What great news! This is the gift the Shakyamuni Buddha gave to all of us. Tara Khadiravani knows this and wants you to know it too, as hinted at in her mantra.

Exploring Tara Khadiravani's Facets

Tara Khadiravani teaches us to befriend and liberate the fear that pervades our human experience in overt and subtle ways. This might arise as fear of not being good enough, fear of not being loved, fear of losing our loved ones, fear of success, fear of failure, fear of flying, or fear of dying. For many of us, the greatest fear of all is the fear of death. The external threats of the eight great dangers—elephants, fire, lions, water, snakes, thieves, demons, and imprisonment—all address this fear of death as threats that might befall beings depending on where and when they lived. But ignorance, aversion, conceit, attachment, jealousy, false views, doubt, and greed all point to the ways in which our obscurations are subtler threats to our well-being. You may recognize that this list includes the five mental afflictions with the addition of false views, doubt, and greed. False views refer to misapprehending the nature of reality, namely clinging to permanence and a separate self. Tara Khadiravani might save us from outer dangers, but her deeper potential lies in reminding us to befriend and heal our fear.

Seeing how pervasive fear is in our lives is not so easy. When I began to dive more deeply into Tara's capacity to befriend and liberate my own fear, I realized how fear lived in me as doubt, undervaluing my feelings, resistance to speaking my truth, fear of loss, and more. There are ways to work with these feelings to release the subtle and less subtle ways that fear separates us from ourselves and our inner wisdom. Eliminating fear is not the goal. In fact, fear is not the enemy; it is one of our greatest teachers. Fear has important messages for us, so listen! Through contemplation, prayer, therapy, journaling, and whatever other techniques work for you, you can hear Tara's whisper like the wind rustling through the leaves of the Khadiravani forest.

Swift like the Wind, a Personal Anecdote

When I was writing this chapter, I found myself in a bit of a writer's slump. One morning during my practice, I said a little prayer out loud: "Tara, please help me move through this resistance and complete my book swiftly!" Later that day, just as I pressed send on the email to my editor with this completed chapter attached, an uncommonly strong gust of wind blew through the trees, rattling my windows. I thought, "That's strange." But I didn't give it any more consideration until an hour or so later when strong gusts began to howl, which was the beginning of three days of extremely high winds causing trees to fall and power outages all around the Bay Area where I live. On the second day of this windstorm, I half-jokingly mentioned my prayer to a friend living in Oakland whose neighbor had just had a large redwood tree fall across their driveway, crushing their minivan. He joked, "Can you ask Tara to chill out?" We had a good laugh, but it was kind of eerie.

Now, I lay no claim to influencing Tara; that is not the point of the story. The reason I share this is that when we are in the flow with Tara, she appears in the most unexpected ways. These are completely unexplainable phenomena, and yet I have found that they are not uncommon. I have gotten many emails from students sharing similar stories, including dreams and tales of healings. Tara is accessible and makes herself known in ways that you can never imagine. I encourage you to notice signs of Tara acting in her mysterious ways in your life. In my opinion, such signs are better left unexplained; rather, they should be appreciated as signs that you are in Tara's graces.

Real-Life Embodiment
Jane Goodall

Enter the emerald forest of our modern-day Green Tara, Jane Goodall (b. 1934), an English primatologist, anthropologist, and environmental activist. Her relationship with nature, animals, and forests showed me that she was a great candidate for our ninth Tara.

In the 1960s, with no formal academic training, Goodall went to the Tanzanian forests to observe chimpanzees in their natural habitat. The discoveries she made challenged conventional scientific theories of the time, reimagining the way we understand our place in the natural order and opening doors for other female scientists. She later founded the Jane Goodall Institute, which educates children on the preservation of and respect for animals and their habitat. Goodall places great import on centering and celebrating the role of young people by educating and empowering them to take action.

Even as a child, she knew that she wanted to live in the forest in Africa. She says that living in the forest and conducting fieldwork in Tanzania was the happiest time of her life; it taught her that everything is interconnected. The spiritual power she felt in the forest reminded her of how she felt in old European churches where people had prayed for centuries.

Goodall's reverence for the natural world and her commitment to helping animals and their habitats embodies Tara Khadiravani's bodhisattva qualities of compassion and care for others. Notably, in the 1980s, Goodall saw that the forests were being destroyed and the live animal trade was worsening due to the trafficking in wild animals and their parts for food, pets, ornaments, "trophies," and "medicines." In response, she and the Jane Goodall Institute increased their advocacy work to end wildlife trafficking—not a straightforward issue. They were forced to address the intense pressures of poverty, governmental corruption, and demand by global consumers. By working with government and community leaders to boost legislation aimed at protecting wildlife and its habitat, Goodall, her organization, and other NGOs have been able to effect change on the ground level.

Goodall's message to the world is that of unflagging hope. She reminds us of nature's resilience, that with time and assistance in many cases even places that have been destroyed "can once again support life, and endangered species can be given a second chance."[8] We can make the world better for people, animals, and the environment because everything is interconnected. Swift and moving like the wind, she is Green Tara, helping others through her tireless activism.

Further Contemplations

How might Green Tara's swift compassion enrich your life and help you befriend your fears? How might we help others find safety and freedom from danger and fear? Perhaps it is through offering shelter to someone in need or laying a loving hand on a fearful child to show them how safety feels. Contemplate the Buddha's teachings on the Noble Eightfold Path. Find ways large and small to help bring Tara's love and protection into this world.

Spend time in nature—a forest, garden, or other greenery. Take hikes and pause to listen to nature's sounds and feel the dappled sunlight through the leaves. Do you have a spot near your home where you can sit or lie down on the earth? If not, you could listen to soundscapes on your headphones or watch a program to remind you of nature's majesty. Meditate on Tara as the power of the forest—she is the greenery all around you; she is the interconnection of all living organisms. Breathe and recite her mantra, then release and merge your mind with nature and the sky as the ultimate recognition of Tara's ever-present love and blessings. Find your unique ways to embody Green Tara's energy and you will naturally help to make this world a pure land of Tara.

Ninth Tara:
Tara Khadiravani Embodiment Meditation

Before you begin, recall the three samadhis of emptiness, compassion, and the union of the two. Remember that all appearances of self and deity are empty of intrinsic existence yet manifest as ceaseless compassion.

Settle into a comfortable meditation seat and take nine relaxation breaths, breathing into any physical tension, then any emotional tension, and finally any mental tension and releasing it all with your exhalations.

Front Visualization

Imagine that from luminous empty space Tara Khadiravani appears in the space in front and slightly above you, peaceful and emerald green in color. With her limitless compassion, she protects beings from adverse circumstances and the eight great dangers, each of which has an inner and outer aspect: the elephant of ignorance, the fire of anger, the lion of arrogant pride, the water of clinging, the snake of jealousy, the thief of false views, the demons of doubt, and the imprisonment of greed. Upon her lotus is the eight-spoked dharma wheel. She is surrounded by numerous wisdom beings.

Recite the Refuge and Bodhichitta Prayer (3 times)

NĀMO
Noble Tara, the essence of all refuges,
you liberate beings from fear and suffering.
I take refuge in your vast, loving compassion.
In order to bring all sentient beings to the state of
  enlightenment,
I generate the twofold bodhichitta of aspiration and action.

Self-Visualization

Sound Tara's seed syllable TĀM three times.

First TĀM: Imagine that your body becomes Tara Khadiravani, peaceful and emerald green in color. Your body is luminous and hollow, with the TĀM in your heart center.

Second TĀM: As Tara Khadiravani, send offerings of rainbow wisdom light to the wisdom beings. Let yourself truly sense this connection between you and them.

Third TĀM: Wisdom beings send rainbow wisdom light back to you, empowering you as Tara Khadiravani, fully activating you. Truly feel what it would be like to be the awakened buddha Tara Khadiravani, a being of radiant light and infinite love and capacity.

Mantra Recitation and Enacting Tara's Enlightened Activities

As you recite the mantra, imagine the TĀṂ and the mantra garland at your heart emanate rainbow wisdom light in all directions. This light and the turbulent wisdom light emanating from the dharma wheel free beings from adverse circumstances and the eight great dangers.

OM TARE TUTTARE TURE DANA TRAYA SVAHA

Recite the mantra as many times as you like—but at least twenty-one times. Genuinely feel yourself as Tara Khadiravani.

Dissolution and Rest in Awareness

When your mantra recitation feels complete, dissolve the visualization: first the world and its inhabitants, then you as Tara Khadiravani converging at the TĀṂ in your heart center. Then everything becomes luminous emptiness.

Rest in spacious awareness—the vast, luminous, and wakeful nature of your own mind. Release into presence. When you are ready, return to your form as Tara Khadiravani and feel yourself fully integrated with her. As you move about your day, recall the compassion and love of Tara Khadiravani within and all around you.

Close the session with a sense of gratitude to Tara and her blessings.

Dedication of Merit

Through this virtue, may I quickly attain the state of Noble Tara.

May I bring each and every being, without exception, to that state.

May all beings be healthy, free from suffering and its causes, and may they awaken to their true nature.

DRÖLMA JIGTEN SUMLE GYALMA
(SKT. TARA TRAILOKA VIJAYA)

The Tenth Tara

Tara Who Is Victorious over the Three Worlds

Homage to you, supremely joyous Mother
Whose majestic crown emanates garlands of light.
With tuttara, smiling and laughing,
You bring demons and worlds under control.

Joyful, laughing Tara Trailoka Vijaya keeps our spiritual practice on track with a playful touch. Her superpower pacifies worldly concerns and distractions that divert us from our spiritual practice. Laughing and smiling, her joie de vivre is contagious; before we know it, we have renewed our commitment to our path and feel invigorated to continue.

She is deep red in color and, you guessed it, in a joyful mood.[1] She displays a touch of fierceness, with an almost mocking expression. This says to me, "I'm waiting for you to step up your game, come on and fulfill your dharma. You'll be happy you did!"

In Sanskrit, Trailoka is a proper name meaning "she who pervades the three worlds," which can also infer "she who pervades the universe," like starlight. [2] *Vijaya* means "she who is victorious." In Tibetan, *jigten* means "world," and *sum* means "three." *Le* is the ablative marker that means "over" or "from," and *gyalma* means "she who is victorious." Therefore, her name can be translated as "Tara Who Is Victorious over the Three Worlds." It's not such a stretch to call her the "queen of the universe" because *gyalmo* also means "queen." I will call her Tara Vijaya ("Victorious Tara") for ease of reading.

Her Mantra

ༀ་ཏུ་རེ་ཏུཏྟ་རེ་ཏུ་རེ་ལོ་ཀ་པ་ཤཾ་ཀུ་རུ་སྭཱ་ཧཱ།

OṂ TĀRE TUTTĀRE TURE LOKA PĀŚAṂ KURU SVĀHĀ

OM TARE TUTTARE TURE LOKA PASHAM KURU SVAHA

OṂ! Tara! Be swift, Tara! Lasso the world! So be it!

In Sanksrit, *pasham* means "lasso"; *loka*, "world"; and *kuru*, as mentioned in "The Fifth Tara," comes from the verbal root √*kṛ*, "to do." Thus, we could interpret "Loka Pasham Kuru" as "Lasso the world!" In Buddhism, the lasso represents the unfailing compassion that brings all sentient beings out of samsara to liberation.

Her Symbol: Victory Banner

Tara Vijaya's symbol atop her lotus is the victory banner,[3] another of the eight auspicious Buddhist symbols. An emblem of enlightenment, the victory banner heralds the triumph of knowledge over ignorance, particularly ignorance that gives rise to the four maras (demons) as laid out in the *Prajnaparamita Sutras*—mara of the aggregates, mara of mental afflictions, mara of death, and mara of the child of the gods (see "The Eighth Tara"). The victory banner symbolizes good fortune, longevity, and prosperity. It uplifts us on our spiritual path and reminds us to not give up when we feel uninspired or challenges arise. The spiritual path is a long and sometimes circuitous route, so at times we may feel disheartened to find ourselves right back where we started. In fact, life can get more challenging before we experience the fruits of practice, so we need encouragement along the way. This is the function of Tara Vijaya and her victory banner.

Exploring Tara Vijaya's Facets
Got Enthusiasm?

In her praise, Tara Vijaya is celebrated as the one who brings "demons and worlds under control." What does this mean? The

Khenpo brothers explain that Tara Vijaya is most concerned with the last of the four maras—mara of the child of the gods—which symbolizes our craving for pleasure, wealth, and fame. While there is nothing inherently wrong with wanting these, if our drive to attain them gets out of control, we are bound to suffer. The Khenpo brothers also teach that this mara represents distraction in meditation. Tara Vijaya encourages us to stay on the spiritual path, in the present moment, reminding us that awakening from the slumber of samsara is how we find lasting happiness, a supreme joy undiminished by the ups and downs of life.

Overcoming distractions on our path to growth and awakening requires skillful effort. This is not just an issue for our modern times: it was addressed by the Buddha 2,600 years ago when he said,

> I have shown you the methods
> Leading to liberation,
> But know that liberation
> Only depends on yourself.[4]

The good and bad news here is that liberation is in our own hands; no one else can do it for us. But this requires us to take responsibility for our liberation and our suffering. We can't medicate or buy our way to nirvana. A common Buddhist saying is that we are like silkworms trapped in our cocoons, imprisoned by the limitations of our own making. Overwhelmed by the mundane activities of material culture that keep us circling in samsara, we may feel too comfortable, stuck, or disheartened to focus on spiritual pursuits. There are times when survival is the best we can do. This is not meant to pass judgment on those who, at certain times in our lives, cannot focus on spiritual practice. However, when we detect that laziness, resistance, disillusionment, or disenchantment have settled in, we should remember that we are not alone and that there are antidotes to stop the wheel from spinning.

One such antidote is the teaching on how to apply "enthusiastic effort," the fourth of the six perfections. Simply put, enthusiastic effort is applying ourselves to spiritual practice with a sense of joy and zeal. To apply ourselves enthusiastically to practice means that we need to find what inspires us to do the work, and this may change from day to day or year to year. One solution that has helped me is to go back to the basics. Whenever learning a new activity or renewing a commitment to a preexisting one—whether it be a new language, exercise, meditation, or music—frequency trumps duration. Doing a new activity for just a few minutes every day is more beneficial than a longer period once a week. Soon, we begin to enjoy it and want more; the initial resistance passes and practicing for longer periods feels natural and unforced. We start to find the satisfaction and nourishment that consistent practice can give us. For example, when I know I need to practice yoga but feel resistance, I tell myself, "Just get on the mat for a few minutes and do what feels good." I know that I usually start to enjoy myself after that and then I don't want to stop.

Test this out for yourself—find creative ways to trick yourself into doing what is good for you. Often we have the resources for practice in the palm of our hand, but we forget and get consumed with other things. Keep your cushion or yoga mat visible and from time to time, just plop down and practice for a few minutes. You may begin to feel enthusiasm suffuse your effort.

Sometimes resistance to trying new things stems from a subtle or gross form of perfectionism. Thinking "I won't be good at that," we don't even attempt it. One helpful and simple trick is to engage in practice for a minute with little or even no expectation of the outcome. Studies show that low expectations toward any endeavor foster greater happiness and compassion.[5] Over time, your expectations can grow as you begin to develop a sense of confidence and stability in your practice. For mastering any activity, high expectations are helpful, but in the beginning, we shouldn't worry about mastery. There will always be someone better than us, so who cares? If you want to become a runner, tell yourself that you will go out running for just one minute, then walk for a bit. Over time, you will want to run for two minutes, three minutes, and so on. Eventually your body will naturally want to do more. Start small and then let the good feeling pull you along. This is an example of how joyful effort feels—it is born from the inside, not forced or imposed from the outside. Over time, the enthusiasm to practice will grow as you feel the benefits take root in you.

A discussion about enthusiastic effort would be incomplete without mentioning that, ultimately, the Dharma is about releasing into your natural state and resting there free of an agenda to better yourself. Maturity as a Dharma practitioner means you know deep down inside that you are enough as you are because you have experienced the peace and beauty within yourself. This may take time, and a lot of healing may need to happen before you can authentically know this truth. In the meantime, we can remember that every moment, every breath, every word, deed, and thought are opportunities for practice.

"Peace is every step" is the essence of true practice, as the late Venerable Thich Nhat Hanh taught. Each breath is a miracle, each moment a gift; and when we infuse our life with mindful awareness, compassion, spaciousness, and humor, we are connected to the Dharma and we are connected to Tara. In Dzogchen, it is said the true meditation is nonmeditation—a natural state of being as you are, uncontrived and at ease in your natural state. But to abide in effortless nonmeditation, we first need to learn how to meditate. As my teacher Lama Tsultrim often says, "You can't have post-meditation without meditation." So we do need to spend some time with our AOC: ass on cushion.

Lastly, another tried-and-true way to overcome obstacles like laziness and resistance is to learn about the lives of other practitioners, great masters, humble yogins, and wise beings who have overcome their own challenges. This is a great way to get inspired to practice the Dharma—or any other activity for that matter.

Three Doorways of Perception Leading to Liberation

Tara Vijaya's praise also says that "she is victorious over the three worlds." Generally, in Buddhism, these three worlds refer to the three realms within samsara in which beings can take rebirth: The first is the desire realm (*kamaloka*) consisting of heaven and hell and everything in between—these are the six realms of hell beings, hungry ghosts, animals, humans, jealous gods, and gods. The second is the form realm (*rupaloka*) consisting of the dhyana[6] dwelling gods. The third is the formless realm (*arupaloka*) consisting of the four heavens, the destination for those who abide in the four formless states.

On a more personal level, these three worlds refer to our body, speech, and mind, called the three doors, gateways, or sometimes avenues of being, that lead us to enlightenment. On an outer level, these three doors are like the notion of righteous deeds (body), words (speech), and thought (mind) that we find in Christianity. In this way, Tara Vijaya reminds us to bring the untrained aspects of ourselves—the actions, words, and thoughts that keep us cycling in samsara—under control for the sake of liberation. The Buddha taught the importance of the mind and our intention with respect to our actions and words in the first lines of the famous text the *Dhammapada*:

> All things have the nature of mind. Mind is chief and takes the lead. If the mind is clear, whatever you do or say will bring happiness that will follow after you like a shadow.
> All things have the nature of mind. Mind is the chief and takes the lead. If the mind is polluted, whatever you do or say leads to suffering which will follow you, as a cart trails a horse.[7]

From a Buddhist contemplative lens, when the body relaxes into stillness, the speech settles into silence (and the breath in its natural rhythm), and the mind releases into spacious awareness—this is called settling the body, speech, and mind in their natural state. On a subtle level, these three doors are the channels, winds, and essence drops that yogins train to bring about awakening via the path of yoga practice. On an even subtler level, when the three doors are purified through spiritual practice, they become what is called the three vajras—the "indestructible" enlightened body, speech, and mind. These three vajras correspond to the three kayas, the three bodies or dimensions of a buddha: (1) form (body), (2) complete enjoyment (speech), and (3) the absolute (mind). The dimension of form (*nirmanakaya*) is associated with the enlightened body, linked with the crown chakra and the seed syllable OM. The dimension of enjoyment (sambhogakaya) is associated with enlightened speech, linked with the throat chakra and the seed syllable ĀH. The absolute dimension (dharmakaya) is associated with the enlightened mind, linked with the heart chakra and the seed syllable HŪM. These seed syllables, OM, ĀH, HŪM, and the chakras are utilized to bring about the experience of our enlightened body, speech, and mind.

The three kayas describe our awakened mind: its essence is empty (dharmakaya), its nature is luminous (sambhogakaya), and its manifestation is unceasing compassion (nirmanakaya). A direct and simple way to understand the three kayas is that the dharmakaya is the sun, the sambhogakaya is the sunlight, and the nirmanakaya is the warmth of the sunlight. When the practice of realizing our natural state as the three kayas is taught by a qualified teacher to a suitable student, this can lead to enlightenment in this very lifetime.

Real-Life Embodiment
Dipa Ma

Dipa Ma (1911–1989) was an extraordinary meditation teacher from the Theravada (Way of the Elders) Buddhist tradition. Born in Chittagong, Bangladesh, of Barua descent,[8] she was a rare example of a mother and grandmother who became a realized Buddhist master. She taught many Western students who traveled to India to learn meditation, some of whom became well-known teachers themselves, such as Sharon Salzberg, Joseph Goldstein, and Jack Kornfield. She is our real-life Tara Vijaya because she triumphed over immense hardship and applied herself to practice with enthusiastic effort, pursuing her liberation all the way to its culmination—realization in this life.

Given the name Nani Barua at birth, she later became known as

Dipa Ma ("Dipa's Mother") in accordance with an Indian custom of naming the mother after her first child. At the age of twelve, she was married off to a young man yet did not live with him until years later. Fortunately, he was a very supportive and loving husband. They moved to Myanmar for his work, and after many years of trying to conceive, Dipa Ma gave birth to their daughter Dipa. Her subsequent two babies died soon after they were born, and not long after, her husband passed away unexpectedly. These tragedies compounded her grief to the point that she was bedridden with illness.

One day, a friend told Dipa Ma about Mahasi Sayadaw, the great Burmese Theravada meditation teacher. In desperation, she made the difficult decision to leave her daughter with family and go study with him in the countryside to begin her path of healing. Eventually, through her commitment and persistent effort, she progressed in meditation, achieving profound states of concentration and showing other extraordinary signs of realization. She uprooted anger, aversion, and clinging from her mind and transformed from a sickly broken woman to a peaceful, independent, and loving one, no longer full of suffering. Some say that she had spiritual powers such as the ability to be in two places at once, to recall past and future lives, and even the capacity to go back to the time of the Buddha to hear his teachings. One of her students, the Western Dharma teacher Amma Thanasanti, says that what she felt when she was around Dipa Ma was the immense power of love emanating from her: "Love was Dipa Ma's superpower."[9]

Dipa Ma eventually left Myanmar for a small Buddhist community in Kolkata in West Bengal, where she lived with her daughter in a modest apartment. She gradually began to share the Dharma with women in her neighborhood and then with students from around the world who came to her for guidance. She taught in a gentle, playful way, sharing her devotion to spiritual practice that was born from her immense suffering and heartbreak.

She was loved by many for her down-to-earth approach to teaching, integrating Buddhist wisdom with everyday life in a way that was accessible to all. I see Dipa Ma as a real-life Tara Vijaya because as a mother she found ways to blend her practice with her daily life. Distractions became doorways to liberation, and she found peace in her very lifetime. Dipa Ma was able to help others do the same, encouraging her students to practice in every moment.

Lastly, Dipa Ma understood the importance of motivation with respect to the three doors of body, speech, and mind when she said, "What is your intention? For any action, physical, verbal, or mental—the Buddha gave the importance to intention. Know your intention in every action."[10] I leave you with her simple yet expansively playful advice, "Anything is possible!"[11] This simple phrase seems like it comes from the lips of Tara Vijaya, with a smile, laughing and nudging us along the path.

Further Contemplations

Good-hearted cheer and playfulness are signs that your spiritual practice is bearing fruit. Bringing joy and loving-kindness into our relationships, work, family, and spiritual practice is a way to feel Tara Vijaya's power moving through us. At the time of my writing this in January 2022, two years into the COVID-19 pandemic coupled with the environmental crisis and political instability and division, I find it is more important than ever to bring a feeling of buoyancy into my life. Tara Vijaya reminds us to not lose hope in the face of adversity. Yes, we need to be aware not to use spiritual practice as a way to bypass our suffering and the suffering of others. Rather, in actions, words, and thoughts, "lasso the world" with compassion and joy, and bring your practice into every moment; transmute adversity into fuel for the road to liberation.

My early Ashtanga yoga teacher Neil Coshever would often say, "Manifest, then take a rest." Do the work, but then know when it is time to restore and replenish. For example, a well-rounded *yogasana* practice includes movement *and* stillness. This is why the corpse pose (*shavasana*) is placed at the end of the movement series. Rest allows us essential time for integration. Find ways to replenish yourself that bring you joy, laughter, and renewal. Perhaps this is through song, dance, art, socializing, naps, massages, meditation, or mantra practice. In a sense, Tara Vijaya is giving us permission to rest after effort, to go inside, replenish, and find joy.

Tenth Tara:
Tara Trailoka Vijaya Embodiment Meditation

Before you begin, recall the three samadhis of emptiness, compassion, and the union of the two. Remember that all appearances of self and deity are empty of intrinsic existence yet manifest as ceaseless compassion.

Settle into a comfortable meditation seat and take nine relaxation breaths, breathing into any physical tension, then any emotional tension, and finally any mental tension and releasing it all with your exhalations.

Front Visualization

Imagine that from luminous empty space Tara Trailoka Vijaya appears in the space in front and slightly above you, joyous and deep red in color. With her joyful laughter, she inspires us to engage in spiritual practice and helps us overcome worldly distractions that prevent us from staying on the path of practice. Her victory banner atop her lotus symbolizes gaining victory over our delusions and ego-fixation, pacifying them into a gentle and calm state. She is surrounded by numerous wisdom beings.

Recite the Refuge and Bodhichitta Prayer (3 times)

NĀMO
Noble Tara, the essence of all refuges,
you liberate beings from fear and suffering.
I take refuge in your vast, loving compassion.
In order to bring all sentient beings to the state of enlightenment,
I generate the twofold bodhichitta of aspiration and action.

Self-Visualization

Sound Tara's seed syllable TĀṂ three times   .

First TĀṂ: Imagine that your body becomes Tara Trailoka Vijaya, deep red and joyful. Your body is luminous and hollow, with the TĀṂ in your heart center.

Second TĀṂ: As Tara Trailoka Vijaya, send offerings of rainbow wisdom light to the wisdom beings. Let yourself truly sense this connection between you and them.

Third TĀṂ: Wisdom beings send rainbow wisdom light back to you, empowering you as Tara Trailoka Vijaya, fully activating you. Truly feel what it would be like to be the awakened buddha Tara Trailoka Vijaya, a being of radiant light and infinite love and capacity.

Mantra Recitation

As you recite the mantra, imagine rainbow wisdom light emanates from the TĀṂ and mantra garland at your heart and the victory banner, helping beings overcome worldly distractions that pull them away from spiritual practice. This light also pacifies delusions and ego-fixation.

OM TARE TUTTARE TURE LOKA PASHAM KURU SVAHA

Recite the mantra as many times as you like—but at least twenty-one times. Genuinely feel yourself as Tara Trailoka Vijaya.

Dissolution and Rest in Awareness

When your mantra recitation feels complete, dissolve the visualization: first the world and its inhabitants, then you as Tara Trailoka Vijaya converging at the TĀṂ in your heart center. Then everything becomes luminous emptiness.

Rest in spacious awareness—the vast, luminous, and wakeful

nature of your own mind. Let your body, speech, and mind settle into their natural state. Release into presence. When you are ready, return to your form as Tara Trailoka Vijaya and feel yourself fully integrated with her. As you move about your day, recall the compassion and love of Tara Trailoka Vijaya within and all around you.

Close the session with a sense of gratitude to Tara and her blessings.

Dedication of Merit

Through this virtue, may I quickly attain the state of Noble Tara.

May I bring each and every being, without exception, to that state.

May all beings be healthy, free from suffering and its causes, and may they awaken to their true nature.

DRÖLMA NORTERMA
(SKT. TARA VASUDA)

The Eleventh Tara

Tara the Wealth-Granting Goddess

Homage to you, Mother [Tara], who has the power to summon
The hosts of all the earth protectors.
Your frowning brow quivering,
you liberate beings from all poverty with the syllable HŪM.

Tara Vasuda bestows wealth and liberates beings from the material and spiritual misery that can result from poverty. Like the third Tara Vasudhara, she is a ratna family deity, associated with the earth element and the qualities of stability, fecundity, and abundance. However, unlike our peaceful golden third Tara, Tara Vasuda's semi-fierce mood and golden red color signify her fiery passion, with a tinge of padma energy, for liberating beings.

Here the Sanskrit and Tibetan translations of her names—Vasuda and Norterma—have the same meaning: "the wealth-granting goddess." In Sanskrit, *vasuda* as a noun means "earth" and as an adjective means "wealth-granting," "treasure-granting," or "generous"; thus her name translates to "Tara, She Who Grants Wealth." In Tibetan, *nor* is short for *norbu*, which means "jewel." The word *ter*[1] as a verb means to "give," "bestow," or "grant." *Ter* with the suffix *ma* means "she who grants." Thus, I translate her name as "Tara the Wealth-Granting Goddess."

Her Mantra

ཨོཾ་ཏཱ་རེ་ཏུཏྟཱ་རེ་ཏུ་རེ་མ་མ་བ་སུ་པུཥྚིཾ་ཀུ་རུ་སྭཱ་ཧཱ།

OṂ TĀRE TUTTĀRE TURE MĀMA VĀSU PUṢṬIM KURU SVĀHĀ
OM TARE TUTTARE TURE MAMA VASU PUSHTIM KURU SVAHA
OṂ! Tara! Be swift, Tara! Please increase my good fortune!
So be it!

This mantra beseeches Tara to increase abundance and wealth for us and all beings. *Mama* means "mine" but can also refer to all beings. *Basu*, as it is written in the Tibetan script, is the Tibetan and Bengalese pronunciation of the Sanskrit term *vasu* for "jewel," "wealth," or "abundance." *Pushtim* means "to increase." *Kuru*, again, is the imperative "to act "or "to do."

Her Symbol: Treasure Vase

Tara Vasuda's symbol atop her lotus is the treasure vase overflowing with jewels,[2] emblematic of the abundant and inexhaustible blessings of the Dharma. Another of the eight auspicious symbols, the treasure vase represents prosperity, health, longevity, harmony, and protection from unwanted circumstances. Often such treasure vases contain precious substances such as gold, silver, turquoise, rubies, lapis, pearls, garnets, and minerals, as well as water, soil, and medicinal herbs from various sacred sites around the world.[3]

Exploring Tara Vasuda's Facets

Tara Vasuda's praise highlights her power to summon the ten protectors of the earth[4] to aid all sentient beings. These local spirits initially resisted Tibet's conversion to Buddhism, creating numerous obstacles for its establishment until the Indian tantric adept Padmasambhava (Guru Rinpoche, circa eighth to ninth centuries) was able to bind them by oath to protect Buddhism similar to the role of Dharma protectors.[5]

Tara Vasuda's quivering eyebrows show her powerful semifierce and joyful nature. We might imagine that she takes no prisoners as she summons the earth protectors and liberates beings from poverty and suffering. In Jigme Lingpa's commentary to the *Praises* found in *The Smile of Sun and Moon,* he writes that the HŪṂ syllable in her heart radiates light that delivers beings from suffering and gathers all the "wealth and glory of the gods, nagas, and men. Showering down whatever one desires."[6] Tara Vasuda invokes HŪṂ—the adamantine nature of mind—as she enacts her enlightened activity to save beings.

Real-Life Embodiment
Oprah Winfrey

Our real-life Tara Vasuda is one of the greatest philanthropists in American history: Oprah Winfrey. North America's first Black multibillionaire, Oprah has used her fame and fortune to help people out of the suffering and limitations of poverty around the world, making her a true treasure-granting goddess. She has donated millions to charities and organizations worldwide to fight HIV/AIDS, climate change, and poverty and to educate and empower children.

Working in the field of television, Oprah's passion and intelligence paired with her spontaneous emotive style—like joyful Tara Vasuda—enabled her to gain popularity and eventually launch her own production company and the popular *Oprah Winfrey Show* in 1986. In the 1990s, she expanded her influence by hosting other shows addressing topics such as health, wellness, spirituality, meditation, and geopolitics.

Oprah embodies Tara Vasuda's enlightened activities because she emphasizes the down-to-earth (ratna) wealth of gratitude for the simple joys and gifts we all have access to in our lives, noting that just waking up each morning "clothed in my right mind, as the old folks used to say"[7] is a priceless gift. This is the abundance of gratitude filled with the overflowing gems of a life lived to its fullest.

Further Contemplations

We can bring Tara Vasuda's gifts into our own lives, no matter who we are. Gratitude is a sign of inner wealth and abundance. When we are grateful, we experience the richness of the earth under our feet and appreciate the abundance of what is here now. When we are thankful for having received something—a gift, smile, compliment—we feel *good*. But sometimes we don't feel *grateful*; sometimes we forget to acknowledge what we do have and focus on what we don't.

We can think of gratitude as having a "greater attitude," a more expansive recognition of the gifts in our life. Even when things seem extraordinarily difficult, there is always something to be grateful for. It might be gratitude for learning how to be more patient, how to be humbler, how to not always need to be right. Or it might be feeling gratitude for this breath and this body, the food we eat, the air we breathe; or for the chirping of the birds and the rising of the sun each morning. The thirteenth-century German Catholic mystic Meister Eckhart (1260-1327) said, "If the only prayer you said was thank you, that would be enough."

When we give a gift—of money or something else—we can try accompanying it with a silent or spoken prayer such as "May this multiply a millionfold." This gesture of abundance helps us counteract constricted or stingy attitudes that we may unknowingly hold around money and other resources. Notice when you might be looping in poverty consciousness—the belief that there isn't enough to go around. Is this moment enough? Is this person enough? Am I enough? If you hear someone put themselves down, offer them the jewel of a compliment. Don't try to fix them or offer them solutions, simply tell them what you appreciate and love about them. Love is inexhaustible, like Tara Vasuda's treasure vase overflowing with jewels.

Connect with the earth guardians, the earth goddess, and Tara Vasuda through prayer, meditation, and simply touching the earth mindfully with love and reverence. Give thanks to them in your daily contemplations. May we all become guardians of the earth for the generations to come.

Here is a simple gratitude practice you can do anytime:

Find a comfortable position either seated or lying down. Take a few moments to breathe deeply and settle in. When you feel settled, relax control of your breath and breathe naturally. With your inhalation, feel the quality of receiving the breath; and with the exhalation, feel the quality of giving the breath. Just sense this simple dynamic of receiving with the inbreath and giving with the outbreath. Notice if the breath has a texture, color, or temperature; notice what is there without imposing anything. Soothe the body and mind into a natural breathing rhythm for a while.

Then, when you are ready, with the inhalation feel gratitude for whatever you cherish—for example, the natural beauty around you, your health, another person, or a pet. Take that in and enjoy it. With the exhalation feel the quality of generosity. Offer love, space, compassion, understanding, whatever you wish to that object of attention. Give out of a sense of abundance. The outbreath is an offering and a letting go. Spend some time with each object of attention, maybe five to ten breaths with each.

Then let go and simply spend some time allowing the mind roam freely, contemplating what you are grateful for. It may be people, experiences, qualities of your life. Feel each one in your body as you breathe. You might simply say in a whisper, "Thank you," again and again as you feel what you are grateful for naturally arising in you.

To conclude, slowly open your eyes. Notice how you feel now compared to how you felt before the practice. Acknowledge the gift you gave yourself in taking the time for practice. Maybe feel gratitude for that.

Eleventh Tara:
Tara Vasuda Embodiment Meditation

Before you begin, recall the three samadhis of emptiness, compassion, and the union of the two. Remember that all appearances of self and deity are empty of intrinsic existence yet manifest as ceaseless compassion.

Settle into a comfortable meditation seat and take nine relaxation breaths, breathing into any physical tension, then any emotional tension, and finally any mental tension and releasing it all with your exhalations.

Front Visualization

Imagine that from luminous empty space Tara Vasuda appears in the space in front and slightly above you, semifierce and golden red in color. Joyful and compassionate, she bestows wealth and liberates beings from all forms of poverty and misery. Rainbow wisdom light streams from her body and the treasure vase atop her lotus, granting all wishes and bestowing the gift of prosperity. She is surrounded by numerous wisdom beings.

Recite the Refuge and Bodhichitta Prayer (3 times)

NĀMO
Noble Tara, the essence of all refuges,
you liberate beings from fear and suffering.
I take refuge in your vast, loving compassion.
In order to bring all sentient beings to the state of enlightenment,
I generate the twofold bodhichitta of aspiration and action.

Self-Visualization

Sound Tara's seed syllable TĀM three times.

First TĀM: Imagine that your body becomes Tara Vasuda, golden red and semifierce. As Tara Vasuda, your body is luminous and hollow, with the TĀM in your heart center.

Second TĀM: As Tara Vasuda, send offerings of rainbow wisdom light to the wisdom beings. Let yourself truly sense this connection between you and them.

Third TĀM: Wisdom beings send rainbow wisdom light back to

you, empowering you as Tara Vasuda, fully activating you. Truly feel what it would be like to be the awakened buddha Tara Vasuda, a being of radiant light and infinite love and capacity.

Mantra Recitation and Enacting Tara's Enlightened Activities

As you recite the mantra, imagine the TĀM and the mantra garland at your heart emanate rainbow wisdom light in all directions. This light and the wisdom light emanating from the treasure vase grant all wishes and bestow the gift of prosperity, liberating beings from all forms of poverty and misery.

OM TARE TUTTARE TURE MAMA VASU PUSHTIM KURU SVAHA

Recite the mantra as many times as you like—but at least twenty-one times. Genuinely feel yourself as Tara Vasuda.

Dissolution and Rest in Awareness

When your mantra recitation feels complete, dissolve the visualization: first the world and its inhabitants, then you as Tara Vasuda converging at the TĀM in your heart center. Then everything becomes luminous emptiness.

Rest in spacious awareness—the vast, luminous, and wakeful nature of your own mind. Release into presence. When you are ready, return to your form as Tara Vasuda and feel yourself fully integrated with her. As you move about your day, recall the compassion and love of Tara Vasuda within and all around you.

Close the session with a sense of gratitude for Tara and her blessings.

Dedication of Merit

Through this virtue, may I quickly attain the state of Noble Tara.
May I bring each and every being, without exception, to that state.
May all beings be healthy, free from suffering and its causes,
    and may they awaken to their true nature.

DRÖLMA TASHI DÖNJEMA
(SKT. TARA MANGALARTHA)

The Twelfth Tara

Tara Who Brings About Auspiciousness

Homage to you, Mother [Tara], so brilliantly adorned,
With a crescent moon as your crown.
Amitabha sits amongst your locks [atop your head]
Ever shining with radiant light.

Tara Mangalartha catalyzes auspicious circumstances such as timely seasons, healthy children, and prosperity. She pacifies natural disasters and brings the five elements into balance. Therefore, Tara Mangalartha is our "Climate Justice Tara." She is peaceful and golden yellow, signaling her ratna buddha family connection.

Tara Mangalartha's name embodies the essence of auspiciousness, therefore I call her "Tara Who Brings About Auspiciousness." In Sanskrit, *mangala* means "prosperity" and "auspicious." *Artha* means "sense" or "meaning." In her Tibetan name Drölma Tashi Dönjema, *tashi* means "auspicious" and is also found in the common greeting *tashi deleg*, which means "auspicious goodness." In Tibetan, *dön* means "meaning," and *je* means "to do" or "to make." Thus, we can translate the compound word *dönje* as "to make meaning" or even "to give meaning."

Her Mantra

ༀ་ཏུ་རེ་ཏུཏྟ་རེ་ཏུ་རེ་མངྒལཾ་ཤྲི་མ་ཧ་པ་ཎི་སྭ་ཧ།

OṂ TĀRE TUTTĀRE TURE MAṄGALAṂ ŚRĪ MAHĀ PĀṆI SVĀHĀ
OM TARE TUTTARE TURE MANGALAM SHRI MAHA PANI SVAHA
OṂ! Tara! Be swift, Tara! Bestow your great gift of auspiciousness. So be it!

Her Symbol: Glorious Endless Knot

Tara Mangalartha's symbol is the endless knot.[1] One of the eight auspicious symbols in Buddhism, the endless knot represents the interdependent nature of all things. This symbol beautifully illuminates the Buddha's teachings on interdependence expressed in the following stanza in many Buddhist scriptures:

> This is because that is.
> This is not because that is not.
> This ceases to be because that ceases to be.[2]

Tara Mangalartha's endless knot is akin to the mythical image of Indra's net[3] that represents the interdependent, interwoven fabric of reality. When the Vedic god Indra created the universe, he wove a cosmic net over the world and placed multifaceted jewels at each juncture. Each jewel reflects every other jewel of this celestial net, revealing a cosmos of infinite realms within realms mutually containing one another. Indra's net symbolizes the infinitely vast and interdependent web of all existence.[4]

Exploring Tara Mangalartha's Facets

Tara Mangalartha's praise depicts her with a crescent moon as her crown. The crescent moon represents the eighth day of the waxing moon of the lunar calendar. It is believed that at this time of the month, the moonlight gives off cooling energy that balances and calms beings, bringing auspicious harmony to the world. This day is associated with Tara and the Medicine Buddha and thus is an auspicious day to do her meditation practice.[5]

The last two lines of Tara Mangalartha's praise highlight a special figure resting on the crown of her head: Amitabha, the Buddha of Infinite Light. The Khenpo brothers point out that Amitabha appears at the crown of each of the twenty-one Taras' heads, even though he is not always depicted there in art. Like Avalokiteshvara—

whose pure land is also found within Amitabha's Blissful pure land—Tara is considered an emanation of Buddha Amitabha. Tara's pure land of Turquoise Leaves is situated within Amitabha's Blissful pure land.

Interdependence and Emptiness

Because Tara Mangalartha embodies the interdependent and auspicious qualities of the natural world, we will explore what is meant by the term *interdependence*, or *tendrel*[6] in Tibetan. The Mahayana scholar-saint Nagarjuna (c. 150–c. 250 C.E.) elaborated on the Buddha's teachings on interdependence and emptiness in his seminal text *Fundamental Verses on the Middle Way*.[7] Nagarjuna states that all experienced phenomena (*dharmas*) are dependently arisen (*tendrel*) and therefore empty of intrinsic existence (*svabhava*).[8] In other words, to say an object is "empty" is synonymous with saying that it is "dependently arisen."[9]

Let's unpack that for a moment. In essence, all dharmas—meaning all phenomena—exist in dependence upon other dharmas. This means that dharmas are devoid of or empty of any intrinsic self-existing nature; they do exist, yet they are *empty of inherent existence*. In other words, phenomena such as a chair or a cloud do exist, but they do not exist objectively from their own side. This means phenomena do not exist independently of causes and conditions *and* do not exist independently of our subjective perception of them. Perceived appearances are filtered through the subjective observer and thus are not separate from our perception of them.

The interdependent nature of all phenomena—tendrel—has become more widely recognized and integrated into modern scientific fields such as the natural, ecological, economic, and psychological sciences.[10] From a quantum physics perspective, scientists including Albert Einstein, Max Planck, and Niels Bohr acknowledged that depending on the instrument of measurement (subjective observation) used, every particle (elementary particles and compound particles like atoms and molecules) may be described as either a particle or a wave. This shows that subjective observation and measurement play a role in our perception. This challenges the assumption that there is a purely objective reality out there that we can understand completely independent of our perception of it.

Biology offers a useful example of the auspicious web of interdependence—the mutually beneficial and benevolent relational cooperation that ensures the flourishing of participating species.[11] Since the 1980s, the biologists David Reed and Suzanne Simard, among others, have proven the hypothesis that there is an "underground network found in forests and other plant communities, created by the hyphae of mycorrhizal fungi joining with plant roots, … [that] connects individual plants … and water, carbon, nitrogen, and other nutrients and minerals between participants."[12] This mycorrhizal (fungus root) network echoes the most fundamental principle of ecology, that of the relationships between organisms, and illustrates the fascinating "wood wide web" of nature (not to be confused with the World Wide Web of the internet). Whereas previously plants were believed to compete for resources, they are more commonly understood to be participating in a "source-sink model," where plants growing under relatively high resources offer carbon and nutrients to plants in less favorable conditions. This reveals that mycorrhizal relationships are more mutualistic than earlier thought with both partners often benefiting in the exchange.

Let's bring this down to earth and tap into the root of our meditation practice. A foundational Dharma practice called the four applications of mindfulness guides us into a personal experience of interdependence. In this practice, we contemplate perception's source, location, and destination in four domains of our personal experience—bodily sensations, emotions, thoughts, and phenomena.[13] This practice brings us to a somatic experience of insight (vipashyana), whereby we come to know intimately the empty, interdependent nature of all phenomena. The Buddha taught that this insight, integrated with the meditative concentration of shamatha, brings about liberation from samsara. When this realization dawns, the illusory "pot" of the separate self shatters; our awareness mixes with space; and we realize that the space outside the pot is no different than the space inside the pot. Our separate sense of ego evaporates, and we realize we are everything and everything is us. We see the multifaceted jewels reflecting everything else in Indra's cosmic net.

When we experience the interdependence of ourselves and the world, we tap into the auspicious web of existence and embody Tara Mangalartha's gift of connection. We no longer feel alone, even in a solitary mountain retreat or a prison cell. Discovering this tendrel is like digging beneath the forest floor to reveal the existence of a glowing web of mutually benefiting networks. We experience firsthand the interrelated web of life, like the mycelia of the natural world. This is Tara Mangalartha's enlightened power manifest in the natural world.

Real-Life Embodiment

Greta Thunberg

Our real-life "Climate Justice Tara" is Greta Thunberg (b. 2003), a Swedish climate and environmental activist known for her advocacy for the environment, children, and future generations. She has catalyzed people worldwide to get involved in the fight for climate justice, a movement that recognizes the causal relationship between historical injustices and our current climate crisis.[14] While Thunberg's story isn't over, we can see how her advocacy embodies Tara Mangalartha's superpower of seeing the connections and implications of our actions in the world and for future generations.

Centering the voices of Indigenous climate activists and climate scientists, Thunberg beseeches politicians to listen to those offering intelligent and concrete ways to solve the climate crisis. She has inspired many people to hold world leaders accountable. This was evident when, in 2018, Thunberg took action by striking outside the Swedish parliament every Friday to pressure lawmakers to address the climate crisis more earnestly. These protests went viral with students from around the world participating in their own *Fridays for Future* to call for climate justice.

A couple of months later, in December 2018, Thunberg gave her famous speech addressing the United Nations COP24 climate talks in Poland in which she criticized world leaders for failing to take sufficient action to address the climate crisis. She galvanized the world, saying that we are never too small to make a difference. Admonishing them for focusing on enriching a small number of people at the expense of future generations, she implored them to do what was right: leave fossil fuels in the ground, focus on equity, and either find solutions or change the system itself.[15] Digging beneath the surface of greed and corruption, Thunberg embodies Tara Mangalartha's enlightened purpose by bringing climate realities to light so that we can begin to heal them.

Understanding that in any crisis the poorest and most vulnerable people often suffer the most, Thunberg partnered with UNICEF in 2020 as the global COVID-19 pandemic forced vital resources to be brought to children in areas of need. Although children were not the primary group at risk for this coronavirus, Thunberg recognized that they suffered the most when schools are shut down, limiting their access to health services, daily nutrition, water, and sanitation. In this way, Thunberg embodies Tara Mangalartha's enlightened activity of supporting children's flourishing on a global scale.

Further Contemplations

How might we embody Tara Mangalartha's qualities of living in harmony with nature and seasonal shifts? Tara Mangalartha is revered for bringing about timely seasons, ensuring that crops will grow and everyone will be fed and prosper. Are you in touch with your own internal seasons? At times we may feel more extroverted, like in the warmth of summer when things are in full bloom. At other times we may feel more introverted, like in the winter when the sap draws closer to the trees' cores. We may have times of going out and meeting new people or staying in and nourishing solitude.

Listen to these seasonal shifts in your own life and adapt accordingly whenever possible; do so with a light touch, free of rigidity. On the eighth lunar day, you may wish to carve out time for meditation practice on your own or with others, or maybe to do a personal home retreat with multiple sessions throughout your day.[16] If you have other practices, you could choose to focus on a Tara practice on the eighth lunar day and do your other practices on different days.

How might you help to bring more harmony and good health to the children in your life? Find time to be out in nature together, talk about what you can do for the environment, and encourage small actionable steps toward ecological and social harmony with your surroundings. You may commit to using less plastic or eating less meat, teaching children how to make good choices with a sense of joy, not guilt or rigidity. It is easy for children to be inspired but overwhelmed by the immensity of the climate crisis, so creatively tap into resources that uplift them. We all can develop a greater capacity to contribute to the interconnected healing of our world and those who live in it.

Let us connect with Tara Mangalartha by nourishing our inner resources through meditation and spiritual practice while also getting out and making our voices heard. When asked about the relationship between activism and mindfulness, Angela Davis (b. 1944), the American political activist, philosopher, scholar, and author, said, "For activists, mindfulness allows us to think deeply about ourselves. For practitioners, mindfulness will show us that work is still to be done."[17] This balance of our active (activism) and contemplative (mindfulness) lives is one way, in my experience, that we can bring about Tara Mangalartha's "auspicious circumstances" in our self and the world. We might contemplate Martin Luther King Jr. (1929-1968) when he said, "Whatever affects one directly, affects all indirectly. I can never be what I ought to be until you are what you ought to be. This is the interrelated structure of reality."[18]

Twelfth Tara:
Tara Mangalartha Embodiment Meditation

Before you begin, recall the three samadhis of emptiness, compassion, and the union of the two. Remember that all appearances of self and deity are empty of intrinsic existence yet manifest as ceaseless compassion.

Settle into a comfortable meditation seat and take nine relaxation breaths, breathing into any physical tension, then any emotional tension, and finally any mental tension and releasing it all with your exhalations.

Front Visualization

Imagine that from luminous empty space Tara Mangalartha appears in the space in front and slightly above you, peaceful and golden yellow in color. Tara Mangalartha brings about auspicious circumstances such as timely seasons, good harvests, healthy children, and prosperity. Internally, she brings about health and well-being. Rainbow wisdom light streams from her body, the crescent moon at her crown, the ruby-red Amitabha in her hair, and the endless knot atop her lotus, bringing blessings and cooling energy to all beings without limit. She is surrounded by numerous wisdom beings.

Recite the Refuge and Bodhichitta Prayer (3 times)

NĀMO
Noble Tara, the essence of all refuges,
you liberate beings from fear and suffering.
I take refuge in your vast, loving compassion.
In order to bring all sentient beings to the state of
    enlightenment,
I generate the twofold bodhichitta of aspiration and action.

Self-Visualization

Sound Tara's seed syllable TĀM three times.

First TĀM: Imagine that your body becomes Tara Mangalartha, peaceful and golden yellow. Your body is luminous and hollow, with the TĀM in your heart center.

Second TĀM: As Tara Mangalartha, send offerings of rainbow wisdom light to the wisdom beings. Let yourself truly sense this connection between you and them.

Third TĀM: Wisdom beings send rainbow wisdom light back to you, empowering you as Tara Mangalartha, fully activating you. Truly feel what it would be like to be the awakened buddha Tara Mangalartha, a being of radiant light and infinite love and capacity.

Mantra Recitation

As you recite the mantra, imagine the TĀM and the mantra garland at your heart emanate rainbow wisdom light in all directions. This light and the wisdom light emanating from the endless knot, crescent moon, and Buddha Amitabha radiate out to all beings in the form of cool healing energy.

OM TARE TUTTARE TURE MANGALAM SHRI MAHA PANI SVAHA

Recite the mantra as many times as you like—but at least twenty-one times. Genuinely feel yourself as Tara Mangalartha.

Dissolution and Rest in Awareness

When your mantra recitation feels complete, dissolve the visualization: first the world and its inhabitants, then you as Tara Mangalartha converging at the TĀM in your heart center. Then everything becomes luminous emptiness.

Rest in spacious awareness—the vast, luminous, and wakeful

nature of your own mind. Release into presence. When you are ready, return to your form as Tara Mangalartha and feel yourself fully integrated with her. As you move about your day, recall the compassion and love of Tara Mangalartha within and all around you.

Close the session with a sense of gratitude to Tara and her blessings.

Dedication of Merit

Through this virtue, may I quickly attain the state of Noble Tara.

May I bring each and every being, without exception, to that state.

May all beings be healthy, free from suffering and its causes, and may they awaken to their true nature.

DRÖLMA YULLE GYALJEMA
(SKT. TARA RIPU CHAKRA VINASHINI)

The Thirteenth Tara

Tara Who Is Victorious Over War

Homage to you, Mother [Tara], seated amidst a
brilliantly radiant garland like the fire at the end of an eon.
Your right leg stretched out and left bent inward,
Immersed in joy, you abolish legions of foes.

Tara Ripu Chakra Vinashini is red and semifierce.[1] Outwardly, Tara Vinashini—as I will call her—protects beings from violence and war, preventing destruction caused by anger and aggression. Inwardly, she destroys the "hosts of human and non-human enemies and harm-doers"[2] that are the two veils or obscurations—(1) emotional obscurations (five poisons of ignorance, aversion, conceit, clinging, and jealousy) and (2) cognitive obscurations (reifying self and phenomena as being intrinsically existent). When we pacify these two veils, we arrive naturally without effort at the threshold of liberation. We are enlightened.

At times Tara Vinashini is depicted seated like the other Taras, and at times she is shown dancing. In both cases, she is amid a "blazing garland of raging wisdom fire, like the fire at...the end of an eon."[3] In her full splendor, she is able to withstand and even harness the heat that brings the end of an eon; she is replenished and renewed by it. This means that any potential hostile forces—inner or outer—should know to show her respect. Through her fierce protective dynamism, she brings joy and peace to all sentient beings.

Tara Vinashini's Sanskrit and Tibetan names vary slightly, but the essential meaning is the same. In Sanskrit, her name can be translated as "she who demolishes (*vinashini*) the ring (*chakra*) of enemies (*ripu*)."[4] In Tibetan, the connotation is the same, but the words differ slightly: "she who (*ma*) is victorious (*gyalje*) over (*le*) war (*yul*)." When shortening her name to Tara Vinashini, we could translate it as "Demolition Tara" because she demolishes, with compassionate skill, all inner and outer enemies.

Her Mantra

ཨོཾ་ཏུ་རེ་ཏུཏྟཱ་རེ་ཏུ་རེ་བཛྲ་ཛྭཱ་ལ་ཕཊཿཕཊཿརཀྵ་རཀྵ་སྭཱ་ཧཱ།

OṂ TĀRE TUTTĀRE TURE VAJRA JVALA PHAṬ PHAṬ RAKṢA
    RAKṢA SVĀHĀ

OM TARE TUTTARE TURE VAJRA JVALA PHAT PHAT RAKSHA
    RAKSHA SVAHA

OṂ! Tara! Be swift, Tara! Blazing vajras! PHAṬ! PHAṬ!
Protection! Protection! So be it!

Her Symbol: Open-Pronged Vajra

Tara Vinashini's symbol is the open-pronged vajra. Usually the vajra's prongs are closed and tapered at the top and bottom, but here they are flared open on both ends, symbolizing her fierce nature and dynamic skillful means to vanquish all that is harmful. The open prongs emit tiny vajras, each multiplying countless sparkling vajras in all directions. These vajras form an indestructible protective tent of rainbow-colored double vajras[5] (like a luminous net) around areas in need, safeguarding beings from war, aggression, and danger. Double vajras represent stability, and the five-colored rainbow lights represent the five wisdoms and the five elements, all unifying to create this elemental indestructible tent.

Exploring Tara Vinashini's Facets

Now let's explore the theme of this thirteenth Tara—to protect beings from the violence of war and all seen and unseen manifestations of harm. Buddhist practitioners often find that particular Taras align uncannily with events in their lives. There are two instances in which Tara Vinashini's presence made itself known in mysterious ways in my life. The first was in September 2020 during the largest wildfire season in California's modern history, with about 4.4 million acres burned by the end of the year. As the smoke from the fires in Northern California began to settle over the San Francisco Bay Area where I live, the air quality became dismal. The morning I was to teach on Tara Vinashini, I awoke at daybreak to an eerily dark sky. As the day progressed, the sky began to glow with a smoldering red, casting an otherworldly Martian-like sepia tone as far as the eye could see. As one journalist put it, the Bay Area woke up and said, "What the f*ck." Amid the dismal political climate of the Trump and COVID-19 era, this doomsday atmosphere increased the feeling of living through the apocalypse, perhaps what it would feel like at "the end of an eon." When I logged into my online twenty-one Taras class, my body and my office were shrouded in a veil of red, creating the surreal feeling of being *within* Tara Vinashini's apocalyptic aura of blazing wisdom flames. The participants and I took a moment to acknowledge the bizarre coincidence we witnessed on this day devoted to Tara Vinashini; it was too strange even to begin to explain. So we practiced Tara Vinashini's meditation and mantra, imagining that we embodied her protective power, visualizing the rainbow vajra tent protecting all those in harm's way, whether in the path of the fire or other war-torn areas worldwide. We also imagined that our compassionate wisdom and power healed and liberated the ways in which we suffered mentally and emotionally. We recognized that, in our essence, we are none other than Tara Vinashini. And then we came to the dissolution stage where we dissolve all effort, all visualization, leaving us in an unfabricated, uncontrived experience of resting in spacious awareness, vast like the sky. The dissolution stage brings us to the ultimate experience of Tara, the nature of our mind, and prepares us for death—as we shed the physical body and return to the clear light of awareness, we come home. In all these ways, we embodied the immediacy of

Tara's blessings and, in some way, made sense of the unexplainable events of that time.

Another spectral coincidence occurred on the very day I began writing this chapter a year and a half later. It was in late February 2022, the day Russia invaded Ukraine. Lama Tsultrim texted me that morning, asking which Tara we should activate for this time in history. I told her that Tara Vinashini is made for this, and we immediately put out a call to practice via Tara Mandala's social media networks, asking people worldwide to mobilize in doing Tara Vinashini's visualization and mantra, imagining a protective rainbow vajra tent surrounding those in danger. We unified our prayers with skillful action by encouraging people to donate to and volunteer for legitimate organizations like the International Rescue Committee (IRC) and UNICEF. Our Polish sangha began raising money for Ukrainians taking refuge across the border.

Then, in March, when Ukrainian president Volodymyr Zelensky's request for the United States and NATO to establish a no-fly zone over parts of Ukraine to protect civilians was denied due to concerns that doing so would potentially lead to nuclear war, I realized that at least we could apply Tara Vinashini's protective vajra tent in a similar way, as a kind of rainbow vajra tent no-fly zone. Instead of feeling utterly powerless, we channeled our prayers, imagining that a rainbow tent of double vajras protected all those threatened by this and other wars around the world. As I write, the war rages on and our global sangha continues to practice in solidarity with Ukrainians and Russians who advocate for peace. To date, our global sangha has collectively recited 9.8 million Tara Vinashini mantras. Any of the twenty-one Taras could have been my focus on that day in February, as she is the "Savioress," but for some serendipitous reason, it was Tara Vinashini.

Ultimate Savior, Ultimate Protection

Because the themes of protection and saving in Tara Vinashini's description and mantra are so prevalent, I would like to spend some time discussing what this means from the perspective of the Dharma. Tara the Savioress ferries beings in a cosmic boat over the ocean of samsara to nirvana. Many of the twenty-one Taras' enlightened activities focus on saving beings from harm, danger, disease, poison, war, untimely death, and so on. This highlights a crucial aspect of the Buddhist path—to release fixation on our sense of individual self that feels the need to be saved or protected by some external power in the first place.

You might wonder, how on earth do we release fixation on the self, let alone overcome the need for protection? Essentially, how do we overcome the fear of death? One way, as taught by the Buddha, is to meet this fear of death head-on. Contemplating death and impermanence is one of the foundational practices of the "four thoughts that turn the mind."[6] The practice is called *maranasati*, "mindfulness of death" or "recollecting death," and it consists of a series of contemplations such as that death is certain yet the time of death is not and the eventual breaking down of the body during the dying process. The purpose is to deepen our appreciation of our mortality to lessen death anxiety and enhance our passion for living.

Research shows that coming to terms with death and impermanence can be quite liberating and essential to living well. Westerners tend to be socialized to avoid discussing or even thinking about death, which can lead to anxiety or even terror of this inevitable event. Through death mindfulness practice we come to realize that nothing is guaranteed, that life doesn't owe us anything. We learn not to take anyone or anything for granted and to be grateful for what we have. For those of us who have witnessed the passing of a loved one, we know that death is the greatest of all teachers, an essential expression of the truth of impermanence. It helps us prioritize what is important in our lives and might even motivate us to practice so that we feel ready when our time comes.

The Buddha emphasized the importance of meditating on death and impermanence as a way to touch the deathless nature beneath the surface illusion of this body and this self—this is our innate wisdom. Contemplating death and impermanence as a path to wisdom is not the sole domain of Buddhists, however. For example, on his deathbed, Socrates urged his students to practice dying as the highest form of wisdom. In quiet contemplation of death and impermanence, we directly access the more expansive awareness that lies beyond the realm of birth and death. This undying nature, our buddha nature, cannot die because it was never born. It transcends the duality of time and space, and like Prajnaparamita, it cannot be defined by words or concepts. We must experience our own wisdom nature firsthand in order to know it with certainty. Through meditation, we learn to befriend our anxiety and fear of death, and we become intimate with the deathless unending nature of mind. All the Tara meditations in this book bring us to this experience—especially the dissolution phase, otherwise known as the completion phase, where we drop all activity and identity and experience our vast buddha nature, unbound and free.

This ability to abide in our natural state with ease and stability *is the ultimate protection* and *is* Tara the Savioress at her innermost essence. Tara is none other than your mind's luminous, primordially pure nature. We must not forget this. Be aware of mistakenly reifying Tara as a solidly, independently existing entity out there somewhere. Instead, understand her infinite forms to be expressions of the luminous nature of your primordial awareness.

In no way do I mean to say that we should disregard real-life safety and protection; we must be safe and provide security for others. There is value in praying to Tara and other deities—as we did during the California wildfires and the war in Ukraine—but in your personal times of contemplation, remind yourself to rest in the deep knowing of your true nature so that you are ready and at peace when your time comes to shed the cloak of this physical form and reunite with the love that is Mother Tara.

This leads us to Tara Vinashini's inner aspect of pacifying our so-called enemy of ego-clinging and mental afflictions that come from that core delusion of grasping to a separate self. Rather than being a problem, these inner enemies are fertile ground for our garden of wisdom. There are times when we may feel we need to employ

Tara Vinashini's joyful yet fierce open-pronged vajra pyrotechnics along with her rainbow protective tent to create a safe container to go within to do our inner healing. In this way, through her mantra and meditation practice, we manifest her compassionate power in service of healing these inner wounds of self-clinging and the subsequent mental afflictions that arise from it.

Now let's explore these themes through the eyes of our real-life Tara Vinashini.

Real-Life Embodiment
Zainab Salbi

Born in Iraq in 1969, Zainab Salbi is an Iraqi American humanitarian, writer, and public speaker who has committed most of her life to helping individuals ravaged by war. Like Tara Vinashini, she has shed light on the untold side of war—how it affects women, children, and families in ways that have often gone unseen and unaddressed by governments and the mainstream media.

Growing up in Baghdad during the Iran–Iraq War showed Salbi the overt and hidden effects of conflict and the fear and danger of living in a dictatorship. Salbi recounts how her mother would try to maintain a semblance of normalcy and stability by playing puppet stories and music with the children during bombing raids. I see the music and puppet stories as rainbow protective tents woven by a mother's love for her children. Stories like these motivated Salbi to found Women for Women International (WfWI) at the age of twenty-three. WfWI is a grassroots humanitarian organization dedicated to serving women survivors of war by offering support, tools, and access to life-changing skills to help them move from crisis and poverty to stability and economic self-sufficiency.

When she learned about the horrors of the rape camps during the war in Bosnia and Herzegovina (1992–95), she launched WfWI's first project creating "sister-to-sister" connections (like a linked double vajra network) between sponsors in the United States and women survivors of this war. She chronicles these women's experiences of rebuilding their lives after going through the violence and abuses of war in her third book, *The Other Side of War*. WfWI also educates men in cultures across the world where spousal abuse is common, helping them develop skills to succeed, feel good about themselves, and understand why abuse of wives and children must stop. Salbi's tremendous global impact on women, children, and families mirrors Tara Vinashini's protective compassion that heals the wounds of war.

Further Contemplations

Perhaps our work is not as grand as Salbi's or as enlightened as Tara Vinashini's. Still, at times we may be able to befriend our obscurations—expressions of fear and confusion—by imagining ourselves and others wrapped in the loving rainbow protective tent of double vajras, both internally and externally, supporting us in our life and liberation. Whenever you feel unsafe, you can imagine Tara Vinashini's protective tent around you, your family, and the world.

If you are privileged with safety and resources, find tangible ways to help protect other beings from violence and harm. You might choose organizations like WfWI, Doctors Without Borders, UNICEF, the International Rescue Committee, and others that assist individuals threatened by or suffering from the effects of war. We can also put our prayers into action by supporting those who work to further nonviolence and employ diplomatic methods to resolve conflict. Like Tara Vinashini, get activated and channel the heat of passion for being of service to others in need.

Thirteenth Tara:
Tara Vinashini Embodiment Meditation

Before you begin, recall the three samadhis of emptiness, compassion, and the union of the two. Remember that all appearances of self and deity are empty of intrinsic existence yet manifest as ceaseless compassion.

Settle into a comfortable meditation seat and take nine relaxation breaths, breathing into any physical tension, then any emotional tension, and finally any mental tension and releasing it all with your exhalations.

Front Visualization

Imagine that from luminous empty space Tara Vinashini appears in the space in front and slightly above you, dark red in color and semifierce, surrounded by blazing wisdom flames. A multitude of tiny vajras radiate out from her open-pronged vajra, each multiplying countless sparkling vajras in all directions. These vajras form an indestructible protective tent of rainbow-colored vajras, protecting beings from war, aggression, and danger. She is surrounded by numerous wisdom beings.

Recite the Refuge and Bodhichitta Prayer (3 times)

NĀMO
Noble Tara, the essence of all refuges,
you liberate beings from fear and suffering.
I take refuge in your vast, loving compassion.
In order to bring all sentient beings to the state of
    enlightenment,
I generate the twofold bodhichitta of aspiration and action.

Self-Visualization

Sound Tara's seed syllable TĀM three times.
    First TĀM: Imagine that your body becomes Tara Vinashini, red and semifierce. As Tara Vinashini, your body is luminous and hollow, with the TĀM in your heart center.
    Second TĀM: As Tara Vinashini, send offerings of rainbow wisdom light to the wisdom beings. Let yourself truly sense this connection between you and them.

Third TĀM: Wisdom beings send rainbow wisdom light back to you, empowering you as Tara Vinashini, fully activating you. Truly feel what it would be like to be the awakened buddha Tara Vinashini, a being of radiant light and infinite love and capacity.

Mantra Recitation

As you recite the mantra, imagine the TĀM and the mantra garland at your heart emanate rainbow wisdom light in all directions. Tiny vajras spark out from your open-pronged vajra, each multiplying countless sparkling vajras in all directions. These vajras form an indestructible protective tent of rainbow-colored vajras, protecting beings from war, aggression, and danger and removing outer and inner obstacles. All beings become free from suffering as they awaken to their true nature.

OM TARE TUTTARE TURE VAJRA JVALA PHAT PHAT RAKSHA RAKSHA SVAHA

Recite the mantra as many times as you like—but at least twenty-one times. Genuinely feel yourself as Tara Vinashini.

Dissolution and Rest in Awareness

When your mantra recitation feels complete, dissolve the visualization: first the world and its inhabitants, then you as Tara Vinashini converging at the TĀM in your heart center. Then everything becomes luminous emptiness.

Rest in spacious awareness—the vast, luminous, and wakeful nature of your own mind. Release into presence. When you are ready, return to your form as Tara Vinashini and feel yourself fully integrated with her. As you move about your day, recall the compassion and love of Tara Vinashini within and all around you.

Close the session with a sense of gratitude to Tara and her blessings.

Dedication of Merit

> Through this virtue, may I quickly attain the state of Noble Tara.
>
> May I bring each and every being, without exception, to that state.
>
> May all beings be healthy, free from suffering and its causes, and may they awaken to their true nature.

DRÖLMA TRONYER CHENMA
(SKT. TARA BHRUKUTI)

The Fourteenth Tara

Tara Who Frowns Fiercely

Homage to Mother [Tara], striking the earth
with the palms of your hands and pounding it with your feet,
Frowning and fierce, you grind the seven underworlds[1]
Into dust with the syllable HŪṂ.

Tara Bhrukuti is very fierce and blue-black in color. She pacifies our innermost subtle delusions and misperceptions that are often the most challenging to see, let alone heal. Her enlightened activity is to liberate these delusions into the true nature of reality, called suchness (dharmata). This does *not* mean that she banishes delusions to hell or prison but rather she releases them from duality and thereby dissolves them into a blissful state of peace.

Tara Bhrukuti's name has essentially the same meaning in Sanskrit and Tibetan. In Sanskrit, *bhrukuti* means "she with the bent brow" or "the frowning goddess" from *bhr/bhru* ("eyebrow") and *kuti* ("twisted," "bent"). In Tibetan, *tro* means "fierce," *nyer* "wrinkle," and *chenma* "she who possesses," thus "Tara Who Frowns Fiercely."

Her Mantra

ཨོཾ་ཏཱ་རེ་ཏུཏྟཱ་རེ་ཏུ་རེ་ཧཱུྃ་ཧཱུྃ་ཧ་ཾ་ཤ་ཾ་ཏྲི་གྷ་ནན་ཕཊ་སྭཱ་ཧཱ།

OṂ TĀRE TUTTĀRE TURE HŪṂ HŪṂ HAṂ ŚAṂ TRIGHNAN
PHAṬ SVĀHĀ
OṂ TARE TUTTARE TURE HUNG HUNG HAM SHAM TRIGHNAN
PHAT SVAHA
OṂ! Tara! Be swift, Tara! HŪṂ HŪṂ HAṂ ŚAṂ! Thrice
suppressing! PHAṬ! So be it!

Her Symbol: Wooden Pestle

Upon Tara Bhrukuti's lotus flower stands a large wooden pestle,[2] which symbolizes her power to pacify, subdue, and grind all obstacles into dust. Traditionally this wooden pestle is used in India to pound nuts and seeds. It is so large that it requires two people to hold it while grinding substances.

Exploring Tara Bhrukuti's Facets

In Jigme Lingpa's commentary to the *Praises*, he describes Tara Bhrukuti as shaking the entire universe, pounding the earth with her hands and feet, chanting HŪṂ, HŪṂ, and grinding our subtlest negativities and delusions into dust—or should we say stardust, given Tara's affiliation with stars. Her fierce HŪṂs and blazing wisdom light liberate our subtlest delusions into suchness, bestowing peace to all beings. As the Khenpo brothers say, she irons out the smallest "wrinkles" in our minds through her pounding. Grinding negativities into dust is a common metaphor in tantric Buddhist practices, such as the Chöd dance in which we imagine that all obstacles and so-called demons are pacified and ground down, no longer able to cause harm.

Tara Bhrukuti's ability to release the subtlest obstacles and delusions into the state of suchness reminds me of the Dzogchen teachings called "natural liberation" (*rangdrol*) whereby our mental afflictions when released from dualistic clinging dissolve of their own accord. A common teaching analogy is to relax the mind, just like a snake tied in knots: when it releases tension, it naturally unravels into its natural state. When our challenges are liberated or released into suchness, it is like clouds dissolving back into the sky, the space from which they came. Dudjom Rinpoche, in his text *The Wish-Fulfilling Gem of Siddhis*, instructs us on how to relate to thoughts in meditation:

> Gazing intently at the very essential nature of whatever arises, without modification, let thoughts descend naturally and flow freely. Joyfully, let them shimmer vividly, without leaving a trace! Let them roll on aimlessly, without restraint, and release them without limits [while] resting spaciously without grasping![3]

This is a refreshing meditative approach, one that might not look like what Tara Bhrukuti does with her HŪṂs and her pounding at first glance but in essence is based on the same understanding: all perceptual appearances[4] whether they are pleasurable or unpleasurable, peaceful or disruptive, arise from and eventually dissolve back into the space of awareness. As we explore embodying Tara Bhrukuti, we might inquire into how to experience this for ourselves. We may at times dance, stomp, and pound a drum, or we may at other times release and rest—or both! Remember the teaching "Manifest, then take a rest"? This oscillation of contraction (manifest) and release (take a rest) helps us to let go more deeply into presence. Tara Bhrukuti is a manifestation of that liberative quality of Tara but with more *oomph*—a fierceness that is needed from time to time when subtle confusion or delusion is stubbornly entrenched.

Shamatha meditation includes a myriad of different techniques to cultivate a relaxed, concentrated, and clear mind. One such approach emphasizes the "release into space" style that is often found within Dzogchen and Mahamudra. My teacher Dr. B. Alan Wallace translated the following teachings by Padmasambhava under the guidance of the Venerable Gyatrul Rinpoche (1925-2023) and taught them to me in 1997. I encourage you to integrate this into your regular practice if you feel it is of benefit:

> Cast your gaze downwards, gently release your mind, and without having anything on which to meditate, gently release both your body and mind into their natural state. Having nothing on which to meditate, and without any modification, place your attention simply without wavering, in its own natural state, its natural limpidity, its own character, just as it is. Remain in clarity and rest the mind so that it is loose and free. Alternate between observing who is concentrating inwardly and who is releasing. If it is the mind, ask: what is that very agent that releases the mind and concentrates the mind? And steadily observe yourself. Then release again. By so doing, fine stability will arise, and you may even identify awareness...[5]

Another approach, as taught by two of the greatest Tibetan Buddhist teachers of all time—Milarepa and Machig Labdrön—is to rest your mind in meditation, like above, and whenever you notice conceptual ideation churning up—distraction or lethargy taking over—sound loudly the seed syllable "PHAṬ!" and then rest in the quietude that follows. This forceful sound of PHAṬ is meant to bring about a feeling of "cutting through" the continual flow of conceptual ideation, opening us to a space of wakeful clarity, the natural state free of distraction and grasping. Give those techniques a try and see what feels most effective to you.

Unpacking Tara Bhrukuti's Mantra

Let's explore Tara Bhrukuti's mantra because it is packed with seed syllables that highlight her purpose. We've seen the first seed syllable, ʜᴜ̄ᴍ, before, which represents the "enlightened mind." In this mantra, ʜᴜ̄ᴍ is the main sound Tara Bhrukuti makes as she stomps the earth to enact her enlightened activities. Given her fierce and dynamic character, "ʜᴜ̄ᴍ! ʜᴜ̄ᴍ!" in this context might mean, "Wake up to your enlightened mind!"[6] The seed syllable ʜᴀᴍ (rhymes with *mom*) represents bliss in Vajrayana teachings. In Tibetan yoga, it signifies the male essence of bliss visualized at the crown of the head. The next seed syllable is ᶊᴀᴍ (also rhymes with *mom*), meaning "being tranquil." It has the same Sanskrit root as *shanti*, meaning "peace."[7] In Vajrayana, shanti refers to the "great peace"[8] synonymous with the state of prajnaparamita, the perfection of wisdom, beyond duality of samsara and nirvana.

The Sanskrit word *trighnan* means "thrice defeating" or "thrice suppressing,"[9] This may sound antithetical to the more peaceful-sounding natural liberation, but they essentially get at the same outcome of liberation. At times there is a more forceful, dynamic approach, like "ʜᴜ̄ᴍ!" and "ᴘʜᴀᴛ!" and at times a more soft, long, and relaxed sound, "ʜᴜ̄ᴍ…" and "ᴘʜᴀᴛ…" Play with it, see how it feels to do both approaches.

Now let's meet the phenomenal real-life Tara Bhrukuti.

Real-Life Embodiment
Qiu Jin

Qiu Jin, a Chinese revolutionary, feminist, writer, and poet, was born in 1875 in Xiamen, Fujian, China, on the Taiwan Strait. Inspired by the life stories of Chinese heroines such as Mulan, she resisted the stifling patriarchal traditions of her era. Qiu Jin's insistence on walking the earth as a free woman, of "[u]nbinding…[her]…feet to pour out a millennium's poisons,"[10] of traveling far and wide to educate herself, of writing and speaking out in support of women's rights, are powerful examples of Tara Bhrukuti's enlightened activity. By unraveling the bonds that kept her tethered to the hearth, Qiu Jin reclaimed her basic human freedoms to move, learn, and lead an uprising in the hopes of liberating other women. Considered China's Joan of Arc, Qiu Jin was posthumously immortalized in the Republic of China's literature and popular consciousness as a martyr of feminism.

Qiu Jin defied Chinese customs by unbinding her feet, which is said to be even more painful than the initial binding process. In so doing, she reclaimed her power to move freely—or as freely as she could under the circumstances—cross-dressed, and temporarily left her husband and children in China to pursue a more progressive education in Japan. While in Japan, she attended a girl's school in Kojimachi (later known as Jissen Women's University), where she gained the skills to participate in revolutionary activities such as the Republican Revolution of 1911, which she did not live to see. While in Tokyo, she helped to promote women's education by cofounding the women's group, Encompassing Love Society. Although she was an accomplished poet and calligrapher, she eventually cast aside the pen to devote her life to politics.

Back in China, Qiu Jin became a leader in the women's rights movement. Known for her eloquent oration, she spoke out for freedom of education, freedom to marry, and the abolishment of the practice of foot-binding. Her courageous voice and passionate activism inspired women to take direct political action and raise their voices to overcome the oppressive Qing dynasty. An embodiment of Tara Bhrukuti's restless dynamism, Qiu Jin used her voice to speak out, hands to write, and feet to "pound the pavement" in her fight for women's rights. She even learned to make bombs to topple the Qing government. Eventually her political activism cost her her life. In 1907, when she was just thirty-one, she was captured by Imperial Forces, who accused her of conspiring to overthrow the Qing dynasty and sentenced to death by decapitation.

Qiu Jin is a powerful example of a woman unbent by patriarchy, who refused to conform and devoted her short life to a cause that continues to demand our devotion and attention. Sometimes we need to be loud and take a stand to iron out the overt and subtle forms of ignorance and delusion within and around us. I hope Qiu Jin inspires you to find creative, meaningful, and even daring ways to embody Tara Bhrukuti's fearless devotion to equity and liberation.

Further Contemplations

Now that you have met Tara Bhrukuti, think of women you know who embody her courageous voice and powerful rhythm. Who inspires an experience of natural liberation (rangdrol) into the nature of suchness through their voice, writing, or artistry of any kind? How might you achieve this? I enjoy walking in nature when I feel bogged down or caged in. It can feel risky to stroll barefoot, but I am often surprised at how the ground is friendlier to our bare feet than we have been taught to believe. Free your feet from your shoes and walk on the earth. Or you might learn how to drum to engage with the sound Tara Bhrukuti makes when she pounds the earth. In my online course for Tara Bhrukuti, I invited my friend and drum teacher Marla Leigh to play the North African frame drum and guide participants in making rhythm together. We danced, pounding the earth with our feet and striking the drum with our hands, to embody Tara Bhrukuti's passion and power.

On a more psychological level, have you ever experienced your neuroses, hopes, and fears release naturally of their own accord? If so, practice this experience in meditations such as the ones I offer in this chapter or in the dissolution phase of the Tara meditations. If you haven't experienced it, when you notice you are caught up in negative self-talk or distractions, say aloud or quietly to yourself, HŪṂ! HŪṂ! PHAṬ! PHAṬ! Or recite Tara Bhrukuti's mantra. While doing this, feel the sound of the seed syllables liberate those negativities, those so-called demons, into space, into suchness. It's a compassionate act of liberation, not an aggressive one. Meditate on and journey with Tara Bhrukuti to bring forth her empowered voice and movement in you.

Fourteenth Tara:
Tara Bhrukuti Embodiment Meditation

Before you begin, recall the three samadhis of emptiness, compassion, and the union of the two. Remember that all appearances of self and deity are empty of intrinsic existence yet manifest as ceaseless compassion.

Settle into a comfortable meditation seat and take nine relaxation breaths, breathing into any physical tension, then any emotional tension, and finally any mental tension and releasing it all with your exhalations.

Front Visualization

Imagine that from luminous empty space Tara Bhrukuti appears in the space in front and slightly above you, extremely fierce and blue-black in color. Wisdom flames of light emanate from her body, and numerous flaming vajras emit from her pestle atop her lotus, destroying all subtle negativities and obstacles. She liberates negativity into the true nature of reality, dharmata. Under her protection, all beings experience peace and tranquility. She is surrounded by numerous wisdom beings.

Recite the Refuge and Bodhichitta Prayer (3 times)

NĀMO
Noble Tara, the essence of all refuges,
you liberate beings from fear and suffering.
I take refuge in your vast, loving compassion.
In order to bring all sentient beings to the state of enlightenment,
I generate the twofold bodhichitta of aspiration and action.

Self-Visualization

Sound Tara's seed syllable TĀM three times.

First TĀM: Imagine that your body becomes Tara Bhrukuti, fierce and blue-black. Your body is luminous and hollow, with the TĀM in your heart center.

Second TĀM: As Tara Bhrukuti, send offerings of rainbow wisdom light to the wisdom beings. Let yourself truly sense this connection between you and them.

Third TĀM: Wisdom beings send rainbow wisdom light back to you, empowering you as Tara Bhrukuti, fully activating you. Truly feel what it would be like to be the awakened buddha Tara Bhrukuti, a being of radiant light and infinite love and capacity.

Mantra Recitation and Enacting Tara's Enlightened Activity

As you recite the mantra, imagine the TĀM and the mantra garland at your heart emanate rainbow wisdom light in all directions. Wisdom flames emanate from your body, and infinite flaming vajras emit from your pestle, destroying all subtle negativities and obstacles. As Tara Bhrukuti, imagine that you stomp the earth with your feet and strike the ground with your hands, vanquishing all negative forces and obstacle makers with the sound of HŪM, liberating them into the state of dharmata. As a result, all beings experience peace and liberation from suffering.

OM TARE TUTTARE TURE HUNG HUNG HAM SHAM TRIGHNAN PHAT SVAHA

Recite the mantra as many times as you like—but at least twenty-one times. Genuinely feel yourself as Tara Bhrukuti.

Dissolution and Rest in Awareness

When your mantra recitation feels complete, dissolve the visualization: first the world and its inhabitants, then you as Tara Bhrukuti converging at the TĀM at your heart center. Then everything becomes luminous emptiness.

Rest in spacious awareness—the vast, luminous, and wakeful

nature of your own mind. Release into presence. When you are ready, return to your form as Tara Bhrukuti and feel yourself fully integrated with her. As you move about your day, recall the compassion and love of Tara Bhrukuti within and all around you.

Close the session with a sense of gratitude to Tara and her blessings.

Dedication of Merit

Through this virtue, may I quickly attain the state of Noble Tara.

May I bring each and every being, without exception, to that state.

May all beings be healthy, free from suffering and its causes, and may they awaken to their true nature.

DRÖLMA RABZHIMA
(SKT. TARA PRASHANTI)

The Fifteenth Tara

Tara the Supremely Peaceful Goddess

Homage to the blissful, joyful, and tranquil Mother [Tara]
Whose domain is the peace of nirvana.
Endowed with the genuinely perfect oṃ and svāhā,
You overcome vast negative actions.

Tara Prashanti is peaceful and white like the full autumn moon. Blissful and calm, her enlightened activity is to alleviate the suffering of samsara, purifying our most entrenched mental afflictions and egregious negative karma. For this reason, she is known as the "Tara of Purification." She is entirely free of negativity and, therefore, free of suffering. She bestows this same level of bliss and happiness upon all beings.

Prashanti in Sanskrit and *rabzhima* in Tibetan both have the same meaning: "supremely peaceful goddess." In Sanskrit, *pra* (Tib. *rab*) means "highest," "supreme," "excellent," or "perfect." In this context, the Tibetan *rab* is short for *rab tu*, which is an intensifier meaning "fully," "supremely," or "totally." In Sanskrit, *shanti* (Tib. *zhima*) means "peaceful one" in the feminine gender as signified by the long *i* in Sanskrit and the suffix *ma* in Tibetan.

Her Mantra

ཨོཾ་ཏུ་རེ་ཏུཏྟུ་རེ་ཏུ་རེ་སཪྦ་པཱ་པ་གཏེ་གཏེ་སྭཱ་ཧཱ།

OṂ TĀRE TUTTĀRE TURE SARVA PĀPAṂ GATE GATE SVĀHĀ
OM TARE TUTTARE TURE SARVA PAPAM GATE GATE SVAHA
OṂ! Tara! Be swift, Tara! All misdeeds, let them be gone! So be it!

Tara Prashanti's mantra functions as a prayer to purify all misdeeds. In Sanskrit, *papam* means "misdeeds" or "evil" and, in this context, refers to the negative karma accumulated through unvirtuous actions. *Gate* (sounds like "got-tay") means "let them be gone,"[1] referring to all misdeeds (*sarva papam*).

Her Symbol: Anointing Vase

Upon Tara Prashanti's lotus flower is an anointing vase filled with purifying ambrosia. Her vase resembles a perfume bottle with a tapered neck that allows liquids to pour out slowly. When we meditate on her, we imagine that she anoints beings with this purifying ambrosia, washing away all negativity to bring bliss and happiness.

The purifying ambrosia in her vase is called *amrita* in Sanskrit and *dütsi* in Tibetan.[2] *Amrita* means "deathless" or "immortality" and is cognate to and shares many similarities with the word *ambrosia*. In Sanskrit and Greek, both amrita and ambrosia are considered the drink of the gods, bestowing longevity or immortality to all who consume it. *Amrita* is another word for the famed soma, the mythical Vedic drink that bestows longevity, wisdom, and the supreme bliss of enlightenment.[3]

Exploring Tara Prashanti's Facets

Buddhism teaches us how to purify our misdeeds through abstaining from negative actions, enacting positive ones, prayer, mantra recitation, and visualization practices. The Buddha taught that it is essential to refrain from engaging in harmful behavior such as lying, stealing, and greed. If you want to clean up a toxic stream, the first step is to stop polluting it. In the same way, we need to stop polluting our minds with negativity to begin the healing process. On that basis, we should adopt virtuous actions that help counteract the polluting behavior. For example, a person with a tendency to lie would first focus on healing the inner and outer conditions that cause them to feel the need to lie. Then they could adopt more virtuous speech, such as speaking honestly and directly with sincerity. Shakyamuni Buddha offered an ethical framework to help us know what to avoid and adopt to cultivate positive states and minimize negative states. Virtue is like amrita; it sustains our well-being and harmonious relationships with the world.

The Ten Nonvirtues and Ten Virtues[4]

1. Avoid killing and harming others; protect life.
2. Avoid stealing; practice generosity.
3. Avoid sexual misconduct (including dishonoring your vows or the vows of another, sexual abuse, and deception); cultivate loving relationships.
4. Avoid lying; speak sincerely and directly.
5. Avoid slander; be a peacemaker.
6. Avoid harsh words; speak calmly and amiably.
7. Avoid useless talk and gossip; speak about meaningful things.
8. Avoid greed; cultivate an open and generous attitude.
9. Avoid covetous thoughts; cultivate goodwill and contentment.
10. Avoid wrong views (such as disregarding cause and effect, believing things to be permanent, and reifying the "self" and "other" as intrinsically existing); cultivate correct views (such as understanding karma, impermanence, interdependence, and emptiness) and practice them.

Changing our behavior can begin in simple ways. We might integrate it with our mindful breathing practices; for example, if we notice we are being judgmental toward someone, we can practice letting go of the critical thought with our exhalation and adopting patience or acceptance with our inhalation. In this way, each breath becomes an opportunity to practice the Dharma, purify our negative karma, and cultivate a healthy environment within and around us. Tara Prashanti represents this benevolent and natural ease aligned with goodwill and a generous heart. By emulating her, we, too, embody the supreme peace that comes from integrity, honesty, and kindness.

Karma—"action" in Sanskrit—comes in all shapes and sizes, but primarily there are said to be three types: positive, negative, and neutral. The complex web of karma is infinite and hard to grasp, but we can at least begin to understand it in terms of cause and effect, seed and fruit. The seed of our motivation is what determines its karmic fruit. As much as possible, imbue your actions, words, and thoughts with bodhichitta, or the care for others' welfare. When we do something out of goodwill, we accrue positive karma. If we do something out of malice, we accrue negative karma. If we do something with a neutral motivation, such as mistakenly stepping on an ant, the karmic repercussions are said to be neutral. It is important to understand that if we say something hurtful out of ignorance, there certainly can be harmful effects, but our karma is less negative than it would be if it were said out of hatred or intended ill will.

This does not excuse us from educating ourselves to minimize the harm we might cause through ignorance. Dharma is all about illuminating the unconscious ways we may cause harm to ourselves and others through our own ignorance. Dharma practices align us with truth or reality, which are both meanings of the word. We do this by understanding that we are all connected through interdependence (tendrel) and, therefore, should care for one another. The Fourteenth Dalai Lama often points out that because our behavior is learned, it can be unlearned. My late Tibetan language mentor Kuno-la would often tell me, "Never stop learning even until the day you die because, in the next life, we pick up right where we left off." It is never too late to make a change, to learn new ways of being that bring harmony into our life.

People often ask, "If our true nature is already enlightened, why do we suffer?" The Buddhist understanding is that we have accumulated positive, negative, and neutral karma through countless lifetimes, and for this reason, we have lost our way and forgotten that we have buddha nature within us. From the perspective of our intrinsic goodness, the vital element is to purify our negative karma and accumulate positive karma, like tuning up the engine, washing the windows, and filling up our gas tank on our trip to enlightenment. Positive actions help us build momentum for the journey ahead.

In this way, Tara Prashanti's purifying power is like the well-known deity Vajrasattva, whose hundred-syllable mantra[5] is recited to purify negative karma in Buddhist tantric practice. When meditating on Vajrasattva, we imagine that he, along with his female counterpart Vajratopa, appear in union (Tib. *yab-yum*) as crystalline white bodies of light in the space above the crown of our head. As we recite the hundred-syllable mantra, we imagine that the mantra circles around their hearts, generating healing white nectar that flows from their point of union, down into the crown of our head, flowing through us and purifying our negative karma. An important element to the purificatory power of this practice is to contemplate what are called the "four powers": regret, reliance, remedy, and restraint. We sincerely regret whatever harm we have caused. We rely upon our spiritual teacher and Vajrasattva as supports. We apply the remedy of virtuous actions. And we commit to restraining from future nonvirtues. Tara Prashanti serves a similar function. When we meditate on her, we imagine that her light and nectar purify the negative karma that obstructs our well-being and liberation. If you would like to include the four powers in your Tara Prashamani meditation, feel free to do so.

Although most, if not all, Buddhist meditations can be understood as purifying, in Vajrayana, visualization and mantra are commonly used to engage our three doors of body (posture), speech (mantra, prana, and breath), and mind (visualization) for the sake of healing. Purification is healing because karma and mental afflictions play a role in our suffering, including illness. This does not mean that we do not need to seek medical help when experiencing illness, but it can't hurt to meditate on purifying ourselves along with any medicine or medical treatment we may need to undergo.

It is not uncommon for tears to come when doing mantra and other meditative practice and prayer. In my experience, when tears flow, they are like a healing and purifying amrita. For example, when we feel the burning of anger, beneath the anger we may find a tender sadness that gives way to a good cry. In those moments, tears can be purifying like Tara Prashanti's nectar flowing from her vase. Tears are medicine that arises from the raw energy of an emotion like anger or jealousy; they are the language of the heart, and at times, they are the expression of the universal heartbreak of being on planet Earth, spinning around the sun in this cyclical existence called samsara.

Real-Life Embodiment of Tara Prashanti
Amma

Amma is a spiritual leader, guru, and humanitarian known as the hugging saint. Her full name, Mata Amritanandamayi, means "Amrita Bliss Goddess." Amma simply means "Honorable Mother." She is my pick for the fifteenth Tara because, like Tara Prashanti, she embodies the healing power of love, which is an elixir or amrita.

Amma was born in 1953 in a remote fishing village in Kerala, South India. As a young girl, she spent many hours in deep meditation, composing devotional songs to Shri Krishna. When Amma was nine, her mother fell ill, which required Amma to go out to gather food for their cows. At that time, she became exposed to the immense poverty and suffering in her area. Despite her own family's limited resources, she began taking food and clothing from her home to offer to those in greater need. She embraced people to comfort them in their sorrow. Though it was considered inappropriate for a young girl in her community and despite protests from her family, Amma continued to embrace those who approached her in despair. When asked about her defiance of the cultural norms ascribed to young women, she said, "I don't see if it is a man or a woman. I don't see anyone different from myself. A continuous stream of love flows from me to all of creation. This is my inborn nature. The duty of a doctor is to treat patients. In the same way, my duty is to console those who are suffering."[6] This reminds me of Wisdom Moon's response to the male monks who told her to pray to be reborn as a man in her next life, she said, "Labeling 'male' or 'female' has no essence but deceives the evil-minded world."

Because Amma chose to lead a life of devotion and service, expressed most notably by her love, motherly embrace, and activism, people began to call her "Amma," Honorable Mother. Amma says that she accepts the Hindu and Buddhist teachings that the individual's suffering is due to their karma (the results of actions performed in the past), but she refuses to accept it as a justification for inaction. Through her realization, she understands that the principle of karma means that we are also tied up with others' experiences. If it is one person's karma to suffer, isn't it our dharma, our duty, to help ease their pain? With this conviction, she teaches that each of us has a responsibility to help those less fortunate. She says, "Love expressed is compassion, and compassion means accepting the needs and sorrows of others as one's own."[7]

Amma's goal is to help beings realize their spiritual unfoldment and enlightenment through her embrace and her blessing. She offers her blessings, but she says that she cannot go against nature, against what is needed for that person in that moment. On the surface, her healing nectar can appear in many ways—from being embraced, ignored, cajoled, caressed, or comforted. Some experience her as simply a nice lady, and others see her as an embodiment of universal consciousness. Often people are brought to tears when in her presence, and many feel that receiving a hug from Amma is a kind of purification. Sometimes sweet and gentle and at other times fierce, like Tara in her many manifestations, Amma may help purify our karma, but not in ways we might expect.

A friend of mine named Susi, who is a student of Amma, once told me a story of how Amma gave her an unusual dose of loving nectar. One day, Susi was at a private home that Amma was to visit. Medically fragile, Susi went in hopes of receiving Amma's *darshan* (vision of a holy being or object). Waiting outside for Amma's arrival, she saw her car approach. She could see Amma in the back seat gazing at her through the darkened window as the car glided to a stop. When Susi tried to approach Amma, she experienced something like a force field that held her back. As she stood there, stunned and disappointed that she couldn't receive Amma's hug, something "sizzled out of her head at the site of an old injury." Susi said that later she understood that Amma had protected her from being overwhelmed by her powerful energy, her *shakti*. Susi felt that Amma gave her just the right dose of her amrita medicine for her own safety.

Amma spreads her healing nectar in many ways, notably through humanitarian initiatives like her commitment to climate justice. In this way, her enlightened activities are like a healing longevity nectar for Mother Earth, helping to sustain life for generations to come.

Further Contemplations

Having met Tara Prashanti and her real-life embodiment Amma, I invite you to contemplate how they come alive for you. How do you access love, peace, and joy in your own life? Amma says, "Love sustains everything."[8] I understand her love to be the amrita that washes away suffering.

You may have already noticed that when you abstain from negativity and water the seeds of positivity in your life, you are happier, more peaceful, and at ease in your own skin. When you do or say something that you don't feel good about, clear it up right away. Expose any "hidden faults" as they say in various Tibetan Buddhist sadhanas. Apologize if you need to; no one is perfect and that is okay. Right any wrongs you may have done so that you can move on with ease in your life and feel good about who you are. And lastly, meditate on Tara Prashanti, feeling her purifying nectar flowing into you and all beings. Then, if you wish, take a journey with her as outlined at the end of the book to explore the wisdom and gifts she has to offer you.

Fifteenth Tara:
Tara Prashanti Embodiment Meditation

Before you begin, recall the three samadhis of emptiness, compassion, and the union of the two. Remember that all appearances of self and deity are empty of intrinsic existence yet manifest as ceaseless compassion.

Settle into a comfortable meditation seat and take nine relaxation breaths, breathing into any physical tension, then any emotional tension, and finally any mental tension and releasing it all with your exhalations.

Front Visualization

Imagine that from luminous empty space Tara Prashanti appears in the space in front and slightly above you, smiling and peaceful. She is white in color like the full autumn moon. Blissful and calm, she alleviates the suffering of samsara by purifying our most entrenched mental obscurations and egregious negative karma. Purifying light streams from her body and her anointing vase upon her lotus, washing away all obscurations and negative karma. She is surrounded by numerous wisdom beings.

Recite the Refuge and Bodhichitta Prayer (3 times)

NĀMO
Noble Tara, the essence of all refuges,
you liberate beings from fear and suffering.
I take refuge in your vast, loving compassion.
In order to bring all sentient beings to the state of
    enlightenment,
I generate the twofold bodhichitta of aspiration and action.

Self-Visualization

Sound Tara's seed syllable TĀṂ three times.

First TĀṂ: Imagine that your body becomes Tara Prashanti, peaceful and white. Your body is luminous and hollow, with the TĀṂ in your heart center.

Second TĀṂ: As Tara Prashanti, send offerings of rainbow wisdom light to the wisdom beings. Let yourself truly sense this connection between you and them.

Third TĀṂ: Wisdom beings send rainbow wisdom light back to you, empowering you as Tara Prashanti, fully activating you. Truly feel what it would be like to be the awakened buddha Tara Prashanti, a being of radiant light and infinite love and capacity.

Mantra Recitation and Enacting Tara's Enlightened Activities

As you recite the mantra, imagine the TĀṂ and the mantra garland at your heart emanate rainbow wisdom light in all directions. A rain of purifying ambrosia pours out of your anointing vase, cleansing all negative karma and obscurations for all beings everywhere, establishing them in supreme calm and bliss.

OM TARE TUTTARE TURE SARVA PAPAM GATE GATE SVAHA

Recite the mantra as many times as you like—but at least twenty-one times. Genuinely feel yourself as Tara Prashanti.

Dissolution and Rest in Awareness

When your mantra recitation feels complete, dissolve the visualization: first the world and its inhabitants, then you as Tara Prashanti converging at the TĀṂ in your heart center. Then everything becomes luminous emptiness.

Rest in spacious awareness—the vast, luminous, and wakeful

nature of your own mind. Release into presence. When you are ready, return to your form as Tara Prashanti and feel yourself fully integrated with her. As you move about your day, recall the compassion and love of Tara Prashanti within and all around you.

Close the session with a sense of gratitude to Tara and her blessings.

Dedication of Merit

Through this virtue, may I quickly attain the state of Noble Tara.

May I bring each and every being, without exception, to that state.

May all beings be healthy, free from suffering and its causes, and may they awaken to their true nature.

DRÖLMA RIGNGAG TOBZHOM
(SKT. TARA VIDYAMANTRA BALA PRASHAMANI)

The Sixteenth Tara

Tara Who Destroys the Power of Evil Spells

Homage to Mother [Tara] who, encompassed by joy,
Completely conquers all adversaries.
You, the Savioress, manifest from the pristine awareness syllable
  HŪṂ
And display your ten-syllable mantra.

Tara Prashamani is red and fierce. She pacifies curses and ill-intended spells resulting from the misuse of mantric power. She also quells the very source of such bad intentions—ego-clinging—that, like an evil spell, intoxicates beings into performing harmful deeds. To aid us in understanding Tara Prashamani's characteristics, I suggest that we interpret this to include the more quotidian use or misuse of words or speech to manipulate others. As a result of pacifying these kinds of deceptions, Tara Prashamani brings peace, love, and compassion into the hearts of all beings.

Her full name, Tara Vidyamantra Bala Prashamani, is translated by the Khenpo brothers as Tara "Who Destroys the Power of Evil Spells."[1] Let's take a closer look at her Sanskrit and Tibetan names to uncover more of her character. First, *vidya* in Sanskrit or *rig* in Tibetan means "gnosis," "understanding," "knowledge," or "awareness," depending on the context. If we were to translate the Sanskrit word *mantra* (Tib. *ngag*), we could say it means "incantation," "magic formula," or "spell." In Sanskrit, *vidyamantra* (Tib. *rigngag*) refers to an incantation that brings about gnosis and, by extension, power.[2] *Bala* in Sanskrit (Tib. *tob*) means "power" or "strength."

Prashamani (Tib. *zhom*) means "to pacify," "to conquer," or "to suppress." Thus, we can literally translate her name as "she who has the power to pacify [the misuse of] gnosis incantations."[3] Why insert "the misuse of" in her name? The spiritual power rendered by *mantrikas* (mantra adepts)—if not motivated and informed by bodhichitta—may lead to the misuse of power for personal gain at the expense of others.

Her Mantra

ༀ་ཏཱ་རེ་ཏུཏྟཱ་རེ་ཏུ་རེ་ཏྲཾ་དུ་ཏྲི་ན་ཏྲཾ་དུ་ཕཊ་སྭཱ་ཧཱ།

OM TĀRE TUTTĀRE TURE TRAM DU TṚNA TRAM DU PHAṬ SVĀHĀ
OM TARE TUTTARE TURE TRAM DU TRINA TRAM DU PHAT SVAHA
OM! Tara! Be swift, Tara! TRAM! Burn trivial things! TRAM!
PHAṬ! So be it![4]

Her Symbol: Double Vajra

Tara Prashamani's symbol is the double vajra, which represents the principle of ultimate stability and the unshakable enlightenment of the Buddha, meaning that he attained irreversible liberation. Consisting of two vajras joined at a central hub with four vajra heads pointing toward the four cardinal directions, the double vajra mirrors the buddha mandala structure with the colors and wisdoms associated with the center and four quadrants and represents the immovable foundation of the mandala.[5] In Buddhist cosmography, a double vajra underlies the entire universe, with Mount Meru at its hub as the mythical center of the world.

Exploring Tara Prashamani's Facets
Power of Speech

Understanding the effects of speech and mantra and how they can be misused or distorted with ill intent is important for our Buddhist practice and connection to the sixteenth Tara. Look around you and notice how people have misused words to twist the truth, spread rumors, gaslight, and create false news for personal gain. Words weave a certain reality and can take on a power of their own, creating ideas that may lead to ideologies that can benefit or harm. When ideologies are misused and abused to maintain power, this is considered a misuse of the power of speech, as we will see in the context of our real-life Tara Prashamani.

Correct speech, one branch of the Noble Eightfold Path, is a crucial aspect of living a life of integrity. The motivation behind our words determines their outcome—the positive, negative, or neutral karmic results of our speech rely on whether our motivation is positive, negative, or neutral. In Buddhist tantra, practitioners are introduced to the "path of mantra" (Mantrayana, synonymous with Vajrayana and Tantrayana) after training in the foundational practices, namely for developing bodhichitta. This sequential approach is necessary because tantric adepts knew that the power coming from mantra practices was tremendous and that a *vidyamantrika* (a practitioner of gnostic mantras) must have a heart and mind imbued with bodhichitta. This explains why one of the twenty-one Taras is devoted to the issue of pacifying any potential misuse of mantras and the power that comes from their practice.

Encompassed by Joy

Tara Prashamani's praise says she is "encompassed by joy" because she is surrounded by wisdom beings, particularly those who have mastered the art of mantra gnosis. In ancient India, one who mastered mantra gnosis was called a *rishi*, a Vedic Sanskrit term for an enlightened being. In India, the correct pronunciation of Sanskrit is critical because it is believed to be a language given to humans by the gods and thus offers a direct conduit to the gods and an expression of reality itself. Rishis hold that power, and they are said to have composed the hymns of the ancient texts of India known as the Vedas. When meditating on Tara Prashamani, we can imagine her surrounded by numerous rishis and other wisdom beings—the other Taras, lineage teachers, buddhas, bodhisattvas, dakinis, dakas, protectors, and knowledge holders—filling all of space like clouds amassed in the sky.

Real-Life Embodiment
Malala Yousafzai

Malala, born on July 12, 1997, to a Yusufzai Pashtun family in Swat, Pakistan, has become an important figure in the fight for girls' education in the face of the oppressive ideology and practices of the Taliban. Malala embodies Tara Prashamani's power to pacify the misuse of speech and ideologies—the terrible and manipulative "spells" cast by extremists in her homeland—by speaking out for peace, equality, and the right of all children to receive an education.

Named after the Afghan national heroine Malalai of Maiwand,[6] Malala gained international recognition after publishing a diary at the age of eleven about her life in Pakistan under Taliban rule. Inspired by her father who was a schoolteacher and advocate for children's education, she began to speak more publicly about the need for girls to have access to a decent and safe education. However, Malala's life changed dramatically in 2012 when she was shot in the head while riding a bus home from school. After healing from a coma in a British hospital, she began to speak out even more, advocating for girls' education around the world, not just in her own country.

We should not underestimate the power of words. When leaders such as the Taliban capture people's imaginations through their charisma and their use of speech, then twist it for their own power, it can cause an immense degree of harm. In the documentary *He Named Me Malala*, her father was asked, "Who shot Malala?"

He replied, "It's not a person. It's an ideology."

He was absolutely right. The documentary shows us how the leader of the Taliban in the Swat Valley cleverly used words to manipulate people, with his speeches broadcast daily to appeal directly to women to gain their trust. Over time, the Taliban enforced their

Sharia law with more force and violence, severely limiting women's freedoms. The Taliban knew that if they first built trust through words, they could then secure power and control people through ideologies that would have more power than guns.

In 2014, at the age of seventeen, Malala became the youngest person to receive the Nobel Peace Prize for her struggle for the rights of all children to education.[7] Malala's fight against harmful ideologies that perpetuate the suppression of children, particularly girls, around the world is a powerful example of Tara Prashamani's enlightened activity. Her advocacy for children's education, which provides tools for critical thinking and building confidence, financial security, equality, and community supports a more just society and minimizes the potential for the misuse of ideologies.

Further Contemplations

Over the years, I have learned through trial and error how vital communication and words can be. Because everyone comes from different circumstances and perspectives, we should not assume that ours will be understood in the precise way we intend. A useful practice is to ask your conversation partner if they are open to mirroring back what they have heard in order to move forward with clarity and avoid unnecessary misunderstandings. Before I speak, I try to check in with my intentions. Am I fishing for a certain response that fits my agenda? Or am I curious and sincerely interested in any answer?

In our Tara meditations, when reciting her mantras, check in with your frame of mind. Are you connected to the meaning and purpose of the practice? Or are you going through the motions? In Tibetan, there is a phrase, *kha tsam tsig tsam ma yin pa*, that means "Don't merely mouth the words." It is a common instruction concerning prayers and mantra recitation. A teacher may say to a student, "Pray with heartfelt devotion; don't just mouth the words." The teaching is to steep in the meaning of the words and let the practice come alive in you. This gives potency to the power behind your prayer and mantra recitation, which should always be imbued with bodhichitta.

Interestingly, just as I began writing this chapter, I experienced the power of words in the form of rumors about me. Even though the rumors were minor, they stung. I then realized, "Oh! This is what Tara Prashamani is for—the feeling of words piercing your heart like an arrow." The Khenpo brothers say that this Tara helps to pacify the misuse of speech that comes from the outside into us. When this happened to me, first I felt righteous indignation and disbelief: Who would say that!? Then came the sense of suffering tied up around the feeling of being wrongly accused. I was ready to investigate and get to the bottom of it. But then I remembered the Dharma teachings that the root of our suffering stems from clinging to a sense of "I" and "mine." The sense of "I" that is so hurt doesn't even really exist, so "my identity" or "my reputation" doesn't have any intrinsic reality either. Because I knew that I had integrity regarding this rumor, I decided not to fixate on what others were saying. I realized there have probably been and will continue to be plenty of misperceptions about me—that's just the nature of being human. This happens to all of us from time to time. I just happened to hear about this one instance. Of course, when we can clear up misunderstandings and rumors, we should do it. But this one was anonymous, and it would have taken a lot of time and effort to do so.

When there is nothing to be done externally, we can do the inner work of releasing the suffering that comes from clinging to a sense of "I" and "mine." Once we do this, the target on our back disappears and no one can harm us. In this way, Tara Prashamani's power to pacify even the root of bad intentions and their hurtful consequences—self-grasping—came alive in me, and it can in you, too.

Sixteenth Tara:
Tara Prashamani Embodiment Meditation

Before you begin, recall the three samadhis of emptiness, compassion, and the union of the two. Remember that all appearances of self and deity are empty of intrinsic existence yet manifest as ceaseless compassion.

Settle into a comfortable meditation seat and take nine relaxation breaths, breathing into any physical tension, then any emotional tension, and finally any mental tension and releasing it all with your exhalations.

Front Visualization

Imagine that from luminous empty space Tara Prashamani appears in the space in front and slightly above you, fierce and red in color. She pacifies negativity and harm caused by the misuse of words and spiritual power. Rainbow wisdom light radiates from her body and the double vajra atop her lotus, bringing peace, love, and compassion into the hearts of all beings. She is surrounded by numerous wisdom beings.

Recite the Refuge and Bodhichitta Prayer (3 times)

NĀMO
Noble Tara, the essence of all refuges,
you liberate beings from fear and suffering.
I take refuge in your vast, loving compassion.
In order to bring all sentient beings to the state of enlightenment,
I generate the twofold bodhichitta of aspiration and action.

Self-Visualization

Sound Tara's seed syllable TĀM three times.

First TĀM: Imagine that your body becomes Tara Prashamani, red and fierce. Your body is luminous and hollow, with the TĀM in your heart center.

Second TĀM: As Tara Prashamani, send offerings of rainbow wisdom light to the wisdom beings. Let yourself truly sense this connection between you and them.

Third TĀṂ: Wisdom beings send rainbow wisdom light back to you, empowering you as Tara Prashamani, fully activating you. Truly feel what it would be like to be the awakened buddha Tara Prashamani, a being of radiant light and infinite love and capacity.

Mantra Recitation

As you recite the mantra, imagine that the mantra garland, TĀṂ syllable, and the double vajra emanate rainbow wisdom light in all directions, completely pacifying all negativity and harm caused by the misuse of words and spiritual power. Imagine the sound of the pristine awareness syllable, HŪṂ, allays the true source of bad intentions, ego-clinging. Imagine the rainbow wisdom light absorbs back into you, removing any remnant of negativity and ego-clinging within you.

OM TARE TUTTARE TURE TRAM DU TRINA TRAM DU PHAT
SVAHA

Recite the mantra as many times as you like—but at least twenty-one times. Genuinely feel yourself as Tara Prashamani.

Dissolution and Rest in Awareness

When your mantra recitation feels complete, dissolve the visualization: first the world and its inhabitants, then you as Tara Prashamani converging at the TĀṂ in your heart center. Then everything becomes luminous emptiness.

Rest in spacious awareness—the vast, luminous, and wakeful nature of your own mind. Release into presence. When you are ready, return to your form as Tara Prashamani and feel yourself fully integrated with her. As you move about your day, recall the compassion and love of Tara Prashamani within and all around you.

Close the session with a sense of gratitude to Tara and her blessings.

Dedication of Merit

> Through this virtue, may I quickly attain the state of Noble Tara.
>
> May I bring each and every being, without exception, to that state.
>
> May all beings be healthy, free from suffering and its causes, and may they awaken to their true nature.

DRÖLMA PAGME NÖNMA
(SKT. TARA APRAMEYAKRAMANI)

The Seventeenth Tara
Tara Who Stops Immeasurable Invading Forces

Homage to Mother Ture, whose feet stomp
And whose seed syllable is HŪM.
You cause the three worlds of
Meru, Mandara, and Vindhya to quake.

Our seventeenth Tara's disposition is peaceful yet strong. She is golden red like the sunrise. She is known for protecting against all external forms of danger—particularly thieves, hunters, and military invasion—to bring safety, calm, and tranquility to all. Because she eradicates all forms of violence and cruelty, she is the "Tara of Nonviolence."

In Sanskrit, *aprameya* (*pagme* in Tibetan) means "immeasurable," "unfathomable," or "countless." *Akramana* can mean "retreat" or "escape" but also "invading forces."[1] The Tibetan *nönma* means "she who stops." Thus I translate her name as "Tara Who Stops Immeasurable Invading Forces." For ease of reading, we can simply call her Tara Aprameya, "Immeasurable Tara," highlighting her immeasurable protective power.

Her Mantra

ཨོཾ་ཏུ་རེ་ཏུཏྟ་རེ་ཏུ་རེ་ཧཱུྃ་ཧཱུྃ་བྃ་ཧོཿསྭཱ་ཧཱ།

OM̩ TĀRE TUTTĀRE TURE HŪM̩ HŪM̩ BAM̩ HO SVĀHĀ
OM TARE TUTTARE TURE HUNG HUNG BAM HO SVAHA
OM̩! Tara! Be swift, Tara! HŪM̩ HŪM̩ BAM̩ HO! So be it!

This mantra offers two new terms: BAM and HO. BAM (sometimes VAM, and rhymes with *mom*) is the seed syllable for the buddha dakini in the center of the mandala structure, representing the element of space and the transformation of ignorance into all-encompassing wisdom. The syllable HO is an interjection that emphasizes what came before, particularly the seed syllables HŪM and BAM.

Her Symbol: Golden Stupa

Upon Tara Aprameya's lotus is a golden stupa,[2] a reliquary monument symbolizing the enlightened mind of the Buddha. Originally stupas were built to enshrine the relics of Shakyamuni Buddha and his prominent disciples. Stupas may be large monuments, built in places to sanctify the landscape and protect it from negative forces, or small personal devotional objects such as those kept on a home or temple altar, often containing the blessed substances and relics of Buddhist masters and sacred words of the Buddha.

Exploring Tara Aprameya's Facets

Tara Aprameya uses her calm yet immovable strength to protect beings from intrusive harm and violence. Even though her disposition is peaceful, she embodies a pertinacious strength indicated by her praise in which the Buddha honors her by saying that her "feet stomp…[causing] the three worlds of Meru, Mandara and Vindhya to quake." Her stomping feet are reminiscent of the fourteenth Tara Bhrukuti, yet she is quite distinct from her fierce sister. I see Tara Aprameya as putting her foot down to say, "Stop here!" drawing a line that negativity cannot cross. Tara Aprameya's stanza also explains that she employs the seed syllable HŪM to make the three worlds quake, protecting beings from invasive negativity. As the sonic symbol for the awakened mind, HŪM is often used to dissolve and disarm negativity and dualistic reification. She has dominion over the three worlds that constitute Buddhist and other

Indian traditions' cosmology called Meru, Mandara, and Vindhya (Binduchal). In essence, this means that she protects beings from harm across these three physical and metaphysical boundaries with her stomping feet and her sounding of HŪṂ.[3]

Real-Life Embodiments

Here I offer two examples of real-life expressions of this Tara's strong protective energy. First, we will look at an individual woman and then a broader movement.

Virginia Hall

Virginia Hall (1906-1982), one of World War II's most heroic female spies, helped save countless Allied lives while working for Great Britain and the United States. This makes her a dynamic manifestation of Tara Aprameya's power to stop invading forces through mostly nonviolent actions. Her calm intelligence coupled with a strength of determination were the ideal qualities needed in the thrilling and dangerous world of wartime intrigue. She conducted espionage, sabotage, and reconnaissance in occupied Europe against the Axis powers, specifically Nazi Germany. This led the Germans to label her as the most dangerous Allied spy in World War II.

During Hitler's rise to power in Germany, Hall knew that she needed to leave the security of her home in Baltimore, Maryland, to help in some way. She applied to the U.S. State Department, hoping to become an officer in the Foreign Service, but was turned down. Based on a chance meeting in 1940 with a British Special Operations Executive (SOE) officer, she decided to apply to the British SOE and was recruited. In 1941, after a short training period, she was sent to occupied France as the SOE's first female operative to help supply resistance groups with much needed weapons and equipment parachuted in from England.

Hall quickly became an expert at these support operations and helped downed airmen to escape the German Gestapo by providing safe houses and medical assistance to wounded agents and pilots. She was respected for her unique and inventive ways of disguising herself and recruiting informants and support networks. She had a prosthetic leg from a childhood hunting accident, which caused her to limp, a characteristic that was not easy to hide while in occupied territory. As her renown spread, the German Gestapo nicknamed her the Limping Lady and Artemis, Greek goddess of the hunt (and the moon).

While in France serving as a wireless radio operator for the U.S. Office of Strategic Services, the precursor to the Central Intelligence Agency, she disguised herself as an elderly milkmaid, dyeing her hair gray. She also wore full skirts to add weight to her frame and shuffled her feet to hide her limp, which reminds me of Tara Aprameya's stomping feet. While undercover, she reported the movements of German troops to London and coordinated parachute drops of arms and supplies for resistance groups. She never stayed in one place for long and slept in barns and attics to avoid the Germans who were frantically trying to track her radio signals. The Gestapo was never able to capture her.

As D-Day loomed, Hall and her team successfully stopped the Germans as they tried to escape (another meaning of *akramani*) by derailing freight trains, severing a key rail line, destroying bridges, and downing telephone lines. As an important part of the resistance circuit, Hall and her team also armed and trained battalions of French resistance fighters to sabotage the retreating Germans. After the war, President Harry Truman awarded her with the Distinguished Service Cross, the second-highest U.S. military award for bravery. In her characteristic humility, like Tara Aprameya's calm immovable strength, Hall downplayed the award, saying, "It was only six years of my life."[4]

Despite her limited training, Virginia Hall was instrumental in gaining momentum for the resistance in France and eventually winning the war. She displayed strength and peace in her relentless commitment to helping others, thus embodying the qualities of the seventeenth Tara. She put her prosthetic foot down, saying

"Stop" to the invading Nazis, bringing her ingenious talents to the front lines of war, and risking her own life to save others. She did this with relative calm and levelheadedness, using intelligence and spy craft to protect lives and help achieve peace. For this reason, we could also nickname Hall "The Limping Tara, She Who Stops Countless Invading Forces."

The #MeToo Movement

We can think of real-life manifestations of the twenty-one Taras not just in terms of individuals but also broader movements. The #MeToo movement is a powerful expression of Tara Aprameya's enlightened activity of protection and healing suffering in the context of sexual abuse. The #MeToo movement raises awareness about sexual violence, working to undermine the cultural norms that protect and perpetuate the abuse as well as giving voice to women, men, and gender-nonconforming individuals who might otherwise feel alone.

One day in 2006, #MeToo founder Tarana Burke (whose name has Tara in it) was motivated to do something about the sexual violence she had experienced as a child and that she saw in her community. She recognized the need to center empathy and solidarity between survivors of sexual violence as a path to healing. Burke took out a piece of paper and wrote "Me Too" across the top and then below it laid out an action plan for a movement. More than fifteen years later, #MeToo has grown into a global movement that is helping to dismantle the power and privilege that are the building blocks of sexual violence.

So much is stolen from those who have experienced sexual assault. Survivors may feel that their bodies are not really their own anymore. While reading about sexual violence and its repercussions, the violation and theft that occurs, I was struck with how this aligned with Tara Aprameya's power to halt and heal violence that attempts to come into us from the outside. Sexual abuse robs us of our sense of autonomy and strips us of our agency over our own bodies. Sexual assault may induce feelings of depression and anxiety, guilt, PTSD, and personality disruptions, such as borderline personality disorder. Survivors may find it challenging to form healthy attachments with others, and they are more likely to use drugs and alcohol to numb the pain of abuse.

The #MeToo movement is a force that says, "Enough is enough," like Tara Aprameya, and seeks to stop sexual abuse through exposing and building solidarity among survivors and allies. As "Taras in training," we must be willing to touch the depths of our own and other's pain so that we can heal and thereby become a refuge for others. In this way, we are all a part of the movement, and we can play a role in protecting all the beings in the three worlds—meaning *everywhere*—from harm. Let's explore further ways to embody Tara Aprameya below, both in our daily lives and in our meditation practice.

Further Contemplations

Let Tara Aprameya come alive in you. For example, how might you put your foot down, say enough is enough, or stick up for yourself when negativity, abuse of power, or disrespect of boundaries occur in your life? How then, do you see with more clarity and empathy when this happens to others? Like a gardener takes measures to protect against invasive plants and insects intruding in and destroying their garden, how do you protect yourself and your community through your words, thoughts, and deeds?

Let's begin to think of the twenty-one Taras in terms of movements. India's nonviolent independence movement led by Mahatma Gandhi, South Africa's Anti-Apartheid movement led by Nelson Mandela, and the U.S. civil rights movement led by Martin Luther King Jr. are all examples of broader social movements that embody the spirit of justice and compassion that Tara represents. Expand your imagination to include creative ways to see Tara's compassion manifesting in the world, whether it be through movements, the natural world, or ideas.

Seventeenth Tara:
Tara Aprameya Embodiment Meditation

Before you begin, recall the three samadhis of emptiness, compassion, and the union of the two. Remember that all appearances of self and deity are empty of intrinsic existence yet manifest as ceaseless compassion.

Settle into a comfortable meditation seat and take nine relaxation breaths, breathing into any physical tension, then any emotional tension, and finally any mental tension and releasing it all with your exhalations.

Front Visualization

Imagine that from luminous empty space Tara Aprameya appears in the space in front and slightly above you, peaceful and golden red like the rising sun. The Tara of Nonviolence, she eradicates all forms of violence and cruelty. In particular, she protects without limit against incoming negativity and danger such as thieves, hunters, and invading forces, bringing all beings to peace and safety. Upon her lotus is a golden stupa, symbolizing the enlightened mind of the Buddha. She is surrounded by numerous wisdom beings.

Recite the Refuge and Bodhichitta Prayer (3 times)

NĀMO
Noble Tara, the essence of all refuges,
you liberate beings from fear and suffering.
I take refuge in your vast, loving compassion.
In order to bring all sentient beings to the state of
    enlightenment,
I generate the twofold bodhichitta of aspiration and action.

Self-Visualization

Sound Tara's seed syllable TĀṂ three times.

First TĀṂ: Imagine that your body becomes Tara Aprameya, peaceful and golden red. Your body is luminous and hollow, with the TĀṂ in your heart center.

Second TĀṂ: As Tara Aprameya, send offerings of rainbow wisdom light to the wisdom beings. Let yourself truly sense this connection between you and them.

Third TĀṂ: Wisdom beings send rainbow wisdom light back to you, empowering you as Tara Aprameya, fully activating you. Truly feel what it would be like to be the awakened buddha Tara Aprameya, a being of radiant light and infinite love and capacity.

Mantra Recitation

As you recite the mantra, imagine masses of rainbow wisdom light emanate from the TĀṂ, mantra garland, and the golden stupa in the form of numerous HŪṂ syllables, protecting beings against incoming negativities such as thieves, hunters, abuse, and all types of harmful invading forces. As a result, all beings are safe and free from harm.

OM TARE TUTTARE HUNG HUNG BAM HO SVAHA

Recite the mantra as many times as you like—but at least twenty-one times. Genuinely feel yourself as Tara Aprameya.

Dissolution and Rest in Awareness

When your mantra recitation feels complete, dissolve the visualization: first the world and its inhabitants, then you as Tara Aprameya converging at the TĀṂ in your heart center. Then everything becomes luminous emptiness.

Rest in spacious awareness—the vast, luminous, and wakeful

nature of your own mind. Release into presence. When you are ready, return to your form as Tara Aprameya and feel yourself fully integrated with her. As you move about your day, recall the compassion and love of Tara Aprameya within and all around you.

Close the session with a sense of gratitude to Tara and her blessings.

Dedication of Merit

Through this virtue, may I quickly attain the state of Noble Tara.

May I bring each and every being, without exception, to that state.

May all beings be healthy, free from suffering and its causes, and may they awaken to their true nature.

DRÖLMA MAJA CHENMO
(SKT. TARA MAHAMAYURI)

The Eighteenth Tara

Tara the Great Peacock Goddess

Homage to Mother [Tara], you hold in your hand
A moon marked with a deer, like a heavenly lake.
With Tara twice and then with PHAṬ,
You completely cleanse all poisons.

Tara Mahamayuri is peaceful and luminously white like a glacier mountain lit by the autumn full moon. She protects the world and all beings from inner and outer poisons. She is renowned for watching over infants and children.

The Great Peacock Goddess's name is similar in Sanskrit and Tibetan. In Sanskrit, Tara Mahamayuri means the "great (*maha*) peacock goddess (*mayuri*)." In Tibetan, Maja Chenmo means the "great goddess (*chenmo*) peacock (*maja*)." In South Asian religious traditions, the peacock is a symbol of the transmutation of poisons into medicine. For this reason, peacocks became a symbol of tantra's alchemical process of transmuting the poisons of our delusions into the medicinal nectar of wisdom.[1]

Her Mantra

ཨོཾ་ཏུ་རེ་ཏུཏྟཱ་རེ་ཏུ་རེ་སརྦ་བི་ཥ་ཏུ་ར་ཕཊ་སྭཱ་ཧཱ།

OṂ TĀRE TUTTĀRE TURE SARVA VIṢA TĀRA PHAṬ SVĀHĀ

OM TARE TUTTARE TURE SARVA VISHA TARA PHAT SVAHA[2]

OṂ! Tara! Be swift, Tara! [Please remove] all poison! PHAṬ! So be it!

Her Symbol: Full Moon Marked with a Rabbit

Tara Mahamayuri's symbol atop her lotus is a full moon marked with a rabbit—or a deer as stated in her stanza.[3] The full moon represents our buddha nature, the self-arisen primordial consciousness (*yeshe*)[4] that is ultimately free from change, free from increasing or decreasing. Like the moon, consciousness may *appear* to change depending on conditions, but in actuality it is always there and always whole. In the same way, primordial consciousness, while not always "visible," is in fact pervading our experience all the time, just like the appearance of our own face. Tara Mahamayuri's mantra and symbol teach us that wisdom naturally arises when the conditions are right, when all poisons that cloud our natural radiance are cleared away.

Exploring Tara Mahamayuri's Facets

Tara Mahamayuri played a key role in the life of the great Indian scholar-saint Nagarjuna from the time of his birth in an elite Brahman family. His parents consulted an astrologer who determined that he would die within a week if they did not supplicate Tara Mahamayuri, who protects children. Because his family were followers of the Hindu tradition, they were initially reluctant to propitiate a Buddhist deity, but they did it anyway, and their son's predicted untimely death was averted. As he grew older, Nagarjuna expressed his desire to ordain in the Buddhist tradition. When he was seven years old, his parents took him to Nalanda, one of the great Buddhist monastic universities in India at the time. It was there that he received a formal initiation and transmission for the practice of Tara Mahamayuri. He practiced her sadhana diligently and quickly accomplished realizing the nonduality of his mind and Tara Mahamayuri. It is popularly believed that he lived for six hundred years because of his practice and devotion to Tara Mahamayuri.

Inner and Outer Pharmakons, Poisonous Medicine, Medicinal Poison

Let's look at the notions of poison and medicine through the lens of Tibetan medicine (Sowa Rigpa) of which there are two types: outer and inner.

Outer poisons are subdivided into two main types: the first is natural outer poison such as poisonous plants or snakes. The second is fabricated outer poison or substances made from combining different properties to intentionally produce poisons such as petro-chemicals, which include plastics, detergents, solvents, drugs, fertilizers, synthetic chemical pesticides, explosives, synthetic fibers and rubbers, and paints.

An inner poison is a substance that may have been benign or even medicinal initially but then becomes a poison. We see this all around us—cases where a good thing, if used in excess, might become a toxin. Often the dose of a substance determines whether it is a medicine or a poison. The labels of "poison" or "medicine" are conditional terms, not intrinsic qualities to the substance itself. This echoes the philosophical notion of *pharmakon*, posited by the philosopher Jacques Derrida (1930-2004), which refers to anything that can either be a poison or a remedy depending on the context.[5]

This philosophical concept of pharmakon can apply to the broader areas of technology, biotechnology, immunology, and addiction. For example, as we well know, digital technology can either be a poison or a medicine with respect to attention and concentration, sometimes leading to conditions like attention deficit disorder, while at other times working as a valuable tool for developing new attentional capacities. This computer on which I am writing my book at times is a medium for creativity, but at other times (or the same time) it can be a source of eye fatigue and headaches. Does this mean the computer itself is intrinsically good or bad? No, of course not. With respect to addiction, Alcoholics Anonymous acknowledges the curative role alcohol may play for an alcoholic who has not yet begun to dry out. Alcohol, for a time, may help to buffer the physical and psychological pain associated with life's challenges as a sort of anesthetic that serves a temporary purpose to allow the alcoholic to move slowly and effectively toward sobriety. Another example of a pharmakon is transitional objects, such as stuffed animals, that create healthy attachments between a parent and child. In the beginning, a stuffed animal serves as a remedy, a link, to support the emotional bond, but eventually it needs to be let go so the child doesn't become overly dependent on it.

My last example of a pharmakon illustrates how a common herbal treat can be a deadly poison. In 2020, a fifty-four-year-old man died from eating too much black licorice, which caused his potassium levels to drop suddenly, leading to cardiac arrest. He had no history of heart problems. The culprit was the glycyrrhizic acid found in black licorice and other foods and supplements that contain licorice root extract. Doctors say that even a small amount of licorice can increase your blood pressure slightly, causing low potassium and imbalances in other minerals, principally electrolytes. This is an example of how dosage of any substance determines whether it is a medicine or a poison. This is also a warning that we should practice care and moderation when consuming food and herbs, or engaging in activities. There is an old saying: "What seems like a blessing may be a curse. What seems like a curse may be a blessing!"

Lastly, in Buddhist spiritual practice, the three mental afflictions of ignorance, clinging, and aversion are commonly called the three poisons. Sometimes conceit and jealousy are added to make a total of five. These are just some of the myriad ways that we can suffer. For example, ignorance can lead to cultural illiteracy and blind complicity in oppression; aversion to anger, hatred, and violence; conceit to arrogance and abuse; clinging to obsessiveness; and jealousy to insecurity, competitiveness, and resentment. But like pharmakons, these poisons may also become medicinal. How? In the Vajrayana teachings, we are told to turn *toward* so-called poisons to learn to transmute the energy held within them into wisdom. When transmuted, these five poisons become ambrosial nectar, the five wisdoms of the all-encompassing wisdom, mirrorlike wisdom,

wisdom of equanimity, discerning wisdom, and all-accomplishing wisdom, respectively.

This is how we take all felicity and adversity on to the path of awakening, as is also taught in Atisha's Mind Training (Lojong) teachings of Mahayana Buddhism. For example, rather than trying to crush our anger, we can learn to channel the energy behind that anger. Perhaps anger stems from the desire for justice and carries within it the clarity and sharp awareness needed to effectively speak up; this is a righteous form of anger. Anger can transform into clarity of mind, like a flash of lightning lighting up the sky or a mirror that reflects appearances without distorting or manipulating them. In this way, we learn to transmute and purify our perceptions rather than obsessing with changing everything around us to make our life "perfect." At times we need to fix things, heal ourselves, clean up toxins, fight for environmental regulations, and so on. At other times, we need to balance our social activism with personal time to heal our body and mind, to purify our internal poisons so that we don't become an internal toxic waste site.

The Buddha taught, when the earth is strewn with thorns, rather than covering the earth with leather, cover your own feet by putting on shoes. Another common Tibetan saying goes, "If dawn does not rise within you, how can you expect the sunshine to come from your neighbors?"

Real-Life Embodiment
Rachel Carson

Rachel Carson (1907-1964) was a scientist, writer, and ecologist who became one of the first instigators of the modern-day environmental movement. Like Tara Mahamayuri, her energies focus on the inner and outer ways poison harms us. Carson's advocacy for environmental justice and for future generations—primarily children—make her a perfect real-life Tara Mahamayuri.

Carson's mother bequeathed her a lifelong love of nature and the living world that she expressed first as a writer and later as a student of marine biology and zoology. Her many articles and books offer insight about the wonder and beauty of the natural world, notably her acclaimed studies on the ocean. Embedded in her work was the view that human beings were but one part of nature distinguished primarily by their power to alter it—in some cases, irreversibly.

During World War II, she was distraught by the widespread use of synthetic chemical pesticides, notably DDT (dichlorodiphenyltrichloroethane), with little or no prior investigation into their health and environmental effects.[6] She challenged the U.S. government and agricultural scientists, calling for research devoted to the environmental impacts correlated with DDT use in agriculture. She raised public awareness of these issues through her writing and warned people about the long-term effects of the misuse of pesticides.

This culminated in her groundbreaking 1962 book *Silent Spring* in which she raised the alarm that DDT and other pesticides caused cancer and their use threatened wildlife, particularly birds. In response, the chemical industry attacked her, calling her a hysterical alarmist. Undeterred, she continued to courageously speak out and remind people that we are a vulnerable part of the natural world, subject to the same damage as the rest of the ecosystem. She did this so that children of future generations could live in a world free of pollution and poison. Speaking about the effects that pesticides have on children's development, she embodied Tara Mahamayuri's mission to protect children. Carson worked to purify and not only save the environment from toxic pollution but also humanity from the toxic and harmful assumptions that we have dominion over nature and thus the right to poison and pillage it. In 1963, just one year before she passed away after a long battle with breast cancer, she testified before Congress, calling for new policies to protect human health and the environment.

Rachel Carson's influence on the modern-day environmental movement cannot be overstated. She beseeched the world to change the way we view the natural world, sparking a public outcry in 1972 to ban DDT for agricultural use in the United States. She took a stand against the corporate poisoning of the people and transmuted corporate greed into the wisdom of public awareness. She helped to transform our perception of a dominant worldview that disregarded the effects of our actions. In this way, she embodied the enlightened intent of Tara Mahamayuri.

Further Contemplations

As protector and transmuter of poison, particularly for children, Tara Mahamayuri's enlightened activity felt particularly poignant during the 2014-16 public health crisis in Flint, Michigan. Tens of thousands of Flint residents were exposed to dangerous levels of lead in the water when, because of a budget crisis, the city changed its water source from the Detroit Water and Sewerage Department to the Flint River. After residents complained about the bad taste, smell, and appearance of the water, it was discovered that officials had failed to apply corrosion inhibitors, resulting in lead from aging pipes leaching into the water supply. Flint switched back to the Detroit water system in 2015 but not in time to avert the horrible crisis that left its citizens, especially children, at high risk of long-term effects of lead poisoning including impacted intellectual functioning and increased chances of Alzheimer's disease.

I can't say enough about the importance of joining our prayers with advocacy for those in need. Prayer helps, and I laud the individuals around the world devoted to a life of contemplation and prayer. But in my opinion, it is not enough to sit on our meditation cushions and pray. We should also find ways to put our prayers into action. Make it personal, make it doable, and if necessary, find small things to have an impact. We don't have to be Rachel Carson, let alone Tara, to make positive changes. Get involved with cleanup days in your neighborhood, volunteer for organizations helping to protect the environment from pollutants, or educate children about our relationship with the natural world.

Eighteenth Tara:
Tara Mahamayuri Embodiment Meditation

Before you begin, recall the three samadhis of emptiness, compassion, and the union of the two. Remember that all appearances of self and deity are empty of intrinsic existence yet manifest as ceaseless compassion.

Settle into a comfortable meditation seat and take nine relaxation breaths, breathing into any physical tension, then any emotional tension, and finally any mental tension and releasing it all with your exhalations.

Front Visualization

Imagine that from luminous empty space Tara Mahamayuri appears in the space in front and slightly above you, peaceful and luminously white like a glacier mountain lit by the autumn full moon. She protects the environment and all beings, particularly infants and children, from poison and pollution. Healing light emanates from her body and the full moon on her lotus, completely removing poison from the environment as well as sentient beings. She is surrounded by numerous wisdom beings.

Recite the Refuge and Bodhichitta Prayer (3 times)

NĀMO
Noble Tara, the essence of all refuges,
    you liberate beings from fear and suffering.
I take refuge in your vast, loving compassion.
In order to bring all sentient beings to the state of enlightenment,
    I generate the twofold bodhichitta of aspiration and action.

Self-Visualization

Sound Tara's seed syllable TĀṂ three times.
    First TĀṂ: Imagine that your body becomes Tara Mahamayuri,

peaceful and luminously white. Your body is luminous and hollow, with the TĀM in your heart center.

Second TĀM: As Tara Mahamayuri, send offerings of rainbow wisdom light to the wisdom beings. Let yourself truly sense this connection between you and them.

Third TĀM: Wisdom beings send rainbow wisdom light back to you, empowering you as Tara Mahamayuri, fully activating you. Truly feel what it would be like to be the awakened buddha Tara Mahamayuri, a being of radiant light and infinite love and capacity.

Mantra Recitation

As you recite the mantra, imagine that rainbow light streams from the TĀM, mantra garland, and full moon on your lotus, cleansing all poisons from the environment and sentient beings, especially protecting infants and children.

OM TARE TUTTARE TURE SARVA VISHA TARA PHAT SVAHA

Recite the mantra as many times as you like—but at least twenty-one times. Genuinely feel yourself as Tara Mahamayuri.

Dissolution and Rest in Awareness

When your mantra recitation feels complete, dissolve the visualization: first the world and its inhabitants, then you as Tara Mahamayuri converging at the TĀM in your heart center. Then everything becomes luminous emptiness.

Rest in spacious awareness—the vast, luminous, and wakeful nature of your own mind. Release into presence. When you are ready, return to your form as Tara Mahamayuri and feel yourself fully integrated with her. As you move about your day, recall the compassion and love of Tara Mahamayuri within and all around you.

Close the session with a sense of gratitude to Tara and her blessings.

Dedication of Merit

Through this virtue, may I quickly attain the state of Noble
Tara.

May I bring each and every being, without exception, to that
state.

May all beings be healthy, free from suffering and its causes,
and may they awaken to their true nature.

DRÖLMA MIPHAM GYALMO DUGKARMO
(SKT. TARA SITATAPATRA)

The Nineteenth Tara

Tara, Invincible Queen of the White Parasol

Homage to you, Mother [Tara], honored by sovereigns,
Divine hosts, gods, and kimnaras
With your full armor of joy and dignity,
You dispel strife and bad dreams.

Tara Sitatapatra is crystal white with a peaceful disposition.[1] Her sublime and regal qualities pacify nightmares, supernatural dangers, misfortune, and religious and mundane conflict and strife. She blesses beings with protective armor—filling us with joy and bliss; making our three doors of body, speech, and mind blaze with radiance; and clearing away everything that disrupts our peace of mind.[2] With her metaphoric and majestic armor of joy, she protects the Dharma and those who teach it from disputes and disharmony, so that the Dharma may flourish and continue to benefit beings.

In Sanskrit, *sita* means "white" and *atapatra* means a large "parasol" or "umbrella," thus "Tara of the White Parasol." In Tibetan, *mipham* means "invincible," *dug* (sounds like *duke*) "parasol," and *kar* "white," while *mo* signifies the female gender. She is also known as the "invincible queen"—Tara Ajitarajni in Sanskrit, Drölma Mipham Gyalmo in Tibetan. The Sanskrit and Tibetan are essentially the same: *ajita* (Tib. *mipham*) and *rajni* (Tib. *gyalmo*) mean "queen." At times her names are combined as Tara the Invincible Queen of the White Parasol.

Her Mantra

ཨོཾ་ཏུ་རེ་ཏུཏྟུ་རེ་ཏུ་རེ་ཧཱུྃ་ཧཱུྃ་ཕཊ་ཕཊ་རཀྵ་རཀྵ་མི་སྭ་ཧ།

OṂ TĀRE TUTTĀRE TURE HŪṂ HŪṂ PHAṬ PHAṬ RAKṢA RAKṢA
  MAṂ SVĀHĀ

OM TARE TUTTARE TURE HUNG HUNG PHAT PHAT RAKSHA
  RAKSHA MAM SVAHA

OṂ! Tara! Be swift, Tara! HŪṂ! HŪṂ! PHAṬ! PHAṬ!
  Protection! Protection! MAṂ! So be it![3]

Her Symbol: White Parasol

Upon Tara Sitatapatra's lotus is a white parasol,[4] a symbol of both
protection and royalty in India. In Buddhism, the parasol is one of
the eight auspicious symbols representing the Buddha's spiritual
sovereignty, meaning his liberation from the bonds of samsara.
The parasol also symbolizes the dome of the sky that casts a protective shadow over the earth, safeguarding beings from harmful
elements such as the blazing sun. The parasol handle represents
the axis mundi, signifying that whoever is beneath the parasol is
the center of the universe. The parasol also indicates the union of
wisdom and compassion—the dome as wisdom and the hanging
skirt lining the parasol as compassion.[5]

Exploring Tara Sitatapatra's Facets

Like Vajra Sarasvati, Ushnisha Vijaya, Kurukulla, and Mahabhairava,
Sitatapatra is also a goddess apart from this twenty-one-Tara pantheon. Some accounts say that she may have roots as far back as the
Jataka tales—the previous life stories of the Buddha—in which she
resided in the white parasols of royalty, speaking to them and guiding
them in their royal affairs. In the Mahayana text *The Noble Dharani
of Sitatapatra Sutra*,[6] she is called Vajra Ushnisha Sitatapatra,[7]
and her origin story is similar to that of the fourth Tara, Ushnisha
Vijaya, because they both arose from Buddha Shakyamuni's crown

protuberance (ushnisha). Vajra Ushnisha Sitatapatra did so when he was teaching in the Trayastrimsha heaven, where his mother Maya came to receive teachings from him after she died. At times Sitatapatra is depicted as a terrifying goddess with thousands of heads, eyes, arms, and legs. At other times she is said to be Avalokiteshvara's counterpart, and like him, she manifests in many elaborate forms such as having many faces, one thousand hands, and one thousand feet.[8]

Her Praise

In her praise, Tara Sitatapatra is honored by sovereign and divine beings, namely Indra and Brahma, two important gods associated with the Vedic and Hindu traditions (see "The Twelfth Tara"). Brahma, the creator god, is a personification of the universal principle of *brahman*, the absolute dimension of reality. The other gods mentioned in the stanza refer to the gods of the mountains, trees, and water who at times bring benefit and at times cause harm. *Kimnaras* are semidivine beings known for their musical abilities, depicted as half-human and half-horse or half-human and half-bird.

The next two lines of the stanza highlight Tara Sitatapatra's armor of joy and dignity that protect our well-being and happiness. In this context, her eight sambhogakaya ornaments are seen as majestic armor, each with its own function to help protect beings from strife and conflict and to bestow peace and dignity. She wears her diadem at her crown to stabilize her bodhichitta; her earrings to prevent slander against spiritual teachers; her shawl, armlets, and anklets to avert the killing of living beings; her necklaces to recollect methods for pacifying concepts; her belt to enact the mudra for binding bodhichitta, and her skirt to cover her lower body.[9] In his commentary to the *Praises*, Jigme Lingpa states that Tara Sitatapatra emits flaming weapons and vajra sparks to protect beings from strife.[10] So while here she is depicted as peaceful, she can also protect beings with an unparalleled ferocity, hence her epithet Invincible Queen.

As her stanza says, Tara Sitatapatra dispels strife and bad dreams. The Tibetan term for "dispel" is *selwa* or simply *sel*. *Sel* is an important Buddhist term that can mean many things. I'd like to emphasize one aspect of sel, which is to "to illuminate." Why? Because to heal strife, we must first illuminate it, shine light on it, acknowledge it. Then based upon that illumination, we can begin to heal it, like the clouds clearing. Tara Sitatapatra shines light upon and dispels strife in its many forms.

Breaking the Spell

How might we understand Tara Sitatapatra's power to dispel negativity, especially supernatural negativity that takes the form of omens, spells, witchcraft, strife, and bad dreams? Today we might benefit from a more secular lens to view spells and witchcraft. Magic and supernatural events are, by definition, beyond science, but isn't supernatural magic also about perception and deception? I see the smoke and mirrors of broadcast media, social media, corporations, political leaders, and others as another form of trickery—they frequently employ formulas, data, and algorithms to sell their products or personas. The algorithms used by social media companies, for example, feed into our biases and foment polarizing viewpoints as clickbait. Such strategies tend to coerce, hypnotize, and cast spells on people such that we neglect important things like civil liberties and the environment and instead focus on less important things like celebrity drama. Is it not true that manipulating our perception is another way of performing magic, like the sleight of hand in a card trick?

Let's explore the meaning of joy for a moment since this Tara wears an armor of it. Joy can be understood and experienced in many ways. The American poet Gay Ross explores the facets of joy in his book *Inciting Joy*, defining it less as the absence of sorrow than as a response to it. In this way, joy has everything to do with our suffering and sorrow; it emerges from it. Joy can be a path to liberation, both personal and collective. Taking a clear-eyed look at injustice, political polarization, and the destruction of the natural world leads us to the necessity of sharing joy amid the sorrow, exploring ways we might resist, and how joy might lead to wild, unpredictable, creative forms of solidarity. Ross posits that it is this solidarity that might just help us survive.[11]

In Buddhism, joy[12] is related to Ross's definition, but it also goes a step further—it leads us into the blissful abliss. In Dharma, joy bubbles up when we tap into the wellspring of the nature of our own mind through meditation and contemplation. Realizing the nature of our mind is like pouring cold water into boiling water—it instantly neutralizes it and stops it from scalding us. In this way, the experience of our innate joy emerges when we calm the boiling water of suffering and despair. The first stage of realization of a bodhisattva is called the "supremely joyful"[13] because it is an experience of the great peace that comes from realizing the nature of mind itself, free of projections and dualistic clinging. Ross is in line with the Dharma in this respect because joy arises in response to our sorrow. Joy exists because sorrow exists in the same way that light exists because dark exists. Without the contrast of the other, each does not come into being. By meeting our sorrow, we access the wellspring of our joy and the shared humanity that it brings. And yet, when we realize the nature of our mind, we taste that supreme bliss *beyond* samsara and nirvana.

In our real-life example of Tara Sitatapatra, we'll explore how such spells and nightmares can be *dispelled* by celebrating the joy and dignity that come from a collective of liberators working together for the benefit of all. Tara's protective parasol is not just for VIPs, sovereigns, gods, and holy men; it is for everyone.

Real-Life Embodiment
Black Lives Matter Movement

My choice for the real-life embodiment of Tara Sitatapatra is the movement Black Lives Matter (BLM), which has sought unique ways to hold a protective shield, like Tara Sitatapatra's parasol, over the lives of those who have been oppressed for too long. Tara's enlightened activity, as we've seen, can manifest as a movement made up of many people working for collective liberation. The BLM mission statement says, "We are a collective of liberators who believe in an inclusive and spacious movement." A collective of liberators is exactly the kind of movement Tara would be a part of because she is *the* Liberatrix, and this nineteenth Tara is the Invincible Queen Liberatrix.

BLM was founded in 2013 by Alicia Garza, Patrisse Cullors, and Opal Tometi in response to the acquittal of Trayvon Martin's murderer. The circumstances of Martin's death sparked a national debate and protest movement addressing racial profiling in the United States. Now BLM is a global organization seeking to eradicate white supremacy, build local power, and intervene in the violence that is afflicted on Black communities by the government, police, and white supremacists.

White supremacy is an overarching issue that includes notions of toxic masculinity and patriarchy, misogyny, and environmental degradation based on "man over the planet" ways of thinking. White supremacy culture, in which whiteness is elevated above other skin colors, teaches us to center the values of one race as superior to all others. In my opinion, because of its power, implications, and reach across the globe, white supremacy is one of the most destructive negative forces we currently face. Healing the ills of white supremacy is important work because it is liberatory work, and Dharma is all about liberation. The Buddha was a justice guy. He went against the caste system, teaching that all people are equal no matter their gender, race, or social status. He taught to value the Earth and nature, to respect that our actions have consequences, and to treat others with love and compassion. One person's liberation is tied up in everyone else's liberation. If others are oppressed, then we are oppressed. This is what is meant by the bodhisattva vow to awaken for the benefit of all beings, because when we really see into the nature of reality, we see that we are all interrelated.

The BLM movement also centers Black joy, imagination, and

innovation by highlighting Black artists, writers, musicians, and thinkers, generating means for liberation and collective healing. I see BLM as donning the armor of joy and dignity that Tara Sitatapatra wears as she dispels negative spells such as racism and white supremacy. In a sense, focusing on Black joy and creativity is a way to find refuge under the cool shade of Tara Sitatapatra's parasol where the collective of liberators can find some rest, safety, and rejuvenation beneath the blazing sun of oppression.

"Black lives matter" does not mean that no one else matters; it means that the Black lives that have historically been excluded and marginalized matter as much as everyone else's. Of course, *all* lives matter. The BLM affirms Black, queer, trans, disabled, and undocumented people, as well as women, people with records, and all lives along the gender spectrum. White supremacy is an issue that affects everyone. It is worthwhile to learn about it and support individuals who have been oppressed due to the color of their skin. If you are a white-bodied individual like me, you can use your privileges to help others. To avoid developing a "white savior complex," let your engagement be well informed and motivated by bodhichitta. As the American author and social activist bell hooks says, the most important way for white people to be of service in the struggle for racial justice is to do their own personal abolitionist work. Through our own journey with this work, we learn how we may knowingly or unknowingly hold white supremacist ways of thinking that cause harm to ourselves and others. We are then able to take steps to dismantle and heal our unperceived biases. It's rewarding and liberating work; it is Dharma work.

Further Contemplations

Each of us holds multiple identities simultaneously that create different intersecting social locations—gender identity, age, socioeconomic, and so on. If you hold a privileged location in society that affords you opportunities and freedoms based on the way you look, how old you are, etc., then look for places to explore and learn about your own conscious and unconscious participation in systems of oppression. Find skillful ways to transform this participation into a commitment to and solidarity with inclusive communities around you. Have conversations, read, take classes, be humble and curious. And please let go of needing to be perfect. There's no reason you have to get it right all the time. If you mess up, acknowledge it, apologize, and get up and keep going. Don't forget to wear the armor of joy and dignity that is Tara Sitatapatra's reminder to us. Enrich your life by stretching your comfort zone to include friends and experiences to which you may not be accustomed. Find ways to expand your sphere of joy.

On a more personal level, ask yourself how you might uplift and counteract negative forces, thoughts, and beliefs that cause harm in your life. What does Tara Sitatapatra's protective parasol and armor of joy feel like to you? How might you create conditions in your life for shade from the blistering sun of negativity? Meditation is one way to become lucid within this waking dream called daily life. How do you find joy—even in the face of adversity? Can you uncover a way to laugh at the preposterous moments? Let humor be your armor of joy.

Nineteenth Tara:
Tara Sitatapatra Embodiment Meditation

Before you begin, recall the three samadhis of emptiness, compassion, and the union of the two. Remember that all appearances of self and deity are empty of intrinsic existence yet manifest as ceaseless compassion.

Settle into a comfortable meditation seat and take nine relaxation breaths, breathing into any physical tension, then any emotional tension, and finally any mental tension and releasing it all with your exhalations.

Front Visualization

Imagine that from luminous empty space Tara Sitatapatra appears in the space in front and slightly above you, peaceful and crystal white in color. With her majestic armor of joy and splendor, Tara Sitatapatra protects beings from bad omens, nightmares, supernatural dangers, conflict, and misfortune—anything that destroys peace of mind and happiness. She also protects the Dharma and those who teach it from disputes and disharmony. Upon her lotus is the white umbrella, which symbolizes her spiritual sovereignty. She is surrounded by numerous wisdom beings.

Recite the Refuge and Bodhichitta Prayer (3 times)

NĀMO
Noble Tara, the essence of all refuges,
you liberate beings from fear and suffering.
I take refuge in your vast, loving compassion.
In order to bring all sentient beings to the state of
    enlightenment,
I generate the twofold bodhichitta of aspiration and action.

Self-Visualization

Sound Tara's seed syllable TĀM three times.

First TĀM: Imagine that your body becomes Tara Sitatapatra, peaceful and crystal white in color. Your body is luminous and hollow, with the TĀM in your heart center.

Second TĀM: As Tara Sitatapatra, send offerings of rainbow wisdom light to the wisdom beings. Let yourself truly sense this connection between you and them.

Third TĀM: Wisdom beings send rainbow wisdom light back to you, empowering you as Tara Sitatapatra, fully activating you. Truly feel what it would be like to be the awakened buddha Tara Sitatapatra, a being of radiant light and infinite love and capacity.

Mantra Recitation and Enacting Tara's Enlightened Activities

As you recite the mantra, imagine rainbow wisdom light streaming from the TĀṂ and the mantra garland in all directions. Sparks of light and vajras emanate from your body and the white umbrella, pacifying all conflict, bad omens, and nightmares and protecting the Dharma and those who teach it from disputes and disharmony. As Tara Sitatapatra, you protect beings from every kind of natural and supernatural danger. Your majestic power and love bring protection, joy, and bliss to all beings.

OM TARE TUTTARE TURE HUNG HUNG PHAT PHAT RAKSHA
RAKSHA MAM SVAHA

Recite the mantra as many times as you like—but at least twenty-one times. Genuinely feel yourself as Tara Sitatapatra.

Dissolution and Rest in Awareness

When your mantra recitation feels complete, dissolve the visualization: first the world and its inhabitants, then you as Tara Sitatapatra converging at the TĀṂ in your heart center. Then everything becomes luminous emptiness.

Rest in spacious awareness—the vast, luminous, and wakeful nature of your own mind. Release into presence. When you are ready, return to your form as Tara Sitatapatra and feel yourself fully integrated with her. As you move about your day, recall the compassion and love of Tara Sitatapatra within and all around you.

Close the session with a sense of gratitude to Tara and her blessings.

Dedication of Merit

Through this virtue, may I quickly attain the state of Noble Tara.
May I bring each and every being, without exception, to that state.
May all beings be healthy, free from suffering and its causes,
    and may they awaken to their true nature.

DRÖLMA RITRÖ LOMA GYÖNMA

(SKT. TARA SHABARI)

The Twentieth Tara

Tara of Mountain Retreat, Clothed in Leaves

Homage to Mother [Tara], your two eyes shine brilliantly
With the fullness of the sun and moon.
With the twice-uttered hara and tuttare
You pacify the most intractable infectious diseases.

Tara Shabari is peaceful and crimson like the color of saffron. She cures contagious diseases and pandemics. She is clothed in medicinal leaves; therefore, I call her the "Medicine Tara," inspired by the well-known Medicine Buddha.

In Sanskrit, Tara Shabari is known as "Tara Who Dwells in the Wilderness." *Shabari* is an interesting term with a wide range of meanings from "variegated color," "wild," to "she who is beyond the caste system." In the Hindu epic *Ramayana*, Shabari is the name of an elderly ascetic who received Rama's blessings due to her intense devotion to him.[1] In the Vedas, Shabari is an epithet used for the four-eyed watchdogs of Yama, the Lord of Death. Later, it was associated with a mountain tribe in the Deccan Plateau in Maharashtra, India.[2]

In Tibetan, *ritrö* means "mountain retreat," *loma* "leaves," and *gyönma* "she who is adorned" or "she who is clothed." Thus, we may translate her Tibetan name as "Tara of Mountain Retreat, Clothed in Leaves." Often her name is shortened to Ritröma, meaning "Lady of Mountain Retreat." The implication is that Ritröma is like a medicine woman who lives in the wilderness, imbued with the wisdom of medicinal plants and the power to heal contagious diseases.

Her Mantra

ༀ་ཏུ་རེ་ཏུཏྟ་རེ་ཏུ་རེ་ནཾ་ཏུ་རེ་མ་ནོ་ཧ་ར་ཧཱུཾ་ཧ་ར་སྭཱ་ཧཱ།

OM TĀRE TUTTĀRE TURE NAMA TĀRE MANO HARA HŪM HARA
SVĀHĀ

OM TARE TUTTARE TURE NAMA TARE MANO HARA HUNG HARA
SVAHA

OM! Tara! Be swift, Tara! Homage, Tara! Steal away the mind
[with] HŪM! So be it!

Her Symbol: Medicinal Vase

Upon Tara Shabari's lotus is a circular medicinal vase or basket[3]
filled with healing ambrosia. Often used by Indian adepts (*siddhas*)
to keep books and ritual objects, the traditional medicinal vase is
at times a basket, a circular container, or a leather bag.

There is an important late fourth-/early fifth-century Mahayana
sutra called *The Medicinal Basket's Display*.[4] The Sanskrit term for
medicinal basket is *karandavyuha* (Tib. *za ma tog*), which is also one
of the 108 names of Avalokiteshvara mentioned in this sutra where
he rises to prominence, enacting various enlightened activities in
different realms contained in the pores of his skin. In this sutra,
it is said that the sun and moon were born from Avalokiteshvara's
eyes,[5] an interesting parallel to Tara Shabari's solar and lunar eyes.[6]

Exploring Tara Shabari's Facets

In his commentary to the *Praises*, Jigme Lingpa describes Tara
Shabari in this way:

> You whose two eyes are like the sun and the full moon. From
> the sun of your right eye shines radiant light, destroying those
> who bring disease like dry grass burnt by fire. From the moon of
> your left eye descends a rich stream of nectar, healing sickness,
> contagious diseases, and their causes and consequences.[7]

Tara Shabari's right sun eye shines sunlight in all directions, destroying disease-bearing beings—microbes, viruses, bacteria, and so on. Her left moon eye streams cooling nectar flowing to all beings, bringing healing and restoring them to health. When we meditate on Tara Shabari, we imagine that "light blazes from the sun and full moon of her eyes, burning contagious disease and those who cause it, and healing sickness."[8]

Tara Shabari's mantra emphasizes how she steals away our dualistic concepts (the term *mano* found in her mantra means "mind") with her healing power and medicinal nectar.[9] In the *Smile of Sun and Moon* commentary, it says that the "Twice-spoken *hara* symbolizes taking away the enemy—the duality of samsara and nirvana—by the unity of bliss and emptiness."[10] HŪṂ, the seed syllable for enlightened mind, removes our dualistic concepts born of ignorance. While Tara Shabari's mantra focuses on her power to steal away the core disease of the mind—dualistic grasping—her symbol—the medicinal vase—focuses on her power to heal contagious diseases of the body.

When the COVID-19 pandemic was first announced in the United States in the winter of 2020, Tara Mandala put out a call to practice devoted to the healing power of the twentieth Tara. I offered online teachings to support this global effort to amplify her energy through mantra recitation and meditation devoted to the well-being of our global community. Since that time, we have accumulated over two million Tara Shabari mantras worldwide.

Now let's learn about two real-life women who have embodied Tara Shabari's healing power through their devotion to curing intractable contagious diseases for their communities.

Real-Life Embodiments
Annie Dodge Wauneka

Dr. Annie Dodge Wauneka (1910-1997), a member of the Diné, was the first woman to sit on the Navajo Tribal Council on which she served as the sole woman for twenty-seven years.[11] Serving as the head of the council's Health and Welfare Committee for three terms, she focused on improving the health and education of her people through eradicating tuberculosis, an infectious disease that generally affects the lungs and was running rampant in the Navajo Nation. She advocated for the Navajo to receive education and opportunities to improve their homes and sanitation, paying particular attention to the young and the elderly. She also wrote a dictionary in which she translated English medical terms in the Navajo language.[12]

Navajo women such as Dr. Wauneka come from a matrilineal clan structure whose culture is based on women's ownership of both residential hogans and herds. Women are responsible for the family land and base their decisions on the natural laws learned from "their spiritual antecedents in this and previous three worlds through which the People have come."[13] Dr. Wauneka became known as the "First Lady of Indian Health" within the National Indian Health Board, an embodiment of Navajo women's legacy of leadership as she fought for the best possible health care for her people.

In 1963, Dr. Wauneka was awarded the Presidential Medal of Freedom by Lyndon B. Johnson, and in 2000, she was inducted into the National Women's Hall of Fame. Stan Steiner, an American historian specializing in Indigenous American peoples and their histories, said that "if there were a queen in the United States, it would have to be this woman."[14] Dr. Wauneka embodies Tara Shabari's enlightened activities through her work to protect the Navajo against infectious disease based on an understanding of the reciprocal web and lineage that she and her people inherited from their ancestors.

Rosemary Gladstar

Rosemary Gladstar (b. 1948) is an internationally renowned herbalist, activist, author, and educator who founded the first herbal school in California in 1978 called the California School of Herbal Studies. In 1987, she moved to Vermont and cofounded Sage Mountain Herbs and United Plant Savers out of her concern for the ecological sustainability of the herb trade. She is respected for her technical knowledge of herbal medicine and for her stewardship in the global herbalist community.

Gladstar grew up on a small dairy farm in Northern California and learned from her maternal grandmother, a survivor of the Armenian genocide, how to craft local wild herbs. Gladstar says that plants began to speak to her at a young age, and luckily no one told her that was impossible. Ever a free spirit, in the summer of 1971 while in her twenties, she set off on a three-and-a-half-month journey on horseback with her toddler son and a friend. They traveled from her home in Sonoma to the Trinity Alps in Northern California, riding every day and sleeping under the stars at night. They ate what they could find in the forests and wildcrafted much of their food, eating seeds, fruit, and vegetables they gathered along the way. She says she felt healthier that summer than at any other time in her life, and her three-year-old son had a great time with tanned skin, rosy cheeks, and golden hair kissed by the sun. It was during those times living so close to plants and nature that she began to realize that she was an herbalist and it was time to give back the wisdom she had received. In 1972 with the help of some friends, she opened a little apothecary in the back of the Guerneville Natural Food store in Guerneville, California.

Gladstar is the author of twelve books on herbalism and the director of the popular educational home study course called The Science and Art of Herbalism. She devotes much of her time to outreach and advocacy as a voice for the plants, defending traditional medicines against corporate trademark all the way to federal court to ensure access for future generations. Gladstar is a national treasure medicine woman, embodying the wisdom of plants as well as of the spirit of Tara Shabari.

Further Contemplations

With a loving expression, Tara Shabari looks upon us as if to say, "My dear, what are you doing for your health? Are you taking care of yourself?" It's easy to forget about our own self-care and how important nature is for our well-being. Recently I put into my calendar an allotted time each week labeled "health focus" when I make calls for doctor's appointments, gather herbs, order supplements— whatever is needed for my well-being. When I look at Tara Shabari, I hear her say, "I care about you. Let's heal." How might you bring the Medicine Tara into your life, into your psyche? If you were to embody her, what self-care would you enact for yourself?

If you don't already, find time to commune with the wisdom of plants and the natural world. Learn how to wildcraft local herbs— what edible plants grow naturally in your area? Go camping, rent a cabin in the woods, do a retreat in nature, listen to the plants and animals. Listen and follow; learn the lessons found within nature. Clothe yourself in leaves literally and metaphorically. Surround yourself in nature, soak in rose-petaled baths, roll around on the leaf-strewn ground. Once while I was teaching on Tara Shabari, I noticed that a large fall-colored leaf had affixed itself to my meditation shawl. It must have stuck to me while I was outside before class. We all had a good laugh, enjoying the playful serendipity of the moment. The Medicine Tara let herself be felt intimately in that moment. Where do you feel her intimately in your life? Find those places and linger there.

Twentieth Tara:
Tara Shabari Embodiment Meditation

Before you begin, recall the three samadhis of emptiness, compassion, and the union of the two. Remember that all appearances of self and deity are empty of intrinsic existence yet manifest as ceaseless compassion.

Settle into a comfortable meditation seat and take nine relaxation breaths, breathing into any physical tension, then any emotional tension, and finally any mental tension and releasing it all with your exhalations.

Front Visualization

Imagine that from luminous empty space Tara Shabari appears in the space in front and slightly above you, peaceful and crimson like saffron. She is clothed in medicinal leaves. From the sun in her right eye shines forth powerful rays that destroy all disease. From the moon of her left eye, a rich stream of nectar descends, returning all beings to perfect health. Upon her lotus is the medicinal vase from which healing nectar flows to all beings. She is surrounded by numerous wisdom beings.

Recite the Refuge and Bodhichitta Prayer (3 times)

> NĀMO
> Noble Tara, the essence of all refuges,
> you liberate beings from fear and suffering.
> I take refuge in your vast, loving compassion.
> In order to bring all sentient beings to the state of
>   enlightenment,
> I generate the twofold bodhichitta of aspiration and action.

Visualization

Sound Tara's seed syllable TĀM three times.

First TĀM: Imagine that your body becomes Tara Shabari, crimson and peaceful. Your body is luminous and hollow, with the TĀM in your heart center.

Second TĀM: As Tara Shabari, send offerings of rainbow wisdom light to the wisdom beings. Let yourself truly sense this connection between you and them.

Third TĀM: Wisdom beings send rainbow wisdom light back to you, empowering you as Tara Shabari, fully activating you. Truly feel what it would be like to be the awakened buddha Tara Shabari, a being of radiant light and infinite love and capacity.

Mantra Recitation

As you recite the mantra, imagine rainbow wisdom light emanating from the mantra garland and TĀṂ to all beings everywhere. Nectar descends from the medicinal vase, healing all disease and epidemics. You are clothed in medicinal leaves. From the sun in your right eye shines forth powerful golden sunlight that purifies all disease. From the moon in your left eye, a rich stream of nectar flows, returning all beings to perfect health.

> OM TARE TUTTARE TURE NAMA TARE MANO HARA HUNG HARA SVAHA

Recite the mantra as many times as you like—but at least twenty-one times. Genuinely feel yourself as Tara Shabari.

Dissolution and Rest in Awareness

When your mantra recitation feels complete, dissolve the visualization: first the world and its inhabitants, then you as Tara Shabari converging at the TĀṂ in your heart center. Then everything becomes luminous emptiness.

Rest in spacious awareness—the vast, luminous, and wakeful nature of your own mind. Release into presence. When you are ready, return to your form as Tara Shabari and feel yourself fully integrated with her. As you move about your day, recall the compassion and love of Tara Shabari within and all around you.

Close the session with a sense of gratitude to Tara and her blessings.

Dedication of Merit

Through this virtue, may I quickly attain the state of Noble Tara.

May I bring each and every being, without exception, to that state.

May all beings be healthy, free from suffering and its causes, and may they awaken to their true nature.

DRÖLMA LHAMO ÖZER CHENMA
(SKT. TARA MARICHI)

The Twenty-First Tara

Tara, Rays of Light

*Homage to you, Mother [Tara], who reveals the three essential
  natures
With your power to pacify.
Supreme Ture, you completely destroy
The throngs of malevolent spirits, zombies, and harm-bringers.*

Tara Marichi is peaceful and white in color. As our Longevity Tara, she protects our vitality and increases longevity, restoring the life force of the sick. She is also renowned for protecting animals and travelers, including refugees, immigrants, and anyone going through transitions. She brings about wisdom and removes obstacles that stand in the way of our spiritual progress.

In Sanskrit, her name, Marichi, means "Tara, Rays of Light." In Tibetan, Drölma Lhamo Özer Chenma means "savioress (*Drölma*), the goddess (*lhamo*) who possesses (*chenma*) light rays (*özer*)." Thus we might translate her name as "Tara, the Rays of Light Goddess." The only difference between the two names is the Tibetan word *lhamo*, which means "goddess."

Her Mantra

ཨོཾ་ཏུ་རེ་ཏུཏྟཱ་རེ་ཏུ་རེ་མ་རཱི་ཙྱཻ་ཚེ་བྷྲཱུྃ་ནྲྀ་ཧཱ་སྭཱ་ཧཱ།

OM̐ TĀRE TUTTĀRE TURE MARICYAI CHE BHRŪṂ NṚJA SVĀHĀ
OM TARE TUTTARE TURE MARICHYAI CHE BHRUM NRIJA SVAHA
OM̐! Tara! Be swift, Tara, Rays of Light! Born from a lotus
[whose seed syllable is] BHRŪṂ, to you [I pray]! So be it![1]

Her Symbol: Golden Fish

Upon Tara Marichi's lotus is a pair of golden fish.[2] Another of the eight auspicious symbols, the golden fish symbolize good fortune, fertility, and liberation from suffering. Specifically, they symbolize fearlessness, particularly freedom from fear of drowning in the ocean of samsara.

Exploring Tara Marichi's Facets

The Three Essential Natures

In her praise, the Buddha says, "Homage to you, Mother [Tara], who reveals the three essential natures / With your power to pacify." What are these three essential natures? They are the enlightened aspects of the body, speech, and mind of the buddhas, namely the three vajra states synonymous with the three kayas (see "The Tenth Tara"). Through her power to pacify obstacles, Tara Marichi clarifies these three aspects of our being that are hidden from view when covered by ignorance. Jigme Lingpa, in his commentary, states that "the practitioners should meditate on the view of their own body, speech, and mind as the primordially pure essential nature of the deity—the enlightened body, speech, and mind of Lady Tārā."[3] He continues to explain that we should visualize the essential nature of Tara's enlightened body as a white OM at our third eye, the essential nature of her enlightened speech as a red ĀḤ at our throat, and the essential nature of her enlightened mind as a blue HŪM at our heart center. By meditating in this way, these three seed syllables will manifest in these three centers as a portal into the experience of abiding in the three essential natures of the deity (enlightened body), mantra (enlightened speech), and samadhi (enlightened mind) of Tara.[4] You will have the chance to experience this in the Tara Marichi embodiment meditation. The next two lines in her stanza emphasize how she "completely destroys / The throngs of malevolent spirits, zombies, and harm bringers." In this context, malevolent spirits[5] refer to the type of spirits that harm humans' bodies and minds.

These malevolent spirits are associated with the planets and astrological influences in our lives. In essence, Tara Marichi has the power to pacify all these negative forces, literally or metaphorically, and to open the doorway into the three essential natures that are our true nature—the enlightened body, speech, and mind of Tara.

Real-Life Embodiment

My approach to the real-life Tara Marichi is not what you might expect. Rather than focusing on health and longevity, which are also the skillful means of Tara Ushnisha Vijaya and Tara Shabari, I highlight an extraordinary woman who has helped preserve the longevity of her culture.

Jetsun Pema

Jetsun Pema (b. 1940), the elder sister of His Holiness the Fourteenth Dalai Lama, has devoted her life to giving refuge and protection to Tibetans in exile, particularly children, through her four decades of work with the Tibetan Children's Village (TCV) in India. She has worked to preserve the longevity of the Tibetan people and their culture.

Jetsun Pema was born in Lhasa, the Tibetan capital, in 1940. She escaped Tibet in 1959 with the Dalai Lama and took refuge in the Himalayan hill station of Dharamsala. She received an education in India, Switzerland, and England before becoming the first elected female minister of the Tibetan government-in-exile. She was awarded the title Mother of Tibet by its national assembly.

Like Tara Marichi, Jetsun Pema has been a protector of travelers during her forty-two-year career as president of the TCV by helping oversee the well-being of thousands of Tibetan children seeking shelter in India, often without their parents. Since the Communist Chinese invasion of Tibet began in 1950, many Tibetans have fled oppressive conditions there in search of freedom in neighboring India, Nepal, and other countries around the world. When the Dalai

Lama was able to establish his government and community in exile in Dharamsala, many Tibetans began to follow him.

Some Tibetan families have made the difficult decision to send their children to India, knowing they could be housed and educated by the TCV. A formidable educational program, the TCV offers those in grades kindergarten through high school courses in Tibetan and international world history, culture, and science, as well as the three languages of Hindi, English, and Tibetan. They study Tibetan cultural and spiritual traditions and have the opportunity to meet the Dalai Lama, a beacon of Tibetan sovereignty and believed to be an embodiment of the Buddha Avalokiteshvara.

With respect to preserving Tibet's cultural heritage, Jetsun Pema has played a key role in Tibetan politics in exile. In 1980, she was sent by the Dalai Lama to visit Tibet to lead the third fact-finding delegation. For three months, she traveled extensively all over the country and gave a sobering assessment of the situation in Tibet upon her return. This helped the Tibetan government-in-exile to propose new solutions and policies in their struggle for autonomy from Chinese rule.

Jetsun Pema embodies Tara Marichi through her commitment to protect refugee children who have come so far, leaving family and homeland behind, to meet their heritage anew and to find fresh opportunities outside of occupied Tibet in hopes of keeping their culture alive. I feel Jetsun Pema's life as a protector and advocate for the longevity of her people is a powerful way to bring this book to a close, for without Tibetan culture and particularly their devotion to the Dharma and to Tara, we would not have these teachings on the twenty-one Taras today and I would not have written this book.

Further Contemplations

How do you preserve the longevity of your ancestry, your cultural memory? What stories and traditions help to create a sense of continuity in your family or for your children and your children's children? Do you know the names of your great-grandparents and further back? If not, look them up and share them along with their histories with those who are younger than you: your children, your nieces and nephews.

More broadly, how can you help people in transition who might not have a stable roof over their head—the travelers, the refugees in need of help? Can you volunteer for or donate to organizations that are assisting those displaced by war, famine, and oppression?

Protecting animals is another aspect of Tara Marichi's enlightened activity, so I encourage you to consider how you might work for them. Some options are to advocate for the humane treatment of animals, reduce your meat and animal product intake, be more conscientious about where you get your animal products. In Buddhist traditions, vegetarianism is advocated to protect animals' lives. Animals are sentient beings like us, and they too wish to live and not to suffer. If we are to really understand the interrelated web of existence, we can appreciate that minimizing our role in causing suffering to any beings, large or small, human or nonhuman, should be an endeavor worth pursuing.[6]

You can embody Tara Marichi's enlightened energy by engaging in her sadhana and the Journey with Tara found at the end of the book to balance and harmonize your nervous system and increase your vitality. Find ways to reduce the amount of stress in your life and enjoy the simple moments of contemplation and devotion to Tara Marichi.

Twenty-First Tara:
Tara Marichi Embodiment Meditation

Before you begin, recall the three samadhis of emptiness, compassion, and the union of the two. Remember that all appearances of self and deity are empty of intrinsic existence yet manifest as ceaseless compassion.

Settle into a comfortable meditation seat and take nine relaxation breaths, breathing into any physical tension, then any emotional tension, and finally any mental tension and releasing it all with your exhalations.

Front Visualization

Imagine that from luminous empty space Tara Marichi appears in the space in front and slightly above you, peaceful and white in color. She protects our vitality and increases longevity. She is renowned for protecting animals and travelers. Upon her lotus is a pair of golden fish that symbolize freedom from fear of drowning in the ocean of samsara. Imagine that white light radiates from the white OM at her brow, red light from the red ĀḤ at her throat, and blue light from the blue HŪM at her heart. The essence of Tara's enlightened body (OM), speech (ĀḤ), and mind (HŪM), these three colored lights summon the life force that has been lost or depleted and increases the vitality for all beings everywhere. She is surrounded by numerous wisdom beings.

Recite the Refuge and Bodhichitta Prayer (3 times)

NĀMO
Noble Tara, the essence of all refuges,
you liberate beings from fear and suffering.
I take refuge in your vast, loving compassion.
In order to bring all sentient beings to the state of
  enlightenment,
I generate the twofold bodhichitta of aspiration and action.

Self-Visualization

Sound Tara's seed syllable TĀM three times.

First TĀM: Imagine that your body becomes Tara Marichi, white and peaceful. Your body is luminous and hollow, with the TĀM in your heart center.

Second TĀM: As Tara Marichi, send offerings of rainbow wisdom light to the wisdom beings. Let yourself truly sense this connection between you and them.

Third TĀM: Wisdom beings send rainbow wisdom light back to you, empowering you as Tara Marichi, fully activating you. Truly feel what it would be like to be the awakened buddha Tara Marichi, a being of radiant light and infinite love and capacity.

Mantra Recitation

As you recite the mantra, imagine rainbow wisdom light radiates from the mantra garland, TĀM, and the golden fish, purifying illness and increasing longevity, personally, collectively, and culturally. Imagine that white light streams from the OM at your brow, red light from the ĀH at your throat, and blue light from the HŪM at your heart, summoning the life force that has been lost or depleted and increasing the vitality for all beings everywhere. Feel that all beings, especially travelers and animals, are protected from harm and their life force is strengthened. By meditating in this way, abide in the three essential natures of the deity (enlightened body), mantra (enlightened speech), and samadhi (enlightened mind) of Tara.

OM TARE TUTTARE TURE MARICHYAI CHE BHRUM NRIJA
SVAHA

Recite the mantra as many times as you like—but at least twenty-one times. Genuinely feel yourself as Tara Marichi.

Dissolution and Rest in Awareness

When your mantra recitation feels complete, dissolve the visualization: first the world and its inhabitants, then you as Tara Marichi converging at the TĀM in your heart center. Then everything becomes luminous emptiness.

Rest in spacious awareness—the vast, luminous, and wakeful

nature of your own mind. Release into presence. When you are ready, return to your form as Tara Marichi and feel yourself fully integrated with her. As you move about your day, recall the compassion and love of Tara Marichi within and all around you.

Close the session with a sense of gratitude to Tara and her blessings.

Dedication of Merit

Through this virtue, may I quickly attain the state of Noble Tara.

May I bring each and every being, without exception, to that state.

May all beings be healthy, free from suffering and its causes, and may they awaken to their true nature.

Conclusion

As we bring these chapters on the twenty-one Taras to a close, I invite you to explore, in your own creative way, how your own three doors of body, speech, and mind become the three essential natures of enlightened body, speech, and mind, as explained in "The Twenty-First Tara." As portals for your own liberation, ponder how your actions, words, and thoughts provide opportunities for you to connect with the essence of Tara. If your body, speech, and mind are doorways to the enlightened body, speech, and mind of Tara, how might you walk through those doors? Whether it is through loving and generous deeds; kind, eloquent words or mantra recitation; or cultivating patience, compassion, and other beneficial mental states, find ways to reveal the three essential natures within you in an authentic and personal way. Traditionally it is said that the essence of deity yoga is to see all appearances as the deity, all sounds as mantra, and all thoughts as the dharmakaya ("truth body"). This is the most direct and profound way to actualize the enlightened qualities of the body, speech, and mind of the Taras.

This leads me to a very pithy and profound teaching I learned from a spiritual teacher early in my life regarding the guru within. I pass this very special teaching on to you. Spell *guru* out loud: *G-U-R-U*. It sounds like, "Gee, you are you!" *You* are your guru. Even though we do need to rely on teachers and the wisdom of the Taras from time to time, the best teachers are the ones who instruct you to look within. Ultimately, you find that the wisdom of Tara is within you—that you are none other than Tara.

I encourage you, as you move about your life, to find ways to pass through the three doors and embody the three essential natures in every step, in every moment. In this way, you train yourself for your grand finale, the moment of death, the ultimate release into the abliss—the bliss of the abyss. Go home to Tara and realize the undying nature of your own primordial consciousness.

Journey with Tara

This personal process was adapted for the twenty-one Taras based on Lama Tsultrim's "Journey with the Dakini." The following meditation can be done on its own or after each of your Tara meditations to access insight into that particular Tara's wisdom. For example, if you want to tap into Tara Vajra Sarasvati more intimately, you could add this journey after her embodiment meditation. Or if you only have a short period of time, you could dive directly into this journey, invoking the presence of Tara Vajra Sarasvati, and go through the steps.

Move into the Journey
- Do the nine relaxation breaths.
  - Close your eyes and keep them closed as much as possible until the end of the process.
  - For the first few breaths, breathe into any physical tension you find in your body; then release it with the exhalation.
  - For the next few breaths, breathe into any emotional tension you find in your body, then release it with the exhalation.
  - For the last few breaths, breathe into any mental tension you are holding, feel where you may be carrying mental tension such as worries or concerns in your body, and then release it with the exhalation.
- Generate your motivation.
  - Next generate the motivation to practice for the benefit of yourself and all beings; this is called raising bodhichitta.

Step One: Invoke the presence of the Tara with whom you would like to journey.

· Call on the Tara with whom you would like to have further communication by sounding her seed syllable TĀM once—or if she has a unique seed syllable, you may sound that instead. See this Tara in front of you just as you normally do in the meditation. Focus on the details of this Tara: her size, color, character, her symbol on her lotus, and the look in her eyes. Notice something about this Tara that you did not see before.

· Now notice the environment around Tara. What kind of place is she in? What is the feeling in the environment? Is she in a place you've been? Can you see the time period? Can you see the country she is in? Do you notice any smells or sounds? Is she on this Earth or in another dimension? If it is another dimension, notice the details of that place.

Step Two: Tara takes you on a journey.

· Now imagine that Tara takes you on a journey to a special place.
· You follow, walking behind her. Notice what the path is like and how it changes as you proceed. Do you sense any smells or sounds? What is the feeling in the environment?
· When you arrive at the special place Tara is taking you, notice where it is.
· What are the qualities of the place that surrounds you? What time of day is it? What is the temperature? Are there any particular smells? What era is it? How do you feel in this place? Does it remind you of anywhere you've been before?
· Tara then explains why she has brought you here and why this place is important to you.

Step Three: Ask Tara your questions.

· Now in this place, ask Tara any questions you have concerning the dynamic you would like to work with. This might be about challenges around embodying this particular Tara's energy and enlightened activity in your life. You can ask one or several questions.

Step Four: Take the seat of Tara and answer the question(s).

· Once you have asked the question(s), switch places and take the seat of Tara. Take a moment to settle into Tara's body. Notice how it feels to be in Tara's body. How does your normal self look from Tara's point of view? After settling into Tara's body, answer the question(s) you have asked, speaking as Tara.

Step Five: Return to your original seat.

· You can continue to dialogue with Tara in this way, asking as many questions as you like and switching places with each new question.
· When you are finished, return to your original position. Take a moment to feel the help and protection that Tara has offered you.
· Now Tara turns away, and when she turns back, she is holding a gift for you.
· Tara gives you the gift. Receive it and notice the details of the gift. Tara explains its meaning.
· Then the gift with all its potency dissolves into your heart. Notice the feeling of the gift inside you.
· Now see Tara in front of you. Look into her eyes and feel her energy pouring into your body. As you feel the energy of Tara entering you, it spreads all the way down to the soles of your feet, to your fingertips, and throughout your whole body.
· Now imagine that Tara dissolves into light. Notice the color of this light. Feel the light dissolving into you, integrating this luminosity into every cell of your body. Take note of the feeling of the integrated energy of Tara in your body.
· Now you, with the integrated energy of Tara, also dissolve.

Step Six: Rest in awareness.

· Rest in the state that is present after the dissolution; allow yourself to rest as long as you like.
· Pause until discursive thoughts begin again. Now gradually come back to your body, recalling the feeling of Tara's energy in your body.
· As you open your eyes, maintain the feeling of Tara's energy in your body and see the world through the eyes of Tara.

Dedication of Merit

Dedicate the merit—the accumulation of positive energy that you've generated through this journey with Tara—to the benefit of all beings everywhere.

Post-Meditation

As you go about the rest of your day, imagine that you are Tara and that everyone you meet is a manifestation of your mandala. As you eat, you are feeding Tara; as you dress, you are dressing Tara. Recite her mantra throughout your daily tasks. Imagine that the world is transformed into a luminous dimension; this is called pure perception.

Journaling Practice

In your own journal devoted to your journeys with Tara, record your process using the following framework if you wish.

Date:
Which Tara:

Step One: Invoke the presence of Tara.
Describe some of the details of Tara:

What was her size, color, and character? What was the symbol on her lotus? What was the look in her eyes? What did you notice about her that you didn't see before? What was the environment Tara was in (era, place, smells, sounds, etc.)?

Step Two: Tara takes you on a journey.

What surrounded the path? What was the path itself like?

What was the special place Tara took you like (where it was, qualities of the place, time of day, temperature, smells, era, feeling…)?

Why did Tara bring you here?

Step Three: Ask Tara your question(s).

Question 1, etc.:

Step Four: Take the seat of Tara and answer the question(s).

Answer 1:

Was there a follow-up question and answer? Do as many questions as you like.

Question:

Answer:

Step Five: Return to your original seat.

What was Tara's gift?

What was the meaning of the gift?

What was the feeling of the gift inside you?

What was the feeling of the integrated energy of Tara in your body?

Step Six: Rest in Awareness

How did it feel to rest in awareness?

    How did it feel to recall the integrated energy of Tara in your body?

    How will you bring Tara's wisdom into your daily life?

Additional Resources

You can find further practices and resources related to the Taras at www.chandraeaston.com. These include guided meditations (like the tonglen and shamatha meditations) and recommended books, articles, podcasts, documentaries, and organizations related to each of the real-life Taras found in this book. You can also find a forum for sharing your recommendations for real-life Taras.

Melodies to the twenty-one Tara mantras can be found at www .21tarascollective.org, www.chandraeaston.com, and on Spotify.

Foreign Names and Terms

Below are lists of phoneticized Sanskrit and Tibetan names and terms as they appear in this book, along with their transliterated forms. For Sanskrit names and terms, I give the transliteration with diacritics according to the International Alphabet of Sanskrit Transliteration (IAST) system. For Tibetan names and terms, I give the Wylie transliteration.

Sanskrit

Phonetic	IAST Transliteration
acharya	ācārya
adarsha	ādarśa
adarshajnana	ādarśajñāna
Agni	Agni
alayavijnana	ālayavijñāna
amarana amrita kalasha	amaraṇa amṛta kalaśa
Amitabha	Amitābha
Amitayus	Amitāyus
amrita	amṛta
ananda	ānanda
anatman	anātman
apramana	apramāṇa

Phonetic	IAST Transliteration
arta	ārta
arupaloka	arūpaloka
Arya Tara	Ārya Tārā
asana	āsana
ashtamangala	aṣṭamaṅgala
Atharvaveda	*Atharvaveda*
Atisha Dipamkara	Atiśa Dīpaṃkara
Atiyoga	Atiyoga
atman	ātman
Avalokiteshvara	Avalokiteśvara
avidya	avidyā
ayur	āyur
Bhagavati Arya Tara	Bhagavatī Ārya Tārā
Bhairava	Bhairavā
Bhairavi	Bhairavī
bhakti	bhakti
Bhumidevi	Bhūmidevi
bhumipala	bhūmipāla
bhuta	bhūta
bija mantra	bīja mantra
bindu	bindu
bodhichitta	bodhicitta
bodhisattva	bodhisattva
Brahma	Brahmā
brahman	brāhman
Brahmanas, the	Brāhmana
catvaro brahmavihara	catvāro brahmavihārāḥ

Phonetic	IAST Transliteration
chakra	cakra
chandali	caṇḍālī
chattra	chattra
Chinnamasta	Chinnamastā
chintamani	cintāmaṇi
chitta	citta
chittatva	cittatva
dade	dāde
daka	ḍāka
dakini	ḍākiṇī
dakshinavarti shankhya	dakṣiṇāvarta śaṅkhya
dana	dāna
darshan	darśan
devaputramara	devaputramāra
dhanushkalapaka	dhanuṣkalāpakaḥ
dharani	dhāraṇī
dharma	dharma
dharmachakra	dharmacakra
dharmadhatu	dharmadhātu
dharmakaya	dharmakāya
Dharmakirti	Dharmakīrti
dharmapala	dharmapāla
dharmata	dharmatā
dhatu	dhātu
dhvaja	dhvaja
dhyana	dhyāna
ekarasa	ekarasa

Phonetic	IAST Transliteration
gandharva	gandharva
garbha	garbha
ghanta	ghaṇṭa
gotra	gotra
graha	graha
Indra	Indra
Indrajala	Indrajāla
ishtadevata	iṣṭadevatā
Jaganmata	Jaganmātā
Jna	Jñā
jnana	jñāna
Jnana Chandra	Jñāna Candra
jnanasattva	jñānasattva
Kalachakra	Kālacakra
kamaloka	kāmaloka
karandavyuha	kāraṇḍavyūha
karma	karma
karman	karman
karuna	karuṇā
kila / kilaya	kīla / kīlaya
kimnara	kiṃnara
klesha	kleśa
kleshamara	kleśamāra
kriya	kriyā
Krodhakali	Krodhakālī
kundalini shakti	kuṇḍalini śaktī
Mahamudra	Mahāmudrā

Phonetic	IAST Transliteration
mahashanti	mahāśānti
mahasiddha	mahāsiddha
mahavidya	mahāvidyā
Maheshvara	Maheśvara
maitri	maitrī
mala	mālā
mandala	maṇḍala
Manjushri	Mañjuśrī
mantra japa	mantra japa
Mantrayana	Mantrayāna
mantrika	māntrika
Mara, maras	Māra
maranasati	maraṇasati
Marut	Marut
Matsyendranatha	Matsyendranātha
moha	moha
mrityumara	mṛtyumāra
mudita	muditā
mudra	mudrā
Mulamadhyamakakarika	*Mūlamadhyamakakārikā*
mushala	muśala
naga	nāga
Nagarjuna	Nāgārjuna
nirmanakaya	nirmāṇakāya
nirvana	nirvaṇā
nrija	nṛja
panchaskandha	pañcaskandha

Phonetic	IAST Transliteration
pandit	paṇḍit
paramita	pāramitā
prajna	prajñā
prajna khadga	prajñā khaḍga
prajnaparamita	prajñāpāramitā
Prajnaparamita Sutras	*Prajñāpāramitā Sūtras*
pramuditabhumi	pramuditābhūmi
prana	prāna
pranayama	prānāyāma
pratityasamutpada	pratītyasamutpāda
Prithvi	Pṛthvī
Puranas, the	Purāṇa
Raga Nishudana Tara	Rāga Niṣūdana Tārā
ratna	ratna
Ratnasambhava	Ratnasambhava
rishi	ṛṣi
rupaloka	rūpaloka
sadhana	sādhanā
samadhi	samādhi
samadhisattva	samādhisattva
samayasattva	samayasattva
sambhogakaya	saṃbhogakāya
sampanna-krama	saṃpanna-krama
samsara	saṃsāra
sangha	saṃgha
sarva papam	sarva pāpaṃ
sattva guna	sattva guṇa

Phonetic	IAST Transliteration
Shabari Vidya	Shabari Vidyā
shakti	śaktī
Shaktirupini	Śaktirūpinī
Shakyamuni	Śākyamuni
Shakyashri Bhadra	Śākyaśrībhadra
shamatha	śamathā
shanti	śānti
Shantideva	Śāntideva
shar	śar
shatparamita	ṣaṭpāramitā
shavasana	śavāsana
shila	śīla
Shiva	Śiva
shloka	śloka
shrivatsa	śrīvatsa
shunyata	śūnyatā
siddha	siddha
siddhi	siddhi
skandha	skandha
skandhamara	skandhamāra
soma	sōma
Sukhavati	Sukhāvatī
Suryagupta	Sūryagupta
suvamamatsya	suvamamatsya
svabhava	svabhāva
swastika	svastika
Tantrayana	Tantrayāna

Phonetic	IAST Transliteration
Tara	Tārā
Tara Ajitarajni	Tārā Ajitarājñī
Tara Aparadhrishya	Tārā Aparadhṛṣyā
Tara Aparajita	Tārā Aparājitā
Tara Aprameya / Aprameyakramani	Tārā Aprameyākramaṇī
Tara Bhrukuti	Tārā Bhṛkuṭī
Tara Khadiravani	Tārā Khadiravaṇī
Tara Kurukulla	Tārā Kurukullā
Tara Mahabhairava	Tārā Mahābhairavā
Tara Mahamayuri	Tārā Mahāmāyūrī
Tara Mangalartha	Tārā Maṅgalārthā
Tara Marichi	Tārā Mārīcī
Tara Prashamani	Tārā Praśamanī
Tara Prashanti	Tārā Praśānṭī
Tara Punyottamada	Tārā Puṅyottamadā
Tara Ripu Chakra Vinashini	Tārā Ripu Cakra Vināśinī
Tara Shabari	Tārā Śabarī
Tara Sitatapatra	Tārā Sitātapatrā
Tara Trailoka Vijaya	Tārā Trailoka Vijayā
Tara Turavira	Tārā Turavīrā
Tara Ushnisha Vijaya	Tārā Uṣṇīṣa Vijayā
Tara Vajra Sarasvati	Tārā Vajra Sarasvatī
Tara Vasuda	Tārā Vasudā
Tara Vasudhara	Tārā Vasudhārā
Tara Vidyamantra Bala Prashamani	Tārā Vidyāmantra Bala Praśamanī
tathagata	tathāgata
tathagatagarbha	tathāgatagarbha

Phonetic	IAST Transliteration
traya	trāya
Trayastrimsha	Trāyastriṃśa
trina	tṛṇa
trisamadhi	trisamādhi
upaya	ūpaya
upeksha	upekṣā
ushnisha	uṣṇīṣa
utpala	utpala
utpatti-krama	utpatti-krama
Vac	Vāc
vahana	vāhana
vajra	vajrā
vajradhatu	vajradhātu
Vajrasattva	Vajrasattva
Vajratopa	Vajrāṭopā
Vajrayogini	Vajrayoginī
Vamana Purana	*Vāmana Purāna*
vayv-adhisara	vayv-adhisāra
vetala	vetāla
vidya	vidyā
vidyamantra	vidyāmantra
vidyamantrika	vidyāmāntrika
vighnan	vighnān
Vikramashila	Vikramaśīla
vina	vīṇā
vipashyana	vipaśyanā
Vishnu	Viṣṇu

PHONETIC	IAST TRANSLITERATION
Vishvarupa	Visvarūpā
vishvavajra	viṣvavajra
yaksha	yakṣa
yantra	yantra
yantrayoga	yantrayoga
yoga	yoga
yogasana	yogāsana
yogini	yoginī
yuj	yuj

Tibetan

PHONETIC	WYLIE TRANSLITERATION
Chenrezig	sPyan ras gzigs
Chöd	gCod
Chögyam Trungpa Rinpoche	Chos rgyam drung pa rin po che
chökyi khorlo	chos kyi 'khor lo
chökyong	chos skyong
chönyi	chos nyid
chorten	mchod rten
dadar	mda' dar
Dampa Sangye	Dam pa sangs rgyas
dam tshig sempa	dam tshig sems dpa'
dazhu	mda' gzhu
desheg nyingpo	de gshegs snying po
Dewachen	bDe ba cen
dezhin shegpa	de bzhin gshegs pa

PHONETIC	WYLIE TRANSLITERATION
Dilgo Khyentse Rinpoche	Dil mgo mkhyen brtse rin po che
dön	gdon
dorje	rdo rje
dorje gyadram	rdo rje rgya gram
Dorje tsugtor dug karmo	rDor rje gtsug tor gdugs dkar mo
drilbu	dril bu
Drölma Jigje Chenmo	sGrol ma jigs byed chen mo
Drölma Jigten Sumle Gyalma	sGrol ma 'jig rten gsum les rgyal ma
Drölma Lhamo Özer Chenma	sGrol ma lha mo 'od zer cen ma
Drölma Loter Yang Chenma	sGrol ma blo gter dbyangs cen ma
Drölma Maja Chenmo	sGrol ma rma bya chen mo
Drölma Mipham Gyalmo Dugkarmo	sGrol ma mi pham rgyal mo gdugs dkar mo
Drölma Norterma	sGrol ma nor ster ma
Drölma Nyurma Pamo	sGrol ma myur ma dpa' mo
Drölma Pagme Nönma	sGrol ma dpag med gnon ma
Drölma Rabzhima	sGrol ma rab zhi ma
Drölma Rignag Tobzhom	sGrol ma rig sngags stobs gzhom
Drölma Ritrö Loma Gyönma	sGrol ma ri khrod lo ma gyon ma
Drölma Sengdeng Nag	sGrol ma seng ldeng gnags
Drölma Sermo Sönam Tobkye	sGrol ma ser mo bso nams stobs bskyed
Drölma Tashi Dönjema	sGrol ma bkra shis don byed ma
Drölma Tronyer Chenma	sGrol ma khro gnyer cen ma
Drölma Tsugtor Namgyalma	sGrol ma gtsug tor rnam rgyal ma
Drölma Wangdu Rigje Lhamo	sGrol ma dbang sdud rig byed lha mo
Drölma Yulle Gyaljema	sGrol ma gyul las rgyal byed ma
Drölma Zhen Gyi Mitubma	sGrol ma gzhan gyi mi thub ma

Phonetic	Wylie Transliteration
Drölma Zhen Migyalwai Pamo	sGrol ma gzhan mi rgyal ba'i dpa' mo
Drönma	sGron ma
drubthab	sgrub thabs
dug	gdugs
dung gye khyil	dung gyas 'khyil
dütsi	bdud rtsi
Dzogchen	rDzogs chen
dzogrim	rdzogs rim
gawa	dga' ba
Gelug	dGe lugs
gyalmo	rgyal mo
gyaltsen	rgyal mtshan
jampa	byams pa
Jamyang Khyentse Chökyi Lodrö	'Jam dbyangs mkhyen brtse chos kyi blo gros
Jangchub Ö	Byang chub ye shes 'od
je	byed
Jigme Lingpa	'Jigs med gling pa
Kagyu	bKa' brgyud
Kham	Khams
khandroma	mkha' 'gro ma
khor	'khor
kun zhi nam par shepa	kun gzhi rnam par shes pa
kyerim	bskyed rim
Lojong	bLo sbyong
Longchen Nyingtig	kLong chen snying thig
Longchen Rabjam	kLong chen rab 'byams pa dri med 'od zer

Phonetic	Wylie Transliteration
lu	klu
Machig Labdrön	Ma gcig labs sgron
Machig Labkyi Drönma	Ma gcig labs kyi sgron ma
marigpa	ma rig pa
melong	me long
melong tabü yeshe	me long lta bu'i ye shes
namtar	rnam thar
nangwa	snang ba
nyingje	rnying rje
Nyingma	rNying ma
padma	pad ma
pal beu	dpal be'u
pawo	dpa' bo
pharol tu chinpa drug	pha rol tu phyin pa drug
phurba	phur ba
rabtu gawa	rab tu dga' ba
rangdrol	rang grol
rangzhin	rang bzhin
rig	rigs
rig ngag	rig ngag
rig ngag tobzhom	rig ngag stobs gzhom
rigpa	rig pa
rochig	ro gcig
Sakya	Sa skya
Sakya Pandita Kunga Gyaltsen	Sa skya pan di ta kun dga' rgyal mtshan
samten	bsam gtan

Phonetic	Wylie Transliteration
selwa	sel ba
sem	sems
semnyi	sems nyid
sernya	gser nya
shepa	she pa
Sidpay Gyalmo	Srid pa'i rgyal mo
Songtsen Gampo	Srong btsan sgam po
Sowa Rigpa	gSo ba rig pa
tang nyom	btang snyoms
tashi	bkra shis
tashi tag gye	bkra shis rtags brgyad
tendrel	rten 'brel
terbum	ster bum
terma	gter ma
terma	ster ma
tertön	gter ston
timug	gti mug
ting nge dzin nampa sum	ting nge 'dzin rnam pa gsum
ting nge dzin sempa	ting nge 'dzin sems dpa'
tonglen	gtong len
tongshing	tong shing
Topa Bhadra	Thod pa bhadra
trinle	'phrin las
tro	khro
Tröma	Khros ma
trulkhor	'phrul 'khor / 'khrul 'khor
tsebum	tshe bum

Phonetic	Wylie Transliteration
tsetar	tse thar
tshe me zhi	tshad med bzhi
tshul zhi	tshul bzhi
tummo	gtum mo
umdze	dbu mdzad
Ushnisha Vijaya Dharani	Uṣṇīṣa Vijaya Dhāraṇī
yab-yum	yab yum
yeshe	ye shes
Yeshe Dawa	Ye shes zla ba
yeshe raldri	ye shes ral gri
yeshe sempa	ye shes sems dpa'
yidam	yi dam
yizhin norbu	yid bzhin norbu
Yulokö	gYu lo bkod
Yum Chenmo	Yum chen mo
yungdrung	gyung drung
zamatog	za ma tog
Zangri Khangmar	Zangs ri khang dmar
zhimatro	zhi ma khro
zhiwa	zhi ba
zhiwa chenpo	zhi ba chen po
zhom	zhom

Notes

Introduction

1. Susan A. Landesman, trans., *The Tārā Tantra: Tārā's Fundamental Ritual Text (Tārā-mula-kalpa) Part One: The Root Text* (New York and Somerville, MA: American Institute of Buddhist Studies and Wisdom Publications in association with the Columbia Center for Buddhist Studies and Tibet House, 2020), 5.
2. This by no means is meant to be an exhaustive list of Tara's manifestations and epithets. For further reading, see Landesman, *Tārā Tantra*.
3. Skt. *vidya*; Tib. *rigpa*.
4. Wisdom Moon is Jnana Chandra in Sanskrit and Yeshe Dawa in Tibetan.
5. Dundubhisvara.
6. Martin Wilson, *In Praise of Tārā: Songs to the Saviouress* (Somerville, MA: Wisdom, 1992), 43.
7. Tib. Chenrezig.
8. Tara was venerated primarily by the Pyu people and the tantric Ari monks of Myanmar. Khin Zaw, "Remaining Legacy of Green Tara in Myanmar (Burmese) Traditional Beliefs," in *Vajrayāna Buddhism in the Modern World, Proceedings of the Second International Conference on Vajrayana Buddhism* (Thimphu, Bhutan: Centre for Bhutan Studies & GNH, March 28-30, 2018): 49.
9. Stephen Beyer, *The Cult of Tara: Magic and Ritual in Tibet* (Berkeley: University of California Press, 1978), 5.
10. Bokar Rinpoche, *Tara the Feminine Divine* (San Francisco: ClearPoint Press, 1999), 56-67.
11. Ibid., 59.
12. Judith Simmer-Brown, *Dakini's Warm Breath: The Feminine Principle in Tibetan Buddhism* (Boston: Shambhala, 2001), 81-83.
13. Lama Tsultrim Allione, *Women of Wisdom* (London: Routledge and Kegan Paul, 1984), 101-2.

14. Or Skt. *tathata*; Tib. *chönyi*. *Dharma* means "truth," "reality," "phenomena"; and *ta* is a common suffix that means "-ness." Thus, *dharmata* is often translated as "suchness," meaning the-way-things-are-*ness*.

15. Most likely, the derivative of the term *dakini* is not known. It perhaps came from a regional spoken language. Some scholars, such as David Snellgrove, have tried to trace its etymology to the Sanskrit verbal root √*di* "to fly" (Dr. Vesna A. Wallace, email correspondence, March 8, 2023). Interestingly, the Sanskrit retroflexive sound *ḍ*—like *ṭ* found in the seed syllable PHĀṬ—is the sound of the tongue striking the upper palate that causes an upward thrust of shakti or power. In this way, dakini may be a poetic representation of a goddess or female character (*ni*) who embodies (*ki*) the flight *(di)* of power or energy caused by the sound of the tongue striking the palate (Prof. Christopher Tompkins phone communication, March 7, 2023).

16. By the eighth century, the tantras were being studied and integrated into many of the traditional Vedic and Buddhist monasteries and universities across India and throughout South and Southeast Asia. Thus, tantra as a spiritual tradition takes its name from the texts upon which the teachings were based. In the Buddhist context, tantra also refers to esoteric texts that elucidate the sutras, the early words of the Buddha. The etymology of the word *tantra* can be understood via the two verbal roots √*tan* and √*tra* that make up the term. *Tan* means "propagate," "elaborate on," or "expand upon"; and *tra* means "save" or "protect." Thus we can understand that tantra "spreads" teachings that "save" beings from the suffering of samsara (Wallis, *Tantra Illuminated*, 26).

17. The masculine form of the word *dakini* is *daka*, which is usually translated into Tibetan as *pawo*, meaning "hero."

18. Tib. *drubthab*.

19. Vipassana is the Pali spelling; *vipashyana* is the Sanskrit for "insight" and what I will use going forward.

20. To learn more about dependent origination, read "The Twelfth Tara."

21. Yoga as "spiritual practice" specifically refers to the control of the mind and the senses, a usage first found in the sixth or seventh century B.C.E. text *Taittirīya-Upanishad* (II.4.1).

22. Bokar Rinpoche, *Tara the Feminine Divine*, 24.

23. Skt. *alayavijnana*; Tib. *kun zhi nam par shepa*. The substrate consciousness, sometimes translated as the "all ground consciousness."

24. *The Praise to Tārā with Twenty-One Verses of Homage and the Excellent Benefits of Reciting the Praise* (*Namastāraikavimśatistotragunahitasahita*; Tib. *sGrol ma la phyag 'tshal nyi shu rtsa gcig gis bstod pa phan yon dang bcas pa*). Another version of the name of the root text is *Praise to Tārā with Twenty-One Verses of Homage* (*Namastāraikavimśatistotra*; Tib. *sGrol ma*

la phyag 'tshal nyi shu rtsa gcig gis bstod pa). The *Praises* is situated within the larger text called *Tara's Tantra: The Origin of All Rites* (*Sarvatathāgata-mātṛtārāviśvakarmabhavatantranāma*; Tib. *De bzhin gshegs pa thams ced kyi yul sgrol ma las sna tshogs 'byung ba zhes bya ba'i rgyud*).

25. While this by no means implies that women were treated equally within hierarchical religious systems in South Asia or other locations that Buddhist tantra spread, it does acknowledge the slightly more gender-inclusive landscape in which the *Praises* arose.

26. Bokar Rinpoche, *Tara the Divine Feminine*, 74.

27. Skt. *karman*; Tib. *trinle*.

28. *Tuttara*, as it is written in both the Sanskrit and Tibetan *Praises,* can be understood either as a mantra syllable, like ʜūṃ, or an epithet of Tara. *Tuttāre*, as it is written in her mantras, is simply the vocative form of *tuttara*. I translate it as the former, just as the Khenpo brothers do in Khenchen Palden Sherab and Khenpo Tsewang Dongyal Rinpoche, *Tara's Enlightened Activity* (Ithaca, NY: Snow Lion, 2007), 200.

29. Lama Zopa Rinpoche, trans., *Praises to the Twenty-One Taras* (Portland, OR: Foundation for the Preservation of the Mahayana Tradition, 2008, 2019, 2021), 16.

30. To read the complete *Praises to the Twenty-One Taras*, I recommend the version found in *Tara's Enlightened Activity* by the Khenpo brothers.

31. This is the tradition addressed in Acharya Zasep Tulku Rinpoche, *Tara in the Palm of Your Hand: A Guide to the Practice of the Twenty-One Taras according to the Mahasiddha Surya Gupta Tradition* (Cambridge, UK: Windhorse, 2013).

32. According to the eleventh-century Indian scholar Vajrasana, Suryagupta is one of the eighty-four *mahasiddhas* (great adepts).

33. Common attainments (*siddhis*) consist of paranormal abilities such as mind reading, flying, and shape-shifting. The uncommon attainment is enlightenment.

34. This is the lineage upon which Rachael Wooten's book on the twenty-one Taras, *Tara, The Liberating Power of the Female Buddha* (Boulder, CO: Sounds True, 2020), is based. The iconography and names differ between Atisha's lineage found in her book and the Nyingma lineage found in this book.

35. The Nagarjuna associated with Atisha and the twenty-one Taras is not to be confused with the Mahayana epistemologist and Buddhist teacher who lived sometime within the first few centuries of the Common Era.

36. The Chokgyur Lingpa system is very similar to the Longchen Nyingtig system with respect to their shared iconography, and thus they are closely associated.

37. Within the context of Jigme Lingpa's terma of the twenty-one Taras, on the outer level, the princess Yeshe Tsogyal is the wisdom dakini, the Queen of Great Bliss, but on a subtler level, "inwardly," she is Tara in her twenty-one manifestations.

38. At times, in other iconographic systems, Tara is in full lotus posture or even standing.

39. Peaceful (Tib. *zhi*), fierce (Tib. *tro*), or peaceful and fierce (Tib. *zhimatro*).

40. Lama Tsultrim Allione, phone conversation, June 2022.

41. Deities may also be shown seated or standing on a sun disc, symbolizing wisdom (*jnana*; Tib. *yeshe*), or a sun and moon disc. While at times the disc corresponds to the "expression" of the deity—peaceful deities are on moon discs, fierce deities are on sun discs, and semifierce deities are on the sun and moon discs—this is not the case in this twenty-one-Tara system.

42. For example, the Buddha's teachings on shamatha and vipashyana can be found in the *Jewel Cloud Sutra* (*Ratnamegha-sūtra*; Tib. *dKon mchog sprin gyi mdo*), one of the most important sutras for the explanation of these two practices in the Tibetan tradition.

43. Skt. *utpatti-krama*; Tib. *kyerim*.

44. To learn more about cultivating shamatha and vipashyana, I recommend studying the *Four Applications of Mindfulness Sutra* (Pali. *Satipaṭṭhāna Sutta*), one of the most important discourses in the early Buddhist tradition. It is the foundation for contemporary vipashyana meditational practices.

45. Tib. *semnyi*.

46. Skt. *sampanna-krama*; Tib. *dzogrim*. Jigme Lingpa, in his text *A Wondrous Ocean of Advice for the Practice of Retreat in Solitude*, says, "In the development [creation] stage, the nature of the deity is free from clinging; its expression, which is the deity's form, is luminous; and its compassion is the clear concentration on the radiation and reabsorption of light rays. Only by maintaining an awareness of these will the development [creation] and completion stages be perfected." (Dilgo Khyentse, *Collected Works: Volume 3* [Boston: Shambhala, 2010], 480.) If you would like to learn more about the creation and completion stages of deity yoga, I recommend reading Jamgön Kongtrul and Sarah Harding, *Creation and Completion: Essential Points of Tantric Meditation* (Somerville, MA: Wisdom, 1996); and Jigme Lingpa et al., *Deity, Mantra, and Wisdom: Development Stage Meditation in Buddhist Tantra* (Ithaca, NY: Snow Lion, 2007).

47. Skt. *trisamadhi*; Tib. *ting nge dzin nampa sum*.

48. Dilgo Khyentse, *Collected Works*, 511.

49. Tib. *dam tshig sempa*.

50. Tib. *yeshe sempa*.

51. Tib. *ting nge dzin sempa*.

52. Due to the sometimes opaque nature of the verses, throughout the book I consulted with three other translations of the *Praises*: Lhasey Lotsawa, trans., *The Praise to Tārā with Twenty-One Verses of Homage and the Excellent Benefits of Reciting the Praise* (2019), Venerable Khenchen Palden Sherab Rinpoche and Venenerable Khenpo Tsewang Dongyal Rinpoche ("the Khenpo brothers"), *Tara's Enlightened Activity: An Oral Commentary on the Twenty-One Praises to Tara* (Ithaca, NY: Snow Lion, 2007), and *The Invincible Determination of the Princess Yeshe Dawa* (New York: Dharma Samudra 2022).

The First Tara: Tara the Swift Heroine

1. Skt. *dakshinavarti shankhya*; Tib. *dung gye khyil.*
2. The eight auspicious symbols (*ashtamangala*; Tib. *tashi tag gye*) are (1) conch, (2) endless knot, (3) pair of golden fish, (4) lotus, (5) parasol, (6) vase, (7) dharma wheel, and (8) victory banner. These eight symbols are considered auspicious because the gods offered them to Shakyamuni Buddha after he attained enlightenment.
3. Nagas (Tib. *lu*) are mythical serpentine spirits endowed with magical powers who live under the surface of the water or earth, or in rocks and trees. Nagas first originated from the Indus valley civilization snake cults in India and were then adopted into Buddhism.
4. Khenchen Palden Sherab Rinpoche, *The Smile of Sun and Moon: A Commentary on The Praise to the Twenty-One Taras*, trans. Anna Orlova (Boca Raton, FL: Sky Dancer Press, 2004), 31.
5. Wallace, "Susan Burton to receive the 2022 Harriet Tubman Legacy Award," *West Side Story Newspaper*, March 31, 2022, https://www.westsidestory newspaper.com/susan-burton-to-receive-the-2022-harriet-tubman -legacy-award/.
6. Skt. *maitri*; Tib. *byams pa.*
7. Wisdom beings are jnanasattvas (see the introduction).
8. Bodhichitta in aspiration refers to the four immeasurables of love, compassion, equanimity, and joy. Bodhichitta in action refers to the six perfections of generosity, ethics, patience, enthusiastic effort, concentration, and wisdom. Both are aspects of relative bodhichitta.
9. When you become the deity Tara, you are the samayasattva, the "commitment being."
10. This TĀṂ syllable is the samadhisattva.
11. Colophon: This sadhana was extracted from the practices of the 21 Taras in the inner sadhana of Dechen Gyalmo (Queen of Great Bliss) from the Longchen Nyingtig (Heart Essence of the Vast Expanse) in response to the

great necessity during the extraordinary time of the COVID-19 pandemic. On Mother's Day, May 9, 2021, the Venerable Khenpo Tsewang Dongyal Rinpoche gave his blessings for these concise Tara sadhanas at his center in upstate New York, the Padmasambhava Institute. May any mistakes be forgiven by the Protectors and may it be of vast benefit to sentient beings. Lopön Chandra Easton in accordance with instructions from Lama Tsultrim Allione, Tara Day, April 1, 2020.

The Second Tara: Tara the Melodious One, the Treasure of Intelligence

1. At times, the seed syllable HRĪṂ (pronounced HRING) may also be written as HRIM. I have kept in line with Khenchen Palden Sherab Rinpoche in *The Invincible Determination of Princess Yeshe Dawa* by transliterating it as HRĪṂ.

2. Skt. *Adarsha*; Tib. *melong*. In South Asia, the mirror represents the pure, clear mind within which all is reflected but not contained.

3. Skt. *vidya*; Tib. *rigpa*.

4. The six perfections (*shatparamita*; Tib. *pharol tu chinpa drug*) lay out the gradual path of the bodhisattva training. The first five correspond to the accumulation of merit. The sixth corresponds with the accumulation of wisdom.

5. Khenchen Palden Sherab, *Smile of Sun and Moon*, 39.

6. According to tantric texts such as the *Kubjikāmata-tantra*, HRĪṂ, in addition to being the seed syllable of Maya and Lakshmi, is also considered the seed syllable of Vishnu and associated with the water element. ("Hrim, Hrīṃ: 6 definitions," last modified October 31, 2021, https://www.wisdomlib.org/definition/hrim). This is interesting because the water element is also associated with the eastern vajra buddha family and its "mirrorlike" wisdom (*adarshajnana*; Tib. *melong tabü yeshe*), the wisdom associated with the ritual mirror.

7. Ignorance (*avidya*; Tib. *marigpa*). Sometimes "stupidity" (*moha*; Tib. *timug*) replaces ignorance on the list of five poisons.

8. In the tradition of Shakyashri Bhadra and Sakya Pandita Kunga Gyaltsen, Red Sarasvati is depicted much like Vajra Sarasvati Tara, with two arms, two legs, and one face, seated in the posture of royal ease and wearing the sambhogakaya ornaments. Instead of holding the stem of the utpala in her left hand, she holds the ritual mirror. Her right hand is resting palm up on her right knee holding a wish-fulfilling gem.

9. David R. Kinsley, *Hindu Goddesses: Visions of the Divine Feminine in Hindu Religious Tradition* (Berkeley: University of California Press, 1988), 58.

10. Ibid.
11. Sattva guna is the quality (guna) that is balanced, peaceful, and spiritual (*sattva*).
12. Kinsley, *Hindu Goddesses*, 60.

The Third Tara: Tara the Golden One Who Bestows Merit

1. Khenchen Palden Sherab, *Smile of Sun and Moon*, 45.
2. Skt. *chintamani*; Tib. *yizhin norbu.*
3. Tib. *desheg nyingpo.* Other terms used for buddha nature in Sanskrit are *gotra* (Tib. *rig*), meaning "class," "family," or "lineage"; and *dhatu* (Tib. *kham*), meaning "element."
4. Miranda Shaw, *Buddhist Goddesses of India* (Princeton, NJ: Princeton University Press, 2006), 247.
5. Skt. *ekarasa*; Tib. *rochig.*
6. In early Buddhism, these were called the four brahma viharas or "divine abodes" (*catvaro brahmavihara*). Later, they became known as the "four immeasurables" (*apramana*; Tib. *tshe me zhi*), the common name used in the Tibetan tradition. The four are loving-kindness (*maitri*; Tib. *jampa*), compassion (*karuna*; Tib. *nyingje*), empathetic joy (*mudita*; Tib. *gawa*), and equanimity (*upeksha*; Tib. *tang nyom*).
7. There are many great teachings on the six, and sometimes ten, perfections by past and present teachers such as the eighth-century Mahayana Buddhist master Shantideva, who authored the classic *Bodhisattva Way of Life* (*Bodhisattvacaryāvatāra*).
8. Global Peace Initiative of Women (GPIW) and Vandana Shiva, *Sacred Seed* (Point Reyes Station, CA: The Golden Sufi Center, 2014), 49–50.

The Fourth Tara: Tara, Victorious Queen of Crowning Light

1. Ushnisha Vijaya Tara is one of the three main longevity buddhas; Amitayus and White Tara are the other two (Khenpo Tsewang Dongyal phone correspondence, August 23, 2022).
2. Victorious Queen of Crowning Light is Miranda Shaw's translation in her chapter about Ushnisha Vijaya in the book *Buddhist Goddesses.*
3. The Sanskrit term *ayur* means "longevity" and *dade* (rhymes with "spa day") is the vocative form of the verbal root √*dad*, which means "to give," connected to *dana*. Thus, *ayur dade* means "give life!" BHRŪṂ is the seed syllable for many long-life deities, such as Amitayus and White Tara. As we saw with Tara Vajra Sarasvati, some Taras may have a second seed syllable

in addition to the universal TĀM seed syllable assigned to all the Taras. BHRŪM may be understood to mean "womb" or "birth."

4. Skt. *amarana amrita kalasha*; Tib. *tsebum.*

5. This immortality vase appears in the iconography of the other two main long-life deities, Amitayus and White Tara.

6. Skt. *tathagata*; Tib. *dezhin shegpa.*

7. Her dharani or Buddhist chant is called the *Ushnisha Vijaya Dharani* and is meant to help beings in troubled times. In China, it was translated from Sanskrit to Chinese as early as the seventh century C.E. and became associated with one of the four main Buddhist holy mountains called Wutaishan, home of the bodhisattva of compassion Manjushri, in Shanxi Province. In Tibet, the personal monastery of the Dalai Lamas, Namgyal Monastery, was named after her by the Third Dalai Lama, Gyalwa Sönam Gyatso, in 1571.

The Fifth Tara: Tara, Magnetizing Goddess of Knowledge

1. Evidence of her assimilation into Buddhist tantra first appears in the *Hevajra Tantra* where we find her heart mantra OM KURUKULLE HRĪḤ SVĀHĀ. Her Buddhist root tantra is called *Practices of the Noble Tara Kurukulla,* translated into Tibetan by a disciple of Atisha, Tsultrim Jeya, another example of Atisha's influence on Tibetan's devotion to Tara in her many forms.

2. *Monier-Williams* online dictionary, accessed December 5, 2022, https://sanskritdictionary.com/kurukull%C4%81/59165/1.

3. Khenchen Palden Sherab and Khenpo Tsewang Dongyal Rinpoche, *Tara's Enlightened Activity,* 85.

4. Her name Wangdu Rigje Lhamo can be translated in even more ways, such as "goddess who knows how to magnetize [everything]" or, as the Khenpo brothers say, "Tara who precisely understands the power of magnetizing" (Ibid., 86).

5. *Nrija* means "born from a human" (*nr* means "human"; and *ja*, "born." (Dr. Vesna A. Wallace, email correspondence, September 3, 2021). Translator's note: It is possible that the Tibetan transliteration of this word might also be a distortion of the Sanskrit word *nirija* or *niraj*, which literally means "the one born from water," implying a lotus. This is an epithet for the Hindu goddess Lakshmi. I have chosen to translate it as "born from a lotus" in the mantra as it seems to make more sense in this context.

6. Skt. *dhanushkalapaka*; Tib. *dazhu.*

7. Skt. *shar;* Tib. *dadar.* One of the most famous stories of the use of the arrow as a teaching tool is found in the life of Saraha (c. eighth century C.E.), whose name means "the one who has shot the arrow." The tale tells of his meeting

with the Fletcheress Dakini, who brought him to realization through the analogy of an arrow hitting its mark.

8. The red lotuses that adorn Kurukulla's implements are another unique element in her iconography. In Indian symbolism from the Vedas to the Tantras, the lotus is commonly identified with feminine beauty and sexuality.

9. Later in the *Praises*, the verse devoted to the fourteenth Tara praises her for ruling the seven netherworlds.

10. Her full name of Machig Labkyi Drönma means the "one mother, the light of Lab." Lab was long considered to be the region of her origins, but it is also the name of her clan.

11. The following account of Machig's life draws from her spiritual biography and hagiography (Tib. *namtar*) from Sarah Harding, *Machik's Complete Explanation: Clarifying the Meaning of Chöd* (Ithaca, NY: Snow Lion, 2003).

12. In Tibet, Indians were often referred to as black because their skin tended to be darker than that of Tibetans.

13. Harding, *Machik's Complete Explanation*, 67.

14. The exact number of Machig's children differs according to the source text. I have based the number on her biography found in Harding, *Machik's Complete Explanation*.

15. Ibid., 85.

The Sixth Tara: The Great, Awe-Inspiring Tara

1. In Sanskrit, when a word ends with either a long *i* or a long *a* vowel, it indicates the female gender. Thus, either Bhairava or Bhairavi are correct.

2. *Vighnan* is written as *bighnen* in the Tibetan script, which often writes the Sanskrit *v* as *b*, like in Bengali script (some posit because many of these teachings came to Tibet via Bengal and Bengali teachers). *Vighnan* means "obstacle" or "difficulty." It is likely *vighnani*, the nominative, accusative (and vocative) forms of the neuter noun *vighna*. *Sarva* means "all." BAM, sometimes VAM, is the seed syllable for the central Buddha Dakini in the Five-Wisdom-Dakini Mandala. It represents the element of space and the transformation of ignorance into all-encompassing wisdom. HŪM is another seed syllable that represents the enlightened mind of the buddhas. Generally, in Sanskrit, HŪM may also have a menacing connotation, meaning "wake up!" or "remember!" and is commonly used with fierce deities. PHAṬ is a powerful seed syllable that has its roots in the Vedic traditions and is particularly used in Vajrayana meditation in which it is said to represent the union of skillful means (PHA) and wisdom (Ṭ). When used in meditative practice or mantra, it signifies the power of cutting through and eliminating negative thoughts and emotions, dissolving them into emptiness. When you

recite Tara Bhairava's mantra, particularly when you say PHAṬ! PHAṬ!, you can feel that clearing away distractions, obstacles, for yourself and others.

3. Skt. *kila / kilaya*; Tib. *phurba*. In Buddhist tantra, the *kila* is associated with another well-known wrathful deity—Vajrakilaya, who is believed to be particularly effective at removing obstacles and purifying negativity in our current age. His mantra is very similar to this Tara's mantra: OM VAJRA KĪLI KĪLAYA SARVA VIGHNAN BAM HŪM PHAṬ SVĀHĀ.

4. In the Chöd teachings of Machig Labdrön, demons can also be physical illness such as viruses or bacterial entities that have invaded our body causing disease. In many cases, physical and mental illness is perceived, in part, as some form of possession, whether it be from bacteria, viruses, or something nonmaterial. In this case, the shaman or lama might use the kila to perform a ritual to rid the person, animal, or environment of whatever negative energy has taken root within them/it.

5. In fact, the name for this harmful spirit literally means "corpse raiser," so we can understand them to be like the walking dead, zombies, or even vampires. Interestingly, these spirits are associated with the misuse of mantra and employing dead bodies to do harm to living beings.

6. You may be familiar with the Hindu goddess Bhairavi, the consort of the wrathful form of Shiva. Bhairavi may be translated as the "Terrifying One" or "Awe-Inspiring One." In Hinduism, she is one of the Ten Mahavidyas, a collection of goddesses called the Great Wisdom Mothers (Kinsley, *Hindu Goddesses*, 161-63).

7. Palgrave Macmillan, "The Nawal El Saadawi Reader," December 15, 1997, https://books.google.com/books?id=r9SPVEG3cv0C&q=Nawal+Saad awi+united+nations+advisor+1979&pg=PR1#v=snippet&q=Nawal%20 Saadawi%20united%20nations%20advisor%201979&f=false.

8. Nawal El Saadawi, "Preface: The Gift," in *A Daughter of Isis: The Early Life of Nawal El Saadawi, In Her Own Words*, trans. Sherif Hetata (London: Zed Books, 2009), 10. Accessed November 22, 2022.

The Seventh Tara: Unassailable Tara

1. The Sanskrit word for this is *yantra*, which is a magical diagram or artifice, also defined as a mechanical device, especially used in warfare. For more information on yantras, see Gudrun Bühnemann, "Maṇḍalas and Yantras," in *Brill's Encyclopedia of Hinduism*, vol. 2, ed. Knut A. Jacobsen (Leiden: Brill, 2010), 566-72.

2. Khenchen Palden Sherab Rinpoche, *The Invincible Determination of the Princess Yeshe Dawa: A Commentary on the Twenty-One Verses of Praise and Homage with the Root Mantra of Ārya Tārā* (Sidney Center, NY: Dharma Samudra, 2022), 82.

3. According to Dr. Vesna A. Wallace, *taka, hana,* and *litsa* or *lica* are not Sanskrit words, thus she recommends separating them out and considering them seed syllables, perhaps in Tibetan or Bengali. Thus I have written them as *ta ka ha na li ca.* Also, it is a common occurrence that the Sanskrit syllables *ca* and *cha* are written as *tsa* and *tsha* in Tibetan, thus I transliterated them in the correct Sanskrit (Dr. Vesna A. Wallace, phone communication, October 12, 2020).

4. Skt. *prajna khadga*; Tib. *yeshs raldri.*

5. Sarat Chandra Das, "Mañjuśrī," in *Dictionary of Buddhist Iconography*, vol. 8, ed. Lokesh Chandra (Delhi: Aditya Prakashan, 2003), 2141.

6. Commonly used in Indian and Greek philosophy, a logical tetralemma consists of: A. existence, B. nonexistence, C. both existence and nonexistence, and D. neither existence nor nonexistence.

7. Dalai Lama, *The Essence of the Heart Sutra: The Dalai Lama's Heart of Wisdom Teachings,* trans. Geshe Thupten Jinpa (Boston: Wisdom, 2005), 1060.

8. Skt. *vayv-adhisara.*

9. See Thubten Yeshe, *The Bliss of Inner Fire: Heart Practice of the Six Yogas of Naropa* (Somerville, MA: Wisdom, 2005), 22.

10. Skt. *chitta*; Tib. *sem.*

11. Skt. *vidya*; Tib. *rigpa.*

12. When Dr. Maathai died of complications from ovarian cancer in 2011, her community was concerned that the Green Belt Movement would come to an end, but it survived and continues to thrive. The Green Belt Movement has planted over fifty-one million trees in Kenya, and it continues to work at the grassroots, national, and international levels to promote environmental conservation (Green Belt Movement, "Mission, Vision, Values," accessed April 6, 2022, http://www.greenbeltmovement.org/newsletter -signupwho-we-are).

The Eighth Tara: Tara, Invincible Heroine

1. *Daha* means "to burn down," and *pacha* means "to cook." Together I translate them as "incinerate."

2. Tib. *dorje.*

3. Skt. *ghanta*; Tib. *drilbu.*

4. In the Mahayana teachings of the *Prajnaparamita Sutras*, mara has four aspects that create obstacles in our lives and our Dharma practice.

1. Mara of the aggregates, *skandhamara* in Sanskrit. The first aspect symbolizes our clinging to the five aggregates of form, feeling, perception, volition, and consciousness as our intrinsic self.

2. The mara of mental afflictions, *kleshamara* in Sanskrit. The five kleshas are ignorance, anger, conceit, craving, and jealousy.

3. The mara of death, *mrityumara* in Sanskrit, sometimes called the mara of the lord of death. This mara symbolizes fear of change and death.

4. The mara of the child of the gods, *devaputramara* in Sanskrit. This mara symbolizes our craving for pleasure. The Khenpo brothers translate this fourth mara as the demon of distractions. This mara consists of all those things that take us out of the moment, that distract us in meditation.

5. King James Bible, Matthew 5:43–45. Full verse: "You have heard that it was said, 'Love your neighbor and hate your enemy.' But I tell you, love your enemies and pray for those who persecute you, that you may be children of your Father in heaven."

The Ninth Tara: Tara of the Acacia Forest

1. Acacia (catechu) is a hardwood tree native to central and east Africa, southern Asia, Bhutan, China, India, Myanmar, Nepal, and Pakistan. Its wood, leaves, and shoots are used to make medicine for stomach problems such as diarrhea, colitis, and indigestion. It is also used for osteoarthritis and to treat pain, bleeding, and inflammation. The bark and sap of the acacia tree are used to make tea to treat blood disorders. The acacia is often used for tools, furniture, and instruments, such as the Chöd drum and various flutes. In Buddhist lore, some trees are considered peaceful, and some are wrathful like the acacia, which is why it is used for the Chöd damaru drum.

2. Tib. Yulokö.

3. Green Tara's pure land is situated in Amitabha's Blissful pure land (Sukhavati; Tib. Dewachen) associated with the western dimension of the mandala.

4. Khenpo Tsewang Dongyal, phone correspondence, March 9, 2021.

5. Skt. *dharmachakra;* Tib. *chökyi khorlo.*

6. The Noble Eightfold Path makes up the three trainings of ethics (*shila*), single-pointed absorption (*samadhi*), and wisdom (*prajna*). Correct speech, action, and livelihood belong to ethics; correct effort, mindfulness, and concentration belong to single-pointed absorption; and correct intention and view belong to wisdom.

7. The Four Noble Truths are (1) the truth of suffering: as long we wander in samsara, we will experience suffering; (2) the truth of the source of suffering: ignorance and craving; (3) the truth of the cessation of suffering: there is a way out; and (4) the truth of the Path: the way out is to walk the Noble Eightfold Path.

8. Jane Goodall's 2019 response to the United Nations report on the global threat to biodiversity.

The Tenth Tara: Tara Who Is Victorious Over the Three Worlds

1. Depending on the source, at times Drölma Jigten Sumle Gyalma is joyful and at times she is peaceful. In this book, I focus on her joyful, semifierce mood, which is aligned with Khenpo brothers, *Tara's Enlightened Activity*; and Khenchen Palden Sherab, *Smile of Sun and Moon*.
2. Prof. Christopher Tompkins, phone correspondence, September 22, 2022.
3. Skt. *dhyaja*; Tib. *gyaltsen*.
4. Matthieu Ricard, *On the Path to Enlightenment: Heart Advice from the Great Tibetan Masters* (Boston: Shambhala, 2013), 121.
5. Jeremy E. Sherman, "Secret to Happiness and Compassion: Low Expectations," *Psychology Today*, August 27, 2014, https://www.psychologytoday .com/us/blog/ambigamy/201408/the-secret-happiness-and-compassion -low-expectations.
6. There are said to be four *dhyanas* (Pali: *jhana*; Tib. *samten*), four concentrations that elucidate our transition from external to internal focused attention. These are (1) "detachment from the external world and a consciousness of joy and ease"; (2) "concentration, with suppression of reasoning and investigation"; (3) "the passing away of joy, with the sense of ease remaining"; and (4) "the passing away of ease also, bringing about a state of pure self-possession and equanimity." Encyclopedia Britannica Online, "Buddhist Meditation," accessed May 4, 2021, https://www.britannica.com /topic/Buddhist-meditation.
7. Buddha, *Dhammapada* (Berkeley: Dharma Publishing, 1985), 3.
8. It is said that the Barua Buddhists are the ancient peoples of Bangladesh, having lived there for over five thousand years. In earlier times, they were Mahayana practitioners, but over time and due to sharing practices with their neighbors in Myanmar, they became primarily Theravada Buddhists.
9. Amma Thanasanti, "Dipa Ma: A Teacher for Our Times," *Awakening Truth*, August 31, 2021, https://awakeningtruth.org/blog/dipa-ma-a-teacher-for-our -times.
10. Dipa Ma, "Essential Quotes," www.dipama.org, accessed March 12, 2021, https://dipama.com/essential-quotes/.
11. Ibid.

The Eleventh Tara: Tara the Wealth-Granting Goddess

1. Tib. *terma* (*ster ma*). Spelled differently, terma (*gter ma*) means "treasure."

2. Tib. *terbum*.

3. In Tibetan culture, treasure vases are often given on special occasions such as births, weddings, housewarmings, and new ventures to bring about success and good fortune. Treasure vases may be kept in homes, businesses, or buried in the earth to restore harmony to the four elements of earth, fire, water, and air in the surrounding area. The treasure vase is associated with various prosperity deities such as Jambhala (also known as Dzambhala in Tibetan), a ratna family deity.

4. Skt. *bhumipala*. There are ten protectors corresponding to the ten cardinal directions (sometimes twelve), yet the primary earth protector is the Great Firm Earth Goddess—Sayi Lhamo Tenma Chenmo, in Tibetan. She and her retinue are linked to both the Buddhist and Bön traditions of Tibet. In Himalayan Buddhism these protectors belong to the retinue of Palden Lhamo, one of the eight main Dharma protectors; and in the Tibetan Bön tradition, they belong to the retinue of the goddess Sidpay Gyalmo.

5. Skt. *dharmapala*; Tib. *chökyong*.

6. Khenchen Palden Sherab, *Smile of Sun and Moon*, 95.

7. Oprah Winfrey, *What I Know for Sure* (New York: Flatiron Books, 2014), 6.

The Twelfth Tara: Tara Who Brings About Auspiciousness

1. Skt. *shrivatsa*; Tib. *pal beu*.

2. Thich Nhat Hanh, *Heart of the Buddha's Teachings: Transforming Suffering into Peace, Joy and Liberation* (New York: Harmony Books, 1998), 371.

3. Skt. Indrajala. Around the third century C.E., Indra's net was woven into Buddhist literature, such as the famous *Flower Garland Sutra* (*Avatamsaka Sutra*), one of the most influential Buddhist sutras in East Asia. In this sutra, we find a description of a cosmos of infinite realms within realms, mutually containing one another. See Thomas Cleary, *The Flower Ornament Scripture: A Translation of the Avatamsaka Sutra* (Boston: Shambhala, 1993), 891–92.

4. The endless knot is found engraved into the chest of the Hindu god Vishnu. Interestingly, the Vaishnava Hindu sect believes that Buddha Shakyamuni is the ninth avatar of Vishnu.

5. Some texts say the eighth and some say the ninth day of the lunar month is Tara's day.

6. Skt. *pratityasamutpada*; Tib. *tendrel*.

7. Skt. *Mulamadhyamakakarika*.

8. Tib. *rangzhin*.

9. Nagarjuna makes this link in the following verse:

Whatever arises dependently is explained as empty.
Thus dependent attribution is the middle way.
Since there is nothing whatever that is not dependently existent,
For that reason, there is nothing whatsoever that is not empty.
(Verse 24:18)

10. Lee Davis, "Economic Interdependence: Definition, Causes, and Effects," www.study.com, accessed June 2, 2022, https://study.com/academy/lesson/economic-interdependence-definition-causes-effects.html; Jody L. Davis, Jeffrey D. Green, and Allison Reed, "Interdependence with the Environment: Commitment, Interconnectedness, and Environmental Behavior," *Journal of Environmental Psychology* 29, no. 2 (June 2009): 173–80, https://www.sciencedirect.com/science/article/abs/pii/S0272494408000947; and "Interdependence Theory," *Psychology*, accessed June 2, 2022, http://psychology.iresearchnet.com/social-psychology/social-psychology-theories/interdependence-theory/.

11. To learn more about this biological example of Indra's net, the mycorrhizal network, a.k.a. the "wood wide web," I recommend reading Suzanne Simard, *Finding the Mother Tree: Discovering the Wisdom of the Forest* (New York: Alfred A. Knopf, 2021), and Merlin Sheldrake, *Entangled Life: How Fungi Make Our Worlds, Change Our Minds, and Shape Our Futures* (New York: Random House, 2020).

12. Sheldrake, *Entangled Life*, audiobook, 4:55.

13. The fourth domain, phenomena, refers to the external objects we experience through the five senses of the eyes, ears, nose, mouth, and skin.

14. Climate justice calls for equitable sharing of the burdens of climate change based on the understanding and acceptance of the causes and effects of historical injustices and our current climate crisis. Climate justice integrates principles of human rights, and social and environmental justice in relation to these historical responsibilities for causing our current climate crisis.

15. Greta Thunberg, "Greta Thunberg Full Speech and UN Climate Change COP24 Conference," YouTube video, 3:29, accessed June 15, 2022, https://www.youtube.com/watch?v=VFkQSGyeCWg.

16. It's common to have four sessions per day while on retreat: one each at sunrise, midmorning, afternoon, and sunset.

17. Angela Davis, "Mindfulness and the Possibility of Freedom, a Dialogue with Angela Davis and Jon Kabat-Zin," delivered at Scottish Rite Center, Oakland, CA, January 15, 2015.

18. Martin Luther King Jr., "Remaining Awake through a Great Revolution," Commencement Address for Oberlin College, June 1965, Oberlin, Ohio, https://www2.oberlin.edu/external/EOG/BlackHistoryMonth/MLK/CommAddress.html.

The Thirteenth Tara: Tara Who Is Victorious Over War

1. This is another instance where Tara at times appears semifierce, a.k.a. joyful, or at other times 100 percent fierce, depending on the source. Under Khenpo Tsewang Dongyal's guidance, I have chosen to stay in line with Jigme Lingpa's commentary to the *Praises* as found in the *Smile of Sun and Moon*.
2. Khenchen Palden Sherab, *Smile of Sun and Moon*, 107.
3. Ibid., 107.
4. In Sanskrit, *ripu* more commonly refers to the "inner enemy"—for example, in the *Bhagavadgita*, chapter 6, on dhyana yoga, it says, "Let a man raise himself by his own self; let him not debase himself. For he is himself his friend and foe" (*shloka* 5). However, *ripu* can occasionally be used as a term for outer enemies as well, like in this instance. (Dr. Cogen Bohanec, correspondence, May 11, 2022.)
5. Double vajra (*vishvavajra*; Tib. *dorje gyadram*). The double vajra is the symbol of the karma family in the five-buddha-family mandala.
6. These are discursive meditations on (1) this precious and rare human existence, (2) impermanence and death, (3) karma (cause and effect), and (4) the unsatisfactory nature of samsara (cyclic existence).

The Fourteenth Tara: Tara Who Frowns Fiercely

1. In the *Smile of Sun and Moon*, the Khenpo brothers say, "According to Taranatha, the seven underworlds beneath the earth are, from the bottom up: 1. The Ground of Asuras, 2. the Supreme Ground, 3. the No-Ground, 4. the Ground Itself, 5. the Essence Ground, 6. the Excellent Ground, 7. the Pure Ground" (113). You may recall that the fifth Tara is praised for ruling the seven higher worlds. This verse praises the fourteenth Tara for ruling these seven netherworlds, which are subterranean paradises.
2. Skt. *mushala*; Tib. *tongshing*.
3. Dudjom Rinpoche and Dudjom Lingpa, *Sublime Dharma: Quintessential Instructions on the Breakthrough and Direct Crossing-Over Stages of Dzogchen*, trans. B. Alan Wallace and Chandra Easton (Ashland, OR: Vimala, 2012), 57.
4. Tib. *nangwa*.
5. Gyatrul Rinpoche, commentary, and B. Alan Wallace, trans., *Natural Liberation: Padmasambhava's Teachings on the Six Bardos* (Somerville, MA: Wisdom, 1998), 106.
6. Because HŪM̐ is repeated twice in this mantra and is important to Tara Bhrukuti's practice, it might be helpful to explore it further. The seed syllable HŪM̐ also ignites an experience of dissolving duality and waking up to the

nature of our own mind. When we chant HŪṂ in this mantra—or in any completion-stage practice in which we say HŪṂ three times—we imagine that our actions (body), breath and sounds (speech), and thoughts (mind) are released into the state of "great peace" (Tib. *zhiwa chenpo*). Another way to put it is that HŪṂ represents that release of external perceptual appearances into their original natural state; this is the natural liberation of all phenomena into suchness.

7. Skt. *shanti*; Tib. *zhiwa*.

8. Skt. *mahashanti*; Tib. *zhiwa chenpo*.

9. *Tri* means "three," and *ghnan* means "to overpower" or "to kill." Khenpo Tsewang Dongyal explains that in Tibet, *trighnan* simply is understood to mean "suppressing," without emphasizing the meaning "three." When performing a tantric rite, trighnan means to secure the boundaries, much like the use of the sixth Tara's ritual dagger, in order to suppress, pin down, or corner negativity so that it cannot cause trouble during the ritual. (Khenpo Tsewang Dongyal Rinpoche, phone communication, March 9, 2021).

10. Yilin Wang, "Translation: Poems by Chinese Feminist and Revolutionary Writer Qiu Jin," NüVoices, accessed March 10, 2021, https://nuvoices .com/2021./03/10/translation-poems-by-chinese-feminist-and-revolutionary-writer-qiu-jin/.

The Fifteenth Tara: Tara the Supremely Peaceful Goddess

1. The Sanskrit term *gate* can be interpreted in various ways from the verbal root √*gam*. It may be the feminine vocative or the masculine or neuter locative. In this case, I have translated it as the vocative since it is connected to "all misdeeds" (*sarva papam*). So we can say, "Let [them] be gone!"

2. Skt. *amrita*; Tib. *dütsi*. The Tibetan term with a slightly different etymology is explained in *The Tantra of the Secret Cycle* in this way:

> To samsara which is like mara (Tib. *bdud*)
> When the elixir (Tib. *rtsi*) of the truth of Dharma is applied,
> It is called nectar (Tib. *bdud rtsi*).

In Vajrayana Buddhism, dütsi is a sacramental drink consumed in rituals such as tantric feasts, empowerments, or fire ceremonies.

3. Historians and ethnobotanists have tried to uncover the actual ingredients of this magical potion. Some suggest it might have been a certain kind of hallucinogenic mushroom, while others say it might have been a combination of cannabis with other herbs and substances.

4. These ten are grouped into actions of body, speech, and mind: the three doors we learned about in "The Tenth Tara." The first three (killing, stealing,

and sexual misconduct) are associated with the body; the following four (lying, slander, harsh words, and gossip) are associated with speech; and the last three (greed, covetous thoughts, and wrong views) are associated with the mind.

5. Vajrasattva's hundred-syllable mantra in Sanskrit: *oṃ/vajrasattva samayam anupālaya vajrasattva/ tvenopatiṣṭha dṛḍho me bhava/ sutoṣyo me bhava/ supoṣyo me bhava/ anurakto me bhava/ sarvasiddhiṃ me prayaccha/ sarvakarmasu ca me/ cittaṃ śreyaḥ kuru/ hūṃ/ ha ha ha ha/ hoḥ/ bhagavan sarvatathāgatavajra/ mā me muñca/ vajrī bhava/ mahāsamayasattva/ āḥ/* In English: oṃ is the supreme expression of praise/ Vajrasattva, ensure your samaya remains intact. Be steadfast in your care of me /Grant me unqualified contentment/ Enhance everything that is noble within me/ Look after me/ Grant me all accomplishments /And in everything I do /Ensure my mind is virtuous/ The hūṃ syllable is Vajrasattva's wisdom mind/ These represent the four immeasurables, the four empowerments, the four joys, and the four kāyās/ What joy!/ Blessed One, who embodies all the tathāgatas, Vajra(sattva), Never abandon me!/ Grant me the realization of vajra nature!/ Great samayasattva/ I am one with you. According to Manjugosha (Jamyang Khyentse Wangpo), in *The Light of Wisdom*, vol. 2, "The Hundred Syllable Mantra of Vajrasattva," trans. Erik Pema Kunsang, accessed July 3, 2022, https://www.bodhicittasangha.org/100-syllable-mantra/.

6. "The Humanitarian Initiatives of Sri Mata Amritanandamayi Devi (Mata Amritanandamayi Math)" (PDF), accessed July 5, 2021, 7, https://web.archive.org/web/20120916081829/http:/www.embracingtheworld.org/wp-content/uploads/2012/08/ETW2012.pdf.

7. Ibid.

8. Amma, "Teachings," www.amma.org, accessed July 5, 2022, https://amma.org/teachings/love-0.

The Sixteenth Tara: Tara Who Destroys the Power of Evil Spells

1. A more literal translation for her name would be "Tara, She Who Has the Power to Pacify the [Misuse of] Gnostic Incantations," but the version in the text is aligned with Khenpo Tsewang Dongyal's translation, which is more relatable, so I use it as well. In the *Invincible Determination*, the Khenpo brothers list her Sanskrit name as Raga Nishudana Tara, the Tara who destroys (*nishudana*) passion (*raga*) (270).

2. At times *rig ngag* may also refer to a person who performs spells or charms (that is, a sorcerer), as in *vidyamantrika* in Sanskrit, or *rig ngagpa* (masculine) or *rig ngagma* (feminine) in Tibetan.

3. Tib. *rig ngag tobzhom*.

4. TRAM is a seed syllable most likely stemming from the Sanskrit verbal root √*trai*, meaning "to protect," linking this meaning to Tara's name, which also derives from the same root. *Trina* literally means "grass" or "straw" and refers to insignificant, worthless things. *Du* is a verbal root that means "to be burned" and is connected to *duh*, the root for *duhkha*, meaning suffering. (Dr. Cogen Bohanec, Zoom correspondence, April 19, 2022.)

5. In Tibetan Buddhism, it is common to see the double vajra embroidered on the fabric hanging in front of teachers' thrones, decorated with four small *swastikas* (Tib. *yungdrung*) in the corners. The swastika is an ancient symbol in many cultures. For example, in China, for Taoists it symbolizes eternity; and in India, it conveys the sun's motion through the four seasons. In Buddhist tantra, the swastika represents the unshakable stability of the earth element.

6. Malalai of Maiwand is considered the Afghan Joan of Arc who helped lead the victory at the Battle of Maiwand on July 27, 1880, during the Second Anglo-Afghan War.

7. The other recipient that year was Kailash Satyarthi, a children's rights activist from India.

The Seventeenth Tara: Tara Who Stops Immeasurable Invading Forces

1. Robert Svoboda, in-person communication, September 17, 2020.

2. Tib. *chorten.*

3. The first, Meru, also known as Mount Meru or Sumeru ("excellent Meru"), is considered the center of both the physical and metaphysical universe in the Buddhist, Jain, and Hindu traditions. In Buddhist cosmology, Mount Meru is said to have four faces—the north is made of gold; the east, crystal; the south, lapis lazuli; and the west, ruby.

The second, Mount Mandara, is said to be a spur of Mount Meru that was used to churn the cosmic ocean of milk in one of the Hindu tradition's most central tales of the struggle between good and evil, gods (devas) and demons (asuras). In short, the gods invited the demons to help them recover the elixir of immortality from the depths of the ocean, Mount Mandara was pulled from Mount Meru to be used as a churning stick, steadied by Vishnu in his incarnation as Kumara the tortoise. Then naga Vasuki (half-human, half-cobra) served as the churning rope with the gods holding his tail. When Vasuki vomited the poison that threatened to befoul the elixir, Shiva caught and held it in his throat, causing his throat to turn blue. Interestingly, the next Tara (Mahamayuri) is associated with this theme of transmuting poison into medicine.

The third, Vindhya, refers to the Vindhya Mountain Range (Vindhyachal), a discontinuous chain of mountain ridges and plateaus that run along the Narmada River in west-central India. In Indian mythology, this is the traditional boundary between north and south India.

4. Cate Lineberry, "Wanted: The Limping Lady," *Smithsonian Magazine*, February 1, 2007, https://www.smithsonianmag.com/history/wanted-the-limping-lady-146541513/.

The Eighteenth Tara: Tara the Great Peacock Goddess

1. In India, peacocks were raised to fend off and kill poisonous snakes, mainly cobras, because they are ophiophagous birds—meaning they eat snakes. Urban myth says that peacocks transmute snake venom into their iridescent plumage, but I have not been able to corroborate this.

2. In the Tibetan script, the Sanskrit letter *v* is often written as *b*. This may be because many of the Buddhist teachings that came to Tibet did so via Bengal where the Sanskrit *v* is written as *b*.

3. The woodblock print, as well as the description of her in the *Smile of Sun and Moon,* lists a rabbit image in her full moon. However, in the *Praises* stanza, it says deer. This discrepancy seems to simply be a difference of context, location, or tradition. In India, they say it is either a rabbit or a deer just as Westerners say there is a man in the moon. Of course, it's subjective, depending on your vantage point.

4. Also translated as primordial wisdom (Skt. *jnana*; Tib. *yeshe*), primordial consciousness is the nondual knowing aspect of the nature of mind. *Ye* is short for *ye nas*, which means "from the beginning" or "primordial"; and *she* is short for *shepa*, which means "consciousness." Thus, yeshe implies a consciousness that has always been present from the very beginning; I translate it as "primordial consciousness."

5. Jacques Derrida was the Algerian-born French philosopher who developed this philosophical notion of pharmakon, linking it to the notion of indeterminacy—the philosophical exploration of meaning and definition with roots in a common scientific and mathematical concept of uncertainty and its implications. Indeterminacy refutes the Kantian notion of *noumenon*, the idea that an object or event exists independently of our subjective perception of it. Not unlike Buddhist Madhyamaka philosophy, Derrida posits that objectively independent noumena do not exist, but rather that objects exist in relation to our sensory experience of them—this is *phenomenon*. As we have seen, the doctrine of emptiness (*shunyata*)—introduced by Nagarjuna—posits that nothing exists independently of causes and

conditions, nor of our perception of it. Phenomena do not intrinsically exist from their own side. This relates to the relational and contextual elements that may determine whether any given substance or experience is a medicine or poison, a pharmakon. Perhaps Tara Mahamayuri—since she embodies the tantric principle of transmuting the so-called poison of delusions into the nectar of wisdom that realizes emptiness—played a role in Nagarjuna's understanding of emptiness, the subjectivity of reality, and interdependence.

6. DDT was the first of the modern synthetic insecticides, initially used during World War II to combat malaria, typhus, and other insect-borne human diseases both on and off the battlefield.

The Nineteenth Tara: Tara, Invincible Queen of the White Parasol

1. She is described as having a facial expression that is "passionate—smiling but a little semi-wrathful" in the Khenpo brothers, *Tara's Enlightened Activity*, 164.

2. The commentary includes mention of protection from the misuse of mantric power, which is an interesting echo of a theme that we saw earlier in the sixteenth Tara chapter.

3. *Raksha* means "protection." MAM is a seed syllable found within the Kalachakra Tantra visualization whereby the syllable transforms into the Mount Meru.

4. Skt. *chattra*; Tib. *dug*.

5. In Tibet, silk parasols are associated with religious figures and peacock feather-embroidered parasols are associated with secular leaders. The Dalai Lamas have had both since they were the secular and spiritual leaders of Tibet since the Fifth Dalai Lama in the seventeenth century until 2011, when, at seventy-one, the Fourteenth Dalai Lama decided to relinquish any political and administrative authority.

6. Found within the Tibetan classification of the *Words of the Buddha* (Kangyur) is "The Noble Dharani of Sitatapatra Born from the Tathagata's Ushnisha, Great Dispeller of Invincible Might and Supreme Accomplishment" (*Ārya-tathāgatoṣṇīṣa-sitātapatrāparājita-mahāpratyaṅgirāparama-siddhā-nāma-dhāraṇī sutra*).

7. Tib. Dorje tsugtor dug karmo.

8. "Buddhist Deity: Sitatapatra Iconography," Himalayan Art Resources, 2002, accessed December 1, 2022, https://www.himalayanart.org/search/set.cfm?setID=5746.

9. Please note that this list of the eight sambhogakaya ornaments differs

slightly from the list given in the introduction. It is not uncommon to see slight discrepancies in the ways her ornaments are listed.

10. Khenchen Palden Sherab, *Invincible Determination of the Princess Yeshe Dawa*, 164.

11. Ross Gay, *Inciting Joy: Essays* (Chapel Hill, NC: Algonquin Books, 2022), 3.

12. Skt. *ananda*; Tib. *gawa*.

13. Skt. *pramuditabhumi*; Tib. *rabtu gawa*.

The Twentieth Tara: Tara of the Mountain Retreat, Clothed in Leaves

1. Sadguru Sant Keshavadas, *Ramayana at a Glance* (Delhi: Motilal Banarsidass, 1988), 122.

2. The great yogi Matsyendranatha, known as one of the originators of Hatha Yoga, established a lineage of practice called Shabari Vidya to help ordinary people gain benefits from the more complex practices that were found in tantra. (Robert Svoboda, phone communication, July 10, 2022.)

3. Skt. *karandavyuha*; Tib. *zamatog*.

4. Skt. *Ārya Kāraṇḍavyūha Nāma Mahāyāna Sūtra*; Tib.*'Phags pa za ma tog bkod pa zhes bya ba theg pa chen po'i mdo.*

5. In this sutra, it also says that Maheshvara (Lord Shiva) was born from Avalokiteshvara's brow, Brahma from his shoulders, Sarasvati from his teeth, Narayana from his heart; and the earth from his feet, the sky from his stomach, and the winds from his mouth. For those interested in learning more about Buddhist creation myths, see Alexander Studholme, *The Origins of Om Mani Padme Hum: A Study of the Karandavyuha Sutra* (Albany: State University of New York Press, 2002), 39–40.

6. This sutra is the source of the most prevalent mantra in Tibetan Buddhism: OṂ MANI PADME HŪṂ.

7. Khenchen Palden Sherab, *Smile of Sun and Moon*, 155.

8. Ibid.

9. Her stanza highlights the twice uttered HARA and TUTTĀRE syllables with which she pacifies the most intractable infectious diseases. In her mantra, HARA is written twice, "MANO HARA HŪṂ HARA." Here, MANO means "mind," and HARA means "to take away," "to steal," or "to remove." We can interpret this mantric phrase to mean "steal away the mind [with] HŪṂ," or "remove dualistic concepts [with the] HŪṂ."

10. Ibid., 157.

11. This council is a legislative branch of the Navajo Nation government that consists of twenty-four district delegates elected to represent chapters within Arizona, New Mexico, and Utah.

12. "Wauneka, Annie Dodge | Arizona Health Sciences Library," ahsl.arizona
.edu, last accessed October 6, 2020.

13. S. H. Witt, "An Interview with Dr. Annie Dodge Wauneka," *Frontiers: A Journal of Women Studies* 6, no. 3 (1981): 64-67, https://doi.org/10.2307/3346218.

14. Ibid.

The Twenty-First Tara: Tara, Rays of Light

1. Marichyai is in the dative case, meaning "to," "for," "at," "in," or "on." BHRŪṂ, the seed syllable for other long-life deities such as Tara Ushnisha Vijaya and Buddha Amitayus, means "pregnant," "embryo," or "seed." It can also mean "life force" or even "creation of life," giving it a generative quality like a seed.

2. Skt. *suvamamatsya*; Tib. *sernya*. Some texts mention just one fish as found in Khenpo brothers, *Tara's Enlightened Activity*. But in the *Smile of Sun and Moon*, as well as in the line drawing here, there are two fish. The single fish symbolizes nirvana. In India, the two golden fish were originally associated with the rivers Ganges and Yamuna. In yogic subtle-body anatomy, these two rivers are understood to be the two side channels that run alongside the central channel. When the winds in the two side channels converge in the central channel, we experience the bliss-emptiness of nonduality—nirvana.

3. Khenchen Palden Sherab, *Invincible Determination of Princess Yeshe Dawa*, 176.

4. Ibid.

5. Skt. *grahas*; Tib. *dön*.

6. One common practice in Buddhism is to do "life-liberation" (Tib. *tsetar*), meaning saving animals, especially those destined for slaughter.

Selected Bibliography

Acharya Zasep Tulku Rinpoche. *Tara in the Palm of Your Hand: A Guide to the Practice of the Twenty-One Taras according to the Mahasiddha Surya Gupta Tradition.* Cambridge: Windhorse, 2013.

Allione, Tsultrim. *Feeding Your Demons: Ancient Wisdom for Resolving Inner Conflict.* New York: Little, Brown, 2008.

——. *Wisdom Rising: Journey into the Mandala of the Empowered Feminine.* New York: Simon and Schuster, 2018.

——. *Women of Wisdom.* London: Routledge and Kegan Paul, 1984.

Beyer, Stephen. *The Cult of Tara: Magic and Ritual in Tibet.* Berkeley: University of California Press, 1978.

The Bible. King James version.

Bokar Rinpoche. *Tara the Feminine Divine.* San Francisco: ClearPoint Press, 1999.

Bradford, Sarah H. *Harriet Tubman: Moses of Her People.* New York: George R. Lockwood and Son, 1886.

Braitstein, Lara, trans. *The Adamantine Songs (Vajragīti) by Saraha.* New York: American Institute of Buddhist Studies at Columbia University, 2014.

Buddha. *Dhammapada.* Berkeley: Dharma Publishing, 1985.

Burton, Susan, and Cari Lynn. *Becoming Ms. Burton: From Prison to Recovery to Leading the Fight for Incarcerated Women.* New York: New Press, 2017.

Carson, Rachel. *Silent Spring.* Boston: Houghton Mifflin, 1962.

Cleary, Thomas. *The Flower Ornament Scripture: A Translation of the Avatamsaka Sutra.* Boston: Shambhala, 1993.

Collett, Alice. *Lives of Early Buddhist Nuns: Biographies as History.* Delhi: Oxford University Press, 2016.

Dalai Lama. *The Essence of the Heart Sutra: The Dalai Lama's Heart of Wisdom Teachings.* Translated by Geshe Thupten Jinpa. Boston: Wisdom, 2005.

Dilgo Khyentse. *Collected Works: Volume Three.* Boston: Shambhala, 2010.

——. *Pure Appearance: Development and Completion Stages in Vajrayana Practice.* Translated by Ani Jinba Palmo. Boston: Shambhala, 2016.

Dudjom Rinpoche and Dudjom Lingpa. *Sublime Dharma: Quintessential Instructions on the Breakthrough and Direct Crossing-Over Stages of Dzogchen*. Translated by B. Alan Wallace and Chandra Easton. Ashland, OR: Vimala, 2012.

Easwaran, Eknath, trans. *The Bhagavad Gita*. Tomales, CA: Nilgiri Press, 1985.

———. *The Upanishads*. Tomales, CA: Nilgiri Press, 1987.

Edou, Jérôme. *Machig Labdrön and the Foundations of Chöd*. Ithaca, NY: Snow Lion, 1995.

Garling, Wendy. *Stars at Dawn: Forgotten Stories of Women in the Buddha's Life*. Boston: Shambhala, 2016.

Gay, Ross. *Inciting Joy: Essays*. Chapel Hill, NC: Algonquin Books, 2022.

Gladstar, Rosemary. *Herbal Healing for Women*. New York: Atria, 1993.

Gladstar, Rosemary, and Pamela Hirsch, eds. *Planting the Future: Saving Our Medicinal Herbs*. Rochester, VT: Healing Arts Press, 2000.

Global Peace Initiative of Women (GPIW) and Vandana Shiva. *Sacred Seed*. Point Reyes Station, CA: The Golden Sufi Center, 2014.

Gyatrul Rinpoche, commentary, and B. Alan Wallace, trans. *Natural Liberation: Padmasambhava's Teachings on the Six Bardos*. Somerville, MA: Wisdom, 1998.

Hanh, Thich Nhat, *The Heart of the Buddha's Teaching: Transforming Suffering into Peace, Joy and Liberation*. New York: Harmony Books, 1998.

Harding, Sarah. *Machik's Complete Explanation: Clarifying the Meaning of Chöd*. Ithaca, NY: Snow Lion, 2003.

Jamgön Kongtrul and Sarah Harding. *Creation and Completion: Essential Points of Tantric Meditation*. Somerville, MA: Wisdom, 1996.

Jamyang Khyentse Chökyi Lodrö. *In Praise of the Goddess Sarasvatī* (*Lha mo dbyangs can ma la bstod pa rab dga'i dbyangs snyan bzhugs*). Translated by Adam Pearcey, 2005. https://www.lotsawahouse.org/tibetan-masters/jamyang-khyentse-chokyi-lodro/sarasvati-praise.

Jigme Lingpa et al. *Deity, Mantra, and Wisdom: Development Stage Meditation in Buddhist Tantra*. Ithaca, NY: Snow Lion, 2007.

Keshavadas, Sadguru Sant. *Ramayana at a Glance*. Delhi: Motilal Banarsidass, 1988.

Khenchen Palden Sherab Rinpoche. *The Invincible Determination of the Princess Yeshe Dawa: A Commentary on the Twenty-One Verses of Praise and Homage with the Root Mantra of Ārya Tārā*. Sidney Center, NY: Dharma Samudra, 2022.

———. *The Smile of Sun and Moon: A Commentary on The Praise to the Twenty-One Taras*. Translated by Anna Orlova. Boca Raton, FL: Sky Dancer Press, 2004.

Khenchen Palden Sherab and Khenpo Tsewang Dongyal Rinpoche. *Tara's Enlightened Activity: An Oral Commentary on the Twenty-One Praises to Tara.* Ithaca, NY: Snow Lion, 2007.

Khenpo Tsultrim Lodro Rinpoche. *Gateway to the Vajrayana Path: Demystifying the World of Tantric Buddhism.* Translated by Dekyi Drolma and Lorraine Wu Chen. Taipei: Larong Books, 2019.

Kinsley, David R. *Hindu Goddesses: Visions of the Divine Feminine in the Hindu Religious Tradition.* Berkeley: University of California Press, 1988.

Lama Zopa Rinpoche, trans. *Praises to the Twenty-One Taras (sGrol ma'i bstod pa bzhugs so).* Portland, OR: Foundation for the Preservation of the Mahayana Tradition, 2008, 2019, 2021.

Landesman, Susan A., trans. *The Tārā Tantra: Tārā's Fundamental Ritual Text (Tārā-mula-kalpa) Part One: The Root Text.* New York and Somerville, MA: American Institute of Buddhist Studies and Wisdom Publications in association with the Columbia Center for Buddhist Studies and Tibet House, 2020.

Maathai, Wangari. *Unbowed: A Memoir.* New York: Alfred A. Knopf, 2006.

Monier-Williams, Monier, et al. *A Sanskrit-English Dictionary: Etymologically and Philologically Arranged with Special Reference to Cognate Indo-European Languages.* Oxford: Oxford University Press, 1899.

Paul, Diana Y. *Women in Buddhism: Images of the Feminine in the Mahāyāna Tradition.* Berkeley: University of California Press, 1985.

The Praise to Tārā with Twenty-One Verses of Homage, and the Excellent Benefits of Reciting the Praise (Namastāraikaviṃśatistotraguṇahitasahita; Tib. *sgrol ma la phyag 'tshal nyi shu rtsa gcig gis bstod pa phan yon dang bcas pa).* Degé Kangyur (T 438).

Ricard, Matthieu. *On the Path to Enlightenment: Heart Advice from the Great Tibetan Masters.* Boston: Shambhala, 2013.

Saadawi, Nawal El. *A Daughter of Isis: The Autobiography of Nawal El Saadawi.* London: Zed Books, 1999.

———. *The Nawal El Saadawi Reader.* London: Zed Books, 1997.

Salbi, Zainab. *Freedom Is an Inside Job: Owning Our Darkness and Our Light to Heal Ourselves and the World.* Boulder, CO: Sounds True, 2018.

———. *The Other Side of War: Women's Stories of Survival and Hope.* Washington, DC: National Geographic, 2006.

Salbi, Zainab, and Laurie Becklund. *Between Two Worlds: Escape from Tyranny: Growing Up in the Shadow of Saddam.* New York: Gotham Books, 2005.

Schaeffer, Kurtis R. *Dreaming the Great Brahmin: Tibetan Traditions of the Buddhist Poet-Saint Saraha.* New York: Oxford University Press, 1985.

Shaw, Miranda. *Buddhist Goddesses of India.* Princeton, NJ: Princeton University Press, 2006.

Sheldrake, Merlin. *Entangled Life: How Fungi Make Our Worlds, Change Our Minds, and Shape Our Futures.* New York: Random House, 2020.

Simard, Suzanne. *Finding the Mother Tree: Discovering the Wisdom of the Forest.* New York: Alfred A. Knopf, 2021.

Simmer-Brown, Judith. *Dakini's Warm Breath: The Feminine Principle in Tibetan Buddhism.* Boston: Shambhala, 2001.

Steiner, Stan. *The New Indians.* New York: Harper and Row, 1968.

Studholme, Alexander. *The Origins of Om Manipadme Hum: A Study of the Kārandavyūha Sūtra.* Albany: State University of New York Press, 2002.

Thubten Yeshe. *The Bliss of Inner Fire: Heart Practice of the Six Yogas of Naropa.* Somerville, MA: Wisdom, 2005.

Tsonkyi Rinpoche with Eric Swanson. *Open Heart, Open Mind: Awakening the Power of Essence Love.* New York: Harmony Books, 2012.

Wallis, Christopher D. *Tantra Illuminated: The Philosophy, History and Practice of a Timeless Tradition.* The Woodlands, TX: Anusara Press, 2012.

Wilson, Martin. *In Praise of Tārā: Songs to the Saviouress.* Somerville, MA: Wisdom, 1992.

Winfrey, Oprah. *What I Know for Sure.* New York: Flatiron Books, 2014.

Zaw, Khin. "Remaining Legacy of Green Tara in Myanmar (Burmese) Traditional Beliefs." From Vajrayāna Buddhism in the Modern World. Proceedings of the Second International Conference on Vajrayana Buddhism. Thimphu, Bhutan. Centre for Bhutan Studies & GNH. (March 28-30, 2018): 49-60.

Index